GETTING INTO FILM

GETTING INTO FILM

REVISED EDITION

MEL LONDON

DESIGNED BY

BEA FEITLER

BALLANTINE BOOKS · NEW YORK

Published in the United States by Ballantine Books, a division of Random House, Inc., New York, and simultaneously in Canada by Random House of Canada Limited, Toronto.

Photo credits may be found on pages 176-77

Library of Congress Catalog Card Number: 85-90583

ISBN: 0-345-32640-7

Manufactured in the United States of America
First Edition: October 1977
Revised Edition: January 1986

10 9 8 7 6 5 4 3

TO MY WIFE, SHERYL
When I turned to look, she taught me how to see.

CONTENTS

ACKNOWLEDGMENTS

For every book, there is a list of people "without whom this book could not have been written." This one is no exception. Whatever an author's background in film, whatever the experience he has acquired over thirty or more years, the field is too large for him to have done everything. In fact, all of us are still learning every day of our film lives—and that is one of the joys of the business. I have, in fact, learned much from merely writing this book and then having to update it to keep it timely in a fluctuating industry.

My list is long. I had not realized just *how* long, until the compilation began. But each and every person below played a part by giving freely of information and experience for the eventual reader and, hopefully, future filmmaker. Therefore, this is my "without whom..." My thanks to all of them:

To Stephanie Chan, my good right arm, constant critic, and young questioner, who researched, typed, probed, corrected, compiled, and struggled through long hours of interviews and telephone calls, and who, incidentally, laughed at all my stories.

To the people who encouraged and helped: Boone Mancall, my ex-partners Lee Bobker and Helen Radin, and especially Irving Oshman, who knows as much about "getting into film" as I do, but who still painstakingly read through the original text to check for technical accuracy, and to Ron Busch, formerly of Ballantine Books, who was convinced that someone would buy the book when it was completed.

And, for their contributions to individual chapters, thanks:

To Jon Fauer, who should probably write his own book, and to Richard Nelson of Official Airline Guide; and Fred Berner and David Smith, two young men who were just starting out when the first edition of this book went to press.

To Elihu Winer, of Writers Guild of America; Brooke Buhrman of TAT Communications, and Artie Julian of "Maude"—for sage words of advice.

To Joe Longo, Leonard Hirschfield, Peter Henning, Michael Livesay, Bernie Hirschenson, Herbert Raditschnig, Rick March, and Michael Barry for their professional excellence and helpfulness in the area of cinematography—as well as to Ron Berenbeim, of Local 644, Union of Motion Picture Cameramen, IATSE.

To Peter Genung, of Local 771, Motion Picture Editors, IATSE, Peter Rosenbaum, Suzanne Jasper, Ted Kanter, Emil Rodriguez, all of whom have put up with my stubborness in editing rooms over the years. Thanks, too, to Maria Mangu of MM Editing Systems.

To Malcolm Dodds, a composer whom I promised to make "rich and famous" if he cooperated with me; Arthur Custer, Michael Shapiro and Rena Kazurski of ServiSound; and to John Franks of Columbia Special Products (CBS Records) for the EZ Cue Music Library Catalogue.

To Don Matthews, who spent six plane trips talking to me about "what it felt like to be a sound person" and to Cheryl Groff and Bill Shaver, who make traveling with sound people a pleasure and delight.

To Saul Bass, who graciously gave of his animation files and his time, and to Jeff Kleiser of Digital Effects who provided all the lessons on Computer Graphics—as well as to Sid Horn of Phil Kimmelman Associates, Emily Hubley and Dick Rauh of the Optical House, and Carmen D'Avino, the only Renaissance Man I know. Thanks, too, to Gerald Salvio of Local 841, Motion Picture Screen Cartoonists, IATSE.

To all the actors who ever had the misfortune of being on my set—especially to John Sucke of Screen Actors Guild, Joe Cirillo, Cynthia Horton, and to my oldest friend in the profession, Mort Schwartz, who may find a perfectly cast chicken some day.

To the many "unsung heroes and heroines": who should also be known: Dick Smth, who is so supportive of the beginner in the field, to Maurice

Stein, and to Ed Callaghan of Local 798, Make-up Artists and Hairstyling, IATSE. To Fredda Briant of Local 764, Theatrical Wardrobe Attendants, IATSE, and to Jo Ynocencio and Jackie Hickey, for their help in costume design and styling, as well as Cis Corman, for information on casting; Sam Robert of Local 52, Union of Motion Picture Studio Mechanics, IATSE; Billy O'Connell and Chris Allen, two of the best gaffers in the business; Lester Polakov of Studio Forum of Stage Design, and Andy Clores, United Scenic Artists; Paul Meistrich of Camera Mart; Wynn Nathan of RKO Pictures; Miriam Gitomer, Zeny Pascual, and Ben Plump for their business advice; and Lee Coyle of Ohio Bell, particularly for the update on corporate communications opportunities.

To Les Tomalin, formerly of Ogilvy and Mather, and to Bill Chororos, also of the erstwhile agency; Maury Penn and Howard Davis of N.W. Ayer; Bill Beste and Millie Wurster of BBD&O; Jack Sidebotham of McCaffery & McCall. And, in the area of getting things done in twenty four hours when it takes ad agencies four months, to Bill Early of Armstrong World Industries.

To Wayne Whitehill and Harold Klein of Directors Guild of America, and particularly to Stan Ackerman and Ernie Ricka for their update on DGA Programs. To David Bellin and to Alan Lansburg and Merrill Grant for their help in the production material for *The Savage Bees*. At that time, too, the director of the film, Bruce Geller, was also of great assistance to me in putting the chapter together, and I was greatly saddened to hear of his death in a plane crash soon afterward.

To Anne Schlosser, Kaye Cooper-Mead, Sam Grogg, Jr., and Willa Robertson, all of the American Film Institute, and a special word of thanks to Karen D. Arandjelovich and Philip Chamberlin of the Academy of Motion Picture Arts and Sciences.

With the booming of Special Effects as a film career, I must also thank Justin Zizes for his original information for the book and Lucasfilm for their wonderful cooperation in bringing the subject up to date and into the eighties. My thanks also to Allen Zwerdling of Backstage Publications, Mary Jane Coleman of the Sinking Creek Celebration, Karen Cooper and Steve Dobi of Film Forum, Joanne Koch of the Film Society of Lincoln Center, Dennis Bade of Filmex, and to yet another friend who has died since the first edition of this book, Margareta Akermark of the Museum of Modern Art. As a special thank you to her, my most recent film book carries a dedication to her as a friend and a mentor for so many years of my film life.

And, to these people, a special thank-you for all the hours of discussion with this male chauvinist filmmaker: Joan Kuehl, Claudia Weill, Nell Cox, Barbara Martinsons, Bobbie Leigh, Brianna Murphy, Faith Hubley, Deborah Boldt, Grania Gurieveitch, Johnna Levine, and Meredith Burch.

As with all "without whoms," there are always the "last, but not least..."

So—last, but not least, to my editor for this update on the book, Ginny Faber, and most of all to the one who was my original editor—Susan Petersen—who found all the things I had left out, changed all the chapters so they made sense, stopped my tendency to apologize, and made me think whenever I took the easy way out—by writing in the margin: "Who? What? Where? Give examples." Since that early time, she has become the *president* of the publishing company imprinted on the cover of this book—and I like to think that it all happened because of the wonderful job she did editing this book in the first place!

To all—to each and every one—again my thanks and love.

Mel London
New York City, 1985

GETTING INTO FILM... AN UPDATE

My dear old grandmother (see page 1) would have said, "My, how time flies!" or used some other predictable but charming platitude. And how right she would have been. For it barely seems possible that the first edition of this book was published so many years ago and that more than fifty thousand communications students and young filmmakers have actually chosen to read it, hopefully gleaning some valuable information along the way.

For me, however, possibly the most exciting thing that has happened during that time has been the revelation that so many of the people who chose to read this book are now actively working in the film field. Over the years, I have received letters of inquiry and countless résumés from young job hunters. I have interviewed some and tried to offer advice, and I have watched in awe as their credits expanded and they found their way into an industry that once seemed so hostile to them. Using the knowledge of *their* success, I can only tell the burgeoning enrollment of communications students that it can, indeed, be done. This is but one reason for the update on this book.

It is also gratifying to know that many of the people who were in the early stages of their careers when this book was first published have managed to find their places as successful and substantial members of the industry. Jon Fauer, starting as a production assistant, camera assistant, and then cinematographer, has moved into the feature field (camera operator for *Splash*). Stephanie Chan, once my youngest assistant, is now a producer of documentary films. Martha Coolidge, once a struggling independent producer, has since directed three feature films (including *Valley Girls*). Ted Churchill, schooled in the difficult free-lance market of cinematographers, is now one of the best known operators of the Steadicam.

Since the first edition of this book was published, new names have surfaced in the film field (while others have disappeared almost completely): Norman Kasden, John Sayles, Pamela Yates, Gregory Nava, Susan Seidelman, Tom Sigel, Anna Thomas now find their places in the reviews and the columns of film criticism and commentary. This, then, is the second reason for an update on a book about film careers.

Film technology has changed dramatically. Where once the field of special effects was limited to an occasional film about apes or earthquakes or fires, a whole range of productions has made these jobs among the most sought-after and highly paid in the entire industry. Beginning with the remarkable *2001* through *Star Wars* and *E.T.*, *Star Trek*, and *2010*, we have all been passengers on a continuous trip into outer space, made possible by special effects geniuses and the ubiquitous computer.

Computer graphics was barely a pup when the first edition was published. It now offers new job opportunities to the young prodigies who fully understand the bits and bytes of this new generation.

Video tape has spawned a whole new industry, staffed by engineers, graphic artists, editors, and producer/directors, many of whom do not even work in the adjunct world of film. Teleconferencing, once the fair-haired wonder of the new era, faltered along the way, and has now seemed to find its place in corporate communications, with more than 50 major American companies providing over 300 specially-designed video conference rooms for their expanding audio-visual staffs. Music video is with us now. And, most script writers now use a word processor instead of an old battered typewriter. The Steadicam has replaced dolly tracks. Film stock is four times faster. A whole new world has opened up.

Certainly, then, if we can say that the field of the motion picture is in a constant state of flux, we can add one more thing to that observation that is as true today as when this book was first written: You will *never* find it boring!

INTRODUCTION

In the past two decades, motion pictures have become the central art form of our time just as fine arts, painting and sculpture were the central art forms of the Renaissance, attracting the "best and the brightest" of the younger creative artists. So it is with film, whether theatrical films, documentary films, television commercials or any other of the various forms this medium can assume. The influx of dynamic, ambitious and talented young men and women to the field has grown and multiplied. High schools, colleges and universities up to and beyond the graduate level are now offering a wide variety of courses and are exceptionally well-equipped to "teach" the art of film. At the same time, hundreds of young men and women seek to enter the field directly—not only in the traditional film centers such as New York and Los Angeles but in such widely separated places as Chicago, Detroit, Tulsa, other cities and even smaller, more isolated areas.

The attraction of film as a career and a lifestyle is obviously very great. It offers creative work in an art form; it offers the opportunity of excellent financial rewards; it can provide great ego satisfaction (e.g., names on marquees and in the columns of Pauline Kael); it can provide travel to far-off, exotic and interesting places; and it makes possible lifelong associations with other creative, interesting, charismatic and intelligent people.

The key question for most of these young men and women, then, is: "How do I get into film?" Wherever one lectures or teaches or speaks, that is usually the first question. It is this question that this book seeks to answer.

Because film is basically an eclectic field and because it offers many vital and challenging areas of creative work, there are many avenues of approach. Unlike a profession like medicine, which dictates a more rigid and traditional entry method, film and filmmaking can be approached along many different paths. Perhaps what is more important than the precise choice of entry method is the level of commitment the individual develops toward filmmaking. As one reads the very useful and interesting pages of this book, one theme repeats itself over and over again: people who find successful careers in filmmaking, although disparate and diverse in their personalities and backgrounds, share in common a deep passion for the art and the technique.

Film is fun. It is intellectually challenging. And it calls forth a wide range of one's inner resources that enrich the life of the filmmaker. To choose film as a way of life is to choose to work hard, to work creatively, holding back nothing of oneself. It is to choose self-expression and to involve oneself deeply in one's own life and time. Through film it is possible to make philosophical and social statements, to influence the course of events and, in the final analysis, to communicate something of oneself with millions and millions of people all over the world. Many of the key answers to that critical and much-asked question, "How do I get into film?" can be found between the pages of this excellent book, which should be not only pragmatically useful but very important to the future of cinema.

—*Lee R. Bobker*
New York City

Lee R. Bobker is the author of Elements of Film *and* Making Movies . . . From Script to Screen *and he is President of Vision Associates in New York.*

CHAPTER 1

THE WOULD-BE FILMMAKER

"You Take Two Eggs..."

My grandmother was a good cook, and whenever she was asked how she made something, she began by saying, "You take two eggs . . ." Every recipe in her vast middle-European repertoire began with the same formula, whether for two people or for a banquet of twenty. "You take two eggs . . ."

Ever since being asked to do this book, that phrase has been rattling around in my head. Having interviewed hundreds of would-be filmmakers, some of them young and many of them well along in years, I have always wanted to be able to give them a formula for getting into the film business, a recipe for success. "If you want to get into film, you take two eggs . . ."

This was not to be another book on "How to Make a Film." There are hundreds on the market today—including books on how to expose film, how to cut film, criticize film, books on film texts, film scripts, analyses of film scripts, criticism of such analyses, and there are film encyclopedias. There are also enough books that explain how to expose film stock at f2.8 or how Antonioni lit the back of Monica Vitti's head in *Red Desert.*

There are some books on the market that seem essential at first glance, if one is to learn about the film industry. When I was a young filmmaker, everyone recommended Spottiswoode and I dutifully bought it—and put it down after five boring pages. I just couldn't understand it, and the combination of British technical terms and ponderous writing were more than I could take. A year later, I picked up the book and found that I didn't need it. I had learned everything while on the job.

There are other books on the market today that are terribly concerned with the "glamour" aspects of the industry: the feature, the commercial, the TV special, the documentary. And there are hundreds of offshoots, too, that offer opportunity for the beginning filmmaker or the student.

A huge gap seems to appear when we look for information about what it is that *most* film people, other than the director or producer, actually do. What about editors, camera people, production personnel, sales, business, writers? And also, of course, actors, studio mechanics, makeup and hairdressing experts, agency producers and composers?

What's more, the largest area of need seems to be in the seemingly simple but very important aspect of getting a job! And how can you make a living free-lancing? . . . Will the unions accept someone like you? . . . Who are the people you are going to meet? . . . Why will they be so hostile to you when you are so talented? The schools don't teach you how to get a job. And neither do the books. And certainly this book is not going to get the job for you. But it will give you information that you need, advice that you can consider, and a basic, practical point of view.

Who *are* the people who work in our field? And how did they get their jobs? Some began by working hard like Horatio Alger. One friend of mine stood on a balcony in New Orleans as a film crew worked below. The director shouted up to her, "How would you like to work on this film?" and her first job was that of a stand-in in a feature. Others began by working for their fathers or friends, and still others went to film school, graduated, and made a first feature that netted $10,000,000. And many have starved. Some have pounded on doors for weeks and months and made their livings by doing other things totally unrelated to the film field. And some of us got into it by accident. There is no formula.

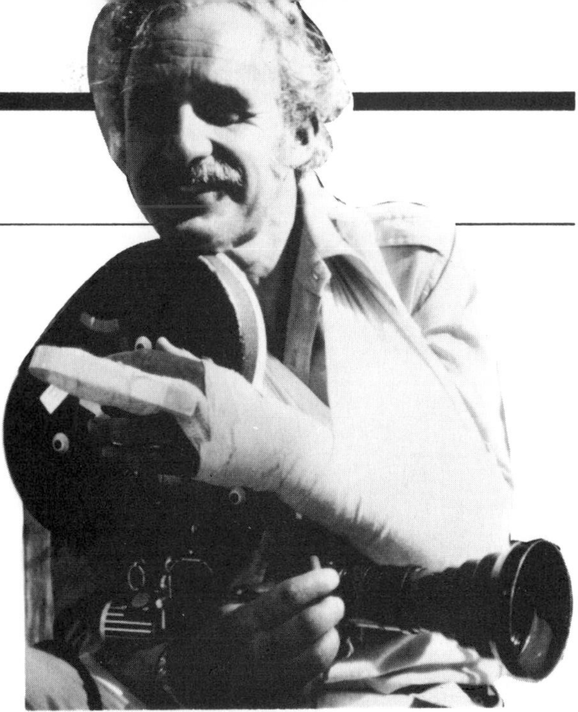

The author, whose grandmother always told him, "No one ever said life would be easy."

But, if there is no magic formula, there are some very practical things that you can learn that will help you break into the industry. Every one of the people I talked to in preparing this book mentioned very much the same things: the love of film, the dedication needed to break in, and the understanding that it's going to be hard work. All the jobs we've described take just those qualities. So, possibly, with that in mind there is a place we can begin.

You want to get into the film field? Let's begin with some very practical things, just as my grandmother did. "You take two eggs . . ."

Curiosity follows the film crew around the world. Cinematographer Jon Fauer with Colombian children, shooting a film in South America for Foster Parents Plan.

CHAPTER 2

THE FILM INDUSTRY

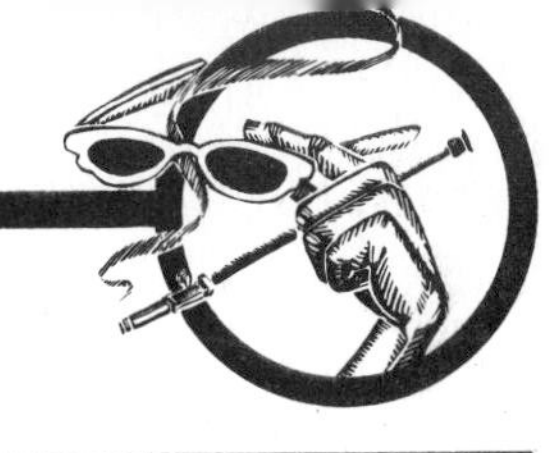

More Than Sunglasses and Autographs

Ever since the early twenties, the film industry has had the reputation of being a glamour field. Nurtured by Hollywood, deliberately sprinkled with tinsel, it flowered during the thirties, when the world needed some escape from the Depression. Hollywood obliged by providing fantasy and stars, larger-than-life people whose names were known to everyone.

The tinsel has not yet disappeared and the image remains. A film crew at an airport will always draw a crowd. "Who's arriving?" is the question most asked. On the street, a documentary unit hears, "What TV station will this be on?" And if you happen upon a feature being shot, notice the crowd hanging from the rafters to catch a glimpse of Robert Redford. How many students now in the schools sit back and dream of their first feature . . . searchlights on opening night . . . millions at the box office?

And yet, the most important thing to recognize is the fact that film is first of all an *industry*. As with most industries, success takes hard work, atrocious hours, and brute labor that would tire a long-distance runner in the Boston Marathon. The difficulties of getting a job in the industry are compounded by the very fact that so many people want to get into it. Let me hasten to add that none of us who have made our careers in the film industry would, for any amount of money, ever leave it. Most, given the opportunity to live their lives over again, would no doubt choose the same career. It is the most exciting, tiring, refreshing, neurotic, thrilling, vital field one could ever find. But it takes work, and commitment.

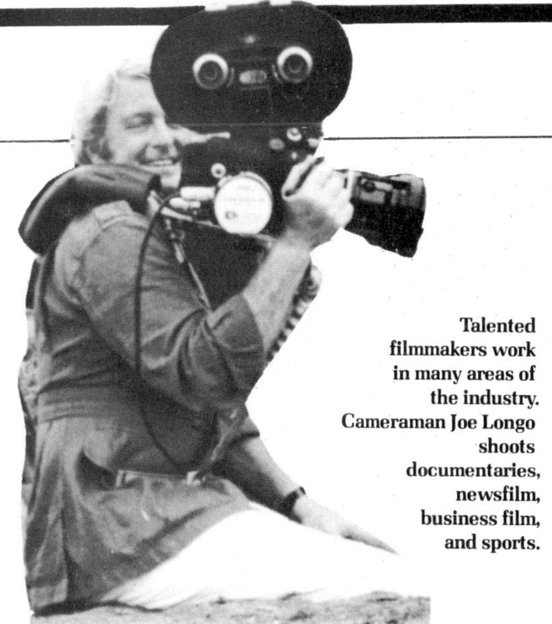

Talented filmmakers work in many areas of the industry. Cameraman Joe Longo shoots documentaries, newsfilm, business film, and sports.

In terms of job opportunities, a broad and diverse field exists out there that transcends the role of the director or producer or writer. Thousands of people are at work in the important supportive roles that help to shape a production, and many of them earn their livings in much smaller towns and cities than New York or Chicago or Hollywood.

Realistically, then, what does the film field look like? Leaving out the glamour, tinsel, and the larger-than-life dolls, let us, first of all, take a look at film as an industry.

THE FEATURE FILM

This part of the film industry is perhaps, in its own way, the most unstructured and haphazard segment. Yet, certain parts of the feature field are rigidly controlled and jobs are categorized by guilds and unions. More union people are employed in this area of filmmaking than in any other.

On the one hand, there is no doubt in anyone's mind that Hollywood is now run by businessmen, by corporations, and by the money-watchers in our society. With few exceptions, the days of the uncontrolled high budget have passed. Every once in a while, the studios smell a trend and pictures are produced quickly and expensively to catch the momentary public fascination with the occult, sharks, or disasters. Make no mistake about the fact that Hollywood has been dollar-conscious for many years now and that the profits on a box-office hit can be phenomenal.

On the other hand, the feature field is also a place where the independent, the foreign production, shoestring budget films, exploitation, and pornography have also made their marks. Also, every so often, a new film-school graduate directs a first film that manages to get distribution and moderately good reviews and a new career is launched. It is rare, when we look at the odds, but it does happen. And every once in a while a major studio overlooks or rejects a story that subsequently is produced independently and then makes nothing but money in the "boondocks," as Hollywood and New York bite their fingernails and ask, "What did we do wrong?" There are, in fact, hundreds of features that never even play the big-city circuits.

The feature film has a vast library of literature, and the neophyte would do well to read some of the books that tell how a feature is put together from script to screen.

Hollywood and New York are the production centers of the country. But the average feature production is less than promising for the beginner, since most crews are fully unionized and most production personnel have worked for producers or directors on other films. The feature film is, of all the film opportunities, the most closed, the most incestuous, the toughest one to crack. But more of that later.

The field has, of course, opened up more and more to the "independent" in the past few years, but even here we must qualify the statement. To produce a feature, you need money—and that money must be raised in the most painful of ways. After all, what bank wants to back a newcomer, no matter how good the idea might be? And, assuming that you have a great script, a rich father, and the best production unit in the field, where are you going to show it? The feature-film field is strewn with the husks of films that were produced for little money and then died on the vine because no one would put them in a theater. The larger chains prefer to deal with the major producers—the smaller ones and the independents are loath to take chances with a beginner. Certainly there have been exceptions. John Sayles, for example, has managed to maintain his independence by raising funds, finding distributors and contributing much of his own income to his productions (*Return of the Secaucus Seven, Baby It's You, The Brother from Another Planet*). But thousands of other independent films have died stillborn.

We are speaking of "producing" your own film—and I mention it early because in every filmmaker's heart of hearts there is the urge to make another *Godfather* or a *Son of The Terminator.*

In terms of job opportunities, the roadblocks are many, as I've mentioned before. In the areas of the major feature productions, all crafts are totally union, and most non-union crews are put together with an eye toward compatibility, experience, and proven talent.

Still, the feature is an important part of the field, and if there are even three budding Selznicks out there, they will never be discouraged—and that is all that matters.

THE DOCUMENTARY

The documentary covers a broad range of film opportunities, for the term really describes a *technique* rather than a particular type of film. In other words, the documentary today is seen even in the feature field, as in *When the Mountains Tremble* or *The Atomic Cafe. Battle of Algiers* used a documentary technique in a semi-fictionalized story. Networks use the documentary to tell their news stories in a longer, hopefully thoughtful form, while people like Frederick Wiseman (*Primate, Hospital*) have developed the television documentary into an art form.

When I use the word "documentary" I am generally referring to the use of what are laughingly called "real people" in "real situations." There usually are no actors, not even a script. The documentarian uses a particular locality as a replacement for the old studio and the set is all around him.

One of the reasons that the documentary grew to such awesome proportions is the fact that film equipment became more portable. At one time, the Mitchell camera was the only one really qualified to do a professional job; to do sound on location took three people; lighting any scene could take a truckload of equipment. All of the technical paraphernalia needed to produce a film was heavy, unwieldy, and difficult to handle. The cameras available needed firm support because of sheer weight and the hand-held camera was far in the future. Even the "small" lights took two people to put them into place and a change of scene in a studio production could take half a day or more. It was all the more amazing that people like Robert Flaherty could operate so well on locations as difficult as the Arctic.

With the invention of the Arriflex BL and then the cameras like the Eclair ACL, Cinema Products CP-16, and Arriflex 16SR—and with the introduction of the Nagra for sound, and small portable quartz lights—location shooting boomed and a crew can now consist of as few as three people. In our company, we have taken world trips that have lasted seven months, covered twenty countries, and have done synchronized sound on the entire job—and yet the crew numbered no more than three: camera, assistant doubling on sound, and director.

There is, certainly, a tendency to use the documentary as a crutch. Frequently, the so-called "documentary" turns out to be a series of "talking heads" without any other method of visualizing the story. And then, some years back, the term "cinéma vérité" became chic, and for some of us in the documentary field it caused extreme tremors. We viewed thousands of feet of film, through hours of screening. More often than not it was an excuse for bad exposures, jiggly unprofessional camera movements, and a quality of hollow sound that seemed to have been recorded in an echo chamber or a bidet. The term "cinéma vérité" has been fading out to some extent and we breathlessly await the newest development of bad documentary techniques.

The documentary, however, does offer job opportunities for the beginner. The mere fact that a film can be made with little equipment (unlike a feature) and with a small crew has encouraged thousands of beginners to produce their own films, or to make reasonably budgeted pictures for companies or foundations who want to spend only a small amount of money for their communications needs. Many smaller films are made outside the realm of the organized company. Some of them are quite good. Some are quite awful. But one thing we have learned over the years is that budget and size of crew have nothing to do with the final effectiveness of the picture. Sometimes one person, working alone, with dedication and talent and an instinctive film sense, can produce a film of sensitivity and quality. And sometimes one person can produce a prime example of disaster. But how many disasters have also been produced on budgets ranging from several hundred thousand to several million dollars?

The documentary is now used in or by the following areas:

- **TELEVISION** Both in news coverage and in the area of the "special," the networks use the form quite frequently.
- **SOCIAL ORGANIZATIONS** Here, the documentary is in one of its strongest areas of use. Produced for information, for fund raising, for training, the subjects range from birth control to prison reform, foster children, community education, United Funds, and the hundreds of disease-research organizations that need a powerful dissemination of information (cerebral palsy, heart disease, cancer, and multiple sclerosis).
- **FOUNDATIONS** Many of the foundation grants for film cover the subjects listed above. Some funds flow into the areas of education. For example, our company has recently completed a film for a local college with funds provided by a large foundation.
- **BUSINESS** We will cover more of this later on in this chapter, but suffice it to say that business and industry have begun to use the documentary with stockholder reports, orientation and recruiting films, sales films, and films about the social consciousness of corporations.
- **TRAVEL** This is really a part of the business area, since most of the travel films are contracted for by the airlines and by the states, countries, and travel organizations who use them most. This is a tricky area of filmmaking, since it is also a "glamour" aspect. Oh, to travel and have someone pay for it!! True, and it's hard work. And fun. And highly competitive. It is a prime example of the documentary technique—real people in real locations. How would you do a travel film in a studio?

Jaime Martin on location at the market in Lilongwee, Malawi, for the World Bank film Reflections on the 21st Century.

COMMERCIALS AND ADVERTISING AGENCIES

The two go together like peanut butter and jelly or Laurel and Hardy. Without the one there is no other. Without the advertising agency, the commercial film company does not exist. Both offer job opportunities. To the documentarian, there will never be an understanding of this most unusual part of the film business. Though my own reaction to it is as volatile as $KClO_3$ mixed with H_2SO_4, I have the utmost respect for a field that can tell an entire story in thirty seconds or one minute and do it professionally and well.

Basically, then, this job market is divided into two parts. The advertising agency is responsible to the client for developing the campaign, both in print and on the air, for purchasing the time and space for the advertising or the commercials, and for supervising the production in both areas. Specifically, in the field of the television commercial, the account executives are the direct contact with the business client, usually the people in the advertising department of the corporation. From that point on, through a series of meetings that determine the direction and thrust of the campaign, the agency copywriters and the art directors begin to develop "storyboards" for the spots—visual aids that help the commercial film company to determine its parameters and thus its final budget. Usually, an agency producer is also assigned to oversee the project—though, more and more, the art director seems to be moving into the area of strongest control. All this is an oversimplification, of course, but it serves to show that jobs are available on many levels in the industry and often forgotten by the film student.

The public-service film is an important part of the industry. Director/cameraman Lenny Hirschfield on location at West Point for an American Cancer Society spot.

For the film company itself, the structure is very much the same as in any other production unit. There is one exception, however: most agencies today seem to choose their production company on the basis of its *directors.* As film has changed, the director has taken over the "star" role in the field. This has been obvious in the feature field, and in the commercial field too. Added to that, the "hot" cameraman or cameraman-director makes a particular production company popular—until someone else replaces him with a new face. It is, to say the least, a very volatile field. By the same token, it also opens many opportunities for new people.

For those of us who do not work in the field of commercials, there is a story that has always described our feelings about it. With so many people involved in the creation and production, we were always convinced that if we saw two people huddled over a Moviola, they were cutting a feature. If we saw twelve people, they were cutting a thirty-second "spot"!

THE BUSINESS FILM

Years ago we called it the "industrial film" and it was just that. They were films made for industry, confined to the manufacturing process, and they generally were filmed right in the huge steaming factories or in a studio that was, for example, a recreated Standard Oil service station.

The distribution of these films took the same path as it does today. A professional distributor is paid by the corporation to see to it that the motion picture is shown before the target groups. There are several companies, but the largest is Modern Talking Picture Service. Their function is to distribute to what we call the nontheatrical audiences: clubs, men's and women's organizations, television, and schools. And that was exactly how they got to all of us back in our grade-school days. How many of us sat through the old Wilding or Jam Handy films while we were in school, looking up at the reel to see how much time remained for sleeping? Somehow the industry managed to survive and even grow to giant proportions—but how many bored victims did it leave in its wake?

Strangely, some of the old industrial clichés are *still* being produced, and now and again we screen one by accident and we laugh—and we even cry a little. Some years ago, in a lecture at Syracuse University, I tried to describe those industrial film clichés and I shall mention them here in the hope that this will be their final epitaph:

"IT ALL BEGAN . . ." (THE CAVEMAN PLOT) Every product, manufactured or homegrown, had its origin with the caveman. From there, our film for the Amalgamated Apple Cider Company progressed to the Egyptians, followed by the discovery of the wheel, which in turn allowed for the development of Electronic Cider Mills.

"THE TRIP THROUGH THE PLANT" This was the standard "nuts-and-bolts" picture—done entirely in medium and long shots. It always began in the receiving department, wandered endlessly past hundreds of workers chained to their machines—and ended with thousands of cartons being loaded on the shipping dock.

As writers became more creative and producers more daring, several variations of these themes began to appear:

A. "WHAT ARE YOU DOING, DADDY?" The extravaganza began in the home of a filmwriter, hard at work, typing his clichés. His young son, tired of torturing the cat, would turn and ask: "What are you doing, Daddy?" The father explained, "I'm trying to write a picture for the Yokohama Incense Company. You'd be surprised at how important incense is in our daily lives." Daddy was just about to take a trip through the plant and invited Junior, giving him a good excuse to talk to the audience on the level of a ten-year-old child.

B. "MELVIN WRITES HIS TERM PAPER" Melvin is a high-school senior and has been given an assignment to write his term paper on the

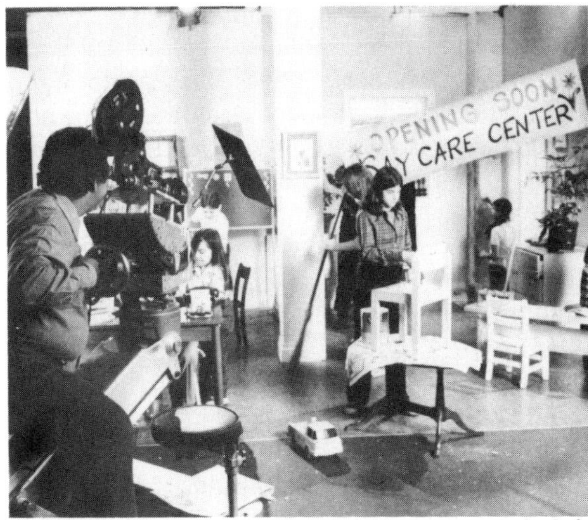

Thousands of organizations use motion pictures as a method of raising funds and gaining public support. Here, a spot is filmed for Girls' Clubs of America.

American Way of Doing Things at his local harness factory. Cordial workmen show Melvin how harnesses contribute to the American Way of Life. Melvin writes his term paper. Incidentally, we were astounded and a bit appalled at how this theme began to crop up again as America's bicentennial year approached.

Staff writers soon began to discuss their themes at length. The trip through the factory was getting dull and too recognizable. So they came up with a few other chestnuts, also dull and recognizable:

"THE SALES MEETING" We watched with bated breath as the dolly moved us closer and closer to a door marked SALES MEETING IN PROGRESS —NO ADMITTANCE. So, of course, we went right in. The sales manager was just beginning to speak: "Let me tell you how this company got to be the largest manufacturer of ten-penny nails in the country. It all began with our president back in 1644 . . ."

"THE LOCAL REPORTER" Assigned to do a story on why the Community Peat Moss Plant is important to our way of life, the Local Reporter told the story. An important costume point was to have the lead actor wear his hat with the brim pushed back.

"MISTER FLUGLE'S SEVEN BUGLES" This was a fantasy story generally produced by the Hollywood industrial film companies. It was generally a plot based upon a dream fantasy and it usually involved a leprechaun, an elf, a sprite, or an angel. It always began in Heaven or on Cloud Number Nine and our hero always looked down on mortal men with pity, for there was so much wrong with the Earth below. St. Peter then sent him on a mission: Reappear on Earth and show those puny mortals that an automatic electric range is so much better than cooking on Sterno. This approach gave a great deal of freedom for the then-budding field of trick photography.

"ANYTOWN, U.S.A." Self-explanatory—it also could be called Middletown or Yourtown or Ourtown and it really resembled Nobody's town.

"A VISIT FROM OLD BILL" In this one, a Young Man was about to be promoted to a job that we, in the audience, knew was much too big for him anyway. Suddenly, just passing through town is Old Bill (also known as "Good Old Bill"), who worked for the company for fifty years before he was forcibly retired. The next hour was spent with these two as the Young Man learned about the company and could now approach his job with confidence, though we still knew it was too big for him.

"WHAT WOULD THE WORLD BE LIKE WITHOUT..." A magnificent catch-all, this film theme could fit any industrial situation. For instance, what would the world be like without paper or rubber?

"CONSOLIDATED PLASTER CAST MANUFACTURING COMPANY IS, AFTER ALL, PEOPLE" This, generally, was a "sitting" picture. It opened with the president (or chairman) sitting at his desk; followed by accountants sitting at their desks; engineers and secretaries sitting at *their* desks; and the audience sitting in their seats and sleeping. It also brought to mind the ultimate title for this theme: "Automation Is, After All, People."

Well, the business film—like the entire film industry—has changed and, for the most part, the clichés outlined above have all disappeared. As early as the thirties, people like John Grierson and Len Lye began to use new techniques quite ahead of their times. The films produced by Grierson for the British General Post Office are still classics. Even today, the films *Color Box* (1935) and *Trade Tattoo* (1937), designed by Len Lye, seem contemporary in their thinking and execution. *Night Mail* (1936), produced by Grierson, directed by Harry Watt and Basil Wright, with an original score by Benjamin Britten and poetry by W. H. Auden, is a film worth seeing and studying. Norman McLaren and the young geniuses of the Canadian Film Board continued the experimentation and these fresh ideas were used in the business film long before the feature industry dared to attempt such innovations as flash-cutting, unusual optical effects, and electronic sound tracks.

Filmmakers began to bring new ideas to the business film and these same people became the leaders in an industry that had a huge potential—for the business film is one major area where funds are allocated before a project is even begun and the financial results are not subject to the vagaries of audiences. Wheaton Galentine, Francis Thompson, Tracy Ward, Charles Guggenheim, Bill Jersey, and my ex-partner, Lee Bobker, began to use and expand upon the techniques that are accepted as standard today: collage on film, micro-photography, and the seemingly mundane technique of just replacing the old medium shot with extreme close-ups. Perhaps most important is the fact that the documentary began to flourish as a new film form under the guidance of these business filmmakers, and new equipment was developed as a result of the changing and expanding business-film field.

Some producers have used the business film as a training ground and then gone into the feature field. Others are active in both parts of the industry at the same time and also produce commercials and television shows. In fact, for many years some of the largest motion picture corporations in the country were also active in the business field, utilizing their sound stages, costumes, writers, and equipment when these were not active in feature production. To this day, we find Paramount and Disney in competition for some of the higher-budgeted films to be produced for corporations.

Peter Vollstadt, cameraman/director for Ohio Bell, checks original footage at the company's editing facilities.

For the new filmmaker, job opportunities exist in a great many cities, though the business-film capital remains New York. But in Chicago, Atlanta, Detroit, St. Louis, Miami, Dallas, San Francisco, and Los Angeles (of course) the industry flourishes and the potential is there for still more growth.

The business film has become ever more sophisticated in the last decade. Almost all of the major corporations use some sort of audiovisual communication and film companies produce motion pictures for "corporate image," marketing, sales-training, fund raising, stockholder orientation, theatrical short-subject release, television, promotion, product introduction, retail clinics, and newsfilm.

IN-PLANT FILM PRODUCTION AND USE As industries grow larger, the tendency is to develop an in-house capability to produce audiovisual materials. For the most part, these departments limit themselves to the design and production of slide-film presentations, training tapes films of sales meetings, and newsfilm. However, many companies—such as the aircraft industry, appliance industry, and some major manufacturing companies—produce everything in-house and therefore need a large and varied staff to do the job: artists, designers, writers, camera operators, sound technicians, etc.

THE FILM INDUSTRY

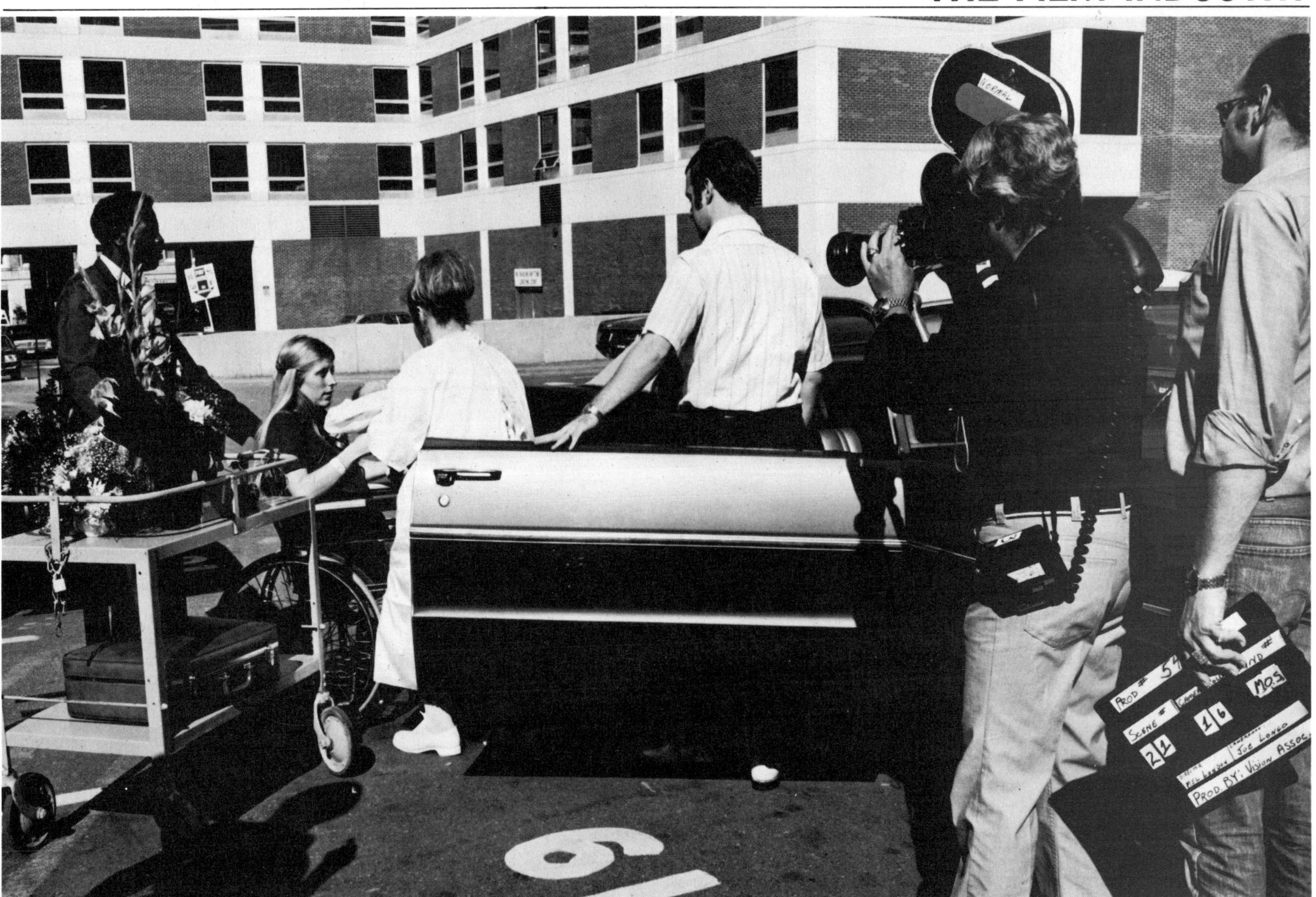

A documentary camera crew on location in Memphis for Reach Out and Touch, a motion picture produced for Methodist Hospitals. Hospitals throughout the United States use the documentary film for fund-raising, training, and public information.

MEDICAL FILMS

This fascinating area of film production has two basic entry opportunities: on the one hand, the business-film sector is quite active in the medical-film field—producing documentaries and training films for pharmaceutical companies, hospitals, or foundations; and a great many people are also employed directly by the hospitals themselves, working on-staff in close cooperation with doctors and surgeons for the purposes of record photography, production of finished training motion pictures, and audiovisual fund-raising programs.

In my own film *To Live Again* (an Academy Award nominee), some of the most dramatic photography in the film was provided by Dr. Irving Cooper of St. Barnabas Hospital and his photographer Rosemary Spitalari. As patients with Parkinson's disease were admitted to the hospital, they were photographed prior to the brain surgery so that their tremors could be studied. A few days following surgery, the patients were photographed again and the dramatic change could be noted. We used the material with great success and much of the acclaim given to the production was due to what would normally be called "record photography."

EDUCATIONAL FILMS

Companies that specialize in the educational field are usually related to book publishing. In other words, the major producers of films used in schools for educational purposes are owned by organizations in allied fields of communications. Certainly, there are exceptions, but if we study the reasons for this, it soon becomes obvious that it is a practical solution to the problem of distribution.

Joe Longo films a newborn infant in the nursery for Reach Out and Touch. Sterile caps and gowns were required, even for the camera crew.

Unlike the business film, the educational film works on infinitesimal budgets. The direct cost of the film is then hopefully recouped by the sale of prints to schools, groups, universities, and foundations around the country. Whereas the budget of a business film is expected to include costs, overhead, and profit for the producer, the educational film does not begin to show a profit until enough prints have been sold to absorb the initial cost.

Producers working in this field therefore make some sort of percentage royalty arrangement with the distributors, and the large sale of a film can bring income for many years. A few words of warning are due at this point—before everyone runs off to cash in on this bonanza of royalty payments. First of all, a film might *not* sell. Nothing more need be said about that. And second of all, the first glimmer of profit usually comes out about three to five years after production of the film—and then only if you have a "best-seller."

TELEVISION FILMS

This specific category is actually a shotgun marriage between the television industry and the feature-film field. Most of the television film fare is turned out by the major producers, but the networks decide through a rating system just what is going to reach our children and their parents. Hollywood still uses most of its back-lot areas and its stages for the production of TV films and pilots, and the coastline is strewn with the mutilated bodies of films that never made it to glory. In addition, a small and successful group of independents, such as Titus Production and David Wolper, have managed to make their way into network programming year after year, but essentially their production companies operate in exactly the same way as the major studios—for if there is a "show biz" category outside the feature film, this is it and the rules for getting work in the field are about the same.

Years ago the trend was to see the live TV director move into feature film. Today, there is no live programming to speak of, so the TV field and the feature have blended into one job market. Hollywood is the phoenix risen from the ashes. The union situation is very much the same in this category as it is in the feature field, and the job classifications are also the same. A beginner with a TV series idea or a script treatment for a specific show is almost always rejected by the industry. Though some TV series do have written specifications available for free-lance writers (sets, numbers of characters, etc.), entry is open only to established professionals or through an agent. In the area of production and the sale of pilots for future series, a few big names control most of the shows.

The picture is not all bleak, however. Even the established professionals of the business had to begin somewhere and at some level. It just looks hopeless if you're starving while your good ideas go unproduced.

The author's TV Special "Celebration" took the crew to fifteen countries. Above: The author with cinematographer Pete Henning and Masai. Below: In Hong Kong.

THE SHORT SUBJECT

Once upon a time there was a day when any moviegoer walked into the dimly lit theater and, before the feature was shown, saw a "Mickey Mouse," a travelogue, a featurette, or a combination of all of them, plus a game of Bingo and then a double feature. At first, these smaller films were produced in-house by the major motion picture companies. In later years, whenever short subjects were needed, they were farmed out to independent producers and then offered to the local movie theaters as a part of a package—mostly as a curtain raiser to let the audience get seated and stop rattling the popcorn boxes. That market began to disappear when the going rate to the producer of a short subject was about one hundred dollars a week. It was no way to make a living, the independents decided, and they went into more profitable fields.

One major distributor is now putting only five short subjects into the field each year. Others have cut back to no short-subject department at all. Most of the short subjects in theaters today are paid for by people who stand to gain by having their story told in a non-commercial and entertaining way. Travel films are now provided free by the airlines and the resort groups. Corporations who can tell their story without apparent commercialism are beginning to find that the theatrical short-subject audience is an untapped market. Some are being distributed by the companies who make features while others are put into theaters on a paid basis by commercial distribution firms such as Modern Talking Picture Service. In other words, the "sponsor" of the film pays the distributor and he, in turn, buys the time in theaters around the country. The short subject, generally about seven to twelve minutes in length, then plays as the curtain raiser in a one-and-a-half-hour program.

One's first reaction to this is that these films must be terribly commercial. Sometimes they are, and I have seen some of them booed out of the theater in vociferous and active places such as Greenwich Village in New York. But many others are incredibly good and quite ingeniously done, so that the commercial aspect is never apparent, except for a small logo at the end. The product is rarely introducted into the body of the film and the entertainment value is generally the criterion by which the film is judged. Certainly, the travel film is the best example that comes to mind and I have made these films for airlines and national organizations, as well as for foreign government tourism departments. In addition, companies as diverse as AT&T, Coca-Cola, the Franklin Mint, and Eastman Kodak have made theatrical short subjects that have been seen by audiences in every part of the United States as well as overseas.

INDEPENDENT AND EXPERIMENTAL FILM

At one time, not too long ago, they were one and the same. But the years and a modicum of popular sophistication have separated the categories. Thus, today, we have successful *independents* in the feature field (Sayles, Seidelman, Nava, Coen) as well as in the documentary (Wiseman, Guggenheim), while the true *experimental*, avant-garde filmmakers toil unheralded, alone, in their attics and basements, unsupported by the commercial world outside.

But, in spite of such anonymity, some interesting and exquisite film techniques have evolved from just such experimentation. Painting on film, computer animation, flash cutting, much of the object animation we see in today's commercials, have all originated with the avant-garde, while the rest of the film industry plodded along with the story of the caveman and the plot of boy-meets-girl. Even today, when—as Jean-Luc Godard commented wryly—Hollywood seems interested in making just *one* film that will be seen by *everybody*, the independents are still the hope for film as expression, self-examination and creativity.

Norman McLaren and Len Lye began their careers as experimental filmmakers. Carmen D'Avino, Kenneth Anger, Gregory Markopolous, Maya Deren, Stan Vanderbeek screened their first efforts at the now-defunct Cinema 16. Some audiences walked out, costs were never recouped, subject matter was outlandish (for the time), but the effort went on. As in any field, some were good, some were bad, and a very few were geniuses.

Many years ago, I worked for a company that was quite avant-garde in its thinking, even though we were working in business films. Many of the films we produced later became classics of the field (such as *Color and Textures* for Alcoa), but our company, unfortunately, went out of business because it strangely failed to grow with the times. Many of us in that company felt that one of our best sources of talent might be the field of the independent filmmakers. We attended the showings of Cinema 16, and we scoured the edges

A still from one of the classics of the documentary film, Nanook of the North, photographed and directed by Robert Flaherty in 1922.

of Greenwich Village and the waterfront of San Francisco for the people who were working on their own things. We finally found one —the savior of the business film, we thought. (He shall remain nameless since he still works as an independent twenty years later.) We brought him to Princeton, New Jersey, and put him in our studios and waited for the miracles to begin.

One day I returned from a location trip to Pittsburgh and happened to pass the editing room as he was working on a project to which he had been assigned. I stood at the door and watched for a while as he continued to work, oblivious of my presence.

He had a huge pair of scissors in one hand and a roll of 35mm color workprint in the other hand. In a series of deft movements he folded the workprint into halves, then quarters, and then cut the folds with the scissors. He did this again and again, while I stood in the doorway with my mouth hanging open. Finally, when the entire four hundred feet had been cut into three-foot lengths, he picked up the pieces, folded them in four parts, and again cut them into smaller pieces. The floor was littered by this time and again he started, folding and cutting, folding and cutting. The pieces of film were now about six inches long and I could stand it no longer. I asked, "Uh, could you tell me what you're doing?" He barely looked up as he began to cut again, and answered, "I'm rhythm-cutting." I watched a while longer and then asked, "Well, what about the Moviola over there?" and I motioned at the idle editing machine standing against the wall. He turned and, with the greatest disdain, say, "Oh, that? I never use one of *those* things!"

Needless to say, the wedding of the experimental film and the business world was short-lived. Every piece of workprint was thrown out and a new workprint was made at the lab and the entire job was turned over to a professional editor who knew how to use a Moviola.

NEWSFILM AND SPORTS-TRAINING FILMS

(For the most part, we are speaking of the cameraman in these film categories and we will cover the job in greater detail in a later chapter.) Not only does a local TV station usually have its own camera and sound crews and editors, but many of them use the material supplied by "stringers"—people who are not on salary, but who sell newsfilm to the stations on a per-assignment basis. A friend of ours down in Memphis owns a production company (Dixie Films, naturally), and he produces commercials, business films, and documentaries for the corporations in the area. But he is also a stringer for the TV stations and his camera is always in his car, so that it is not unusual to be traveling to a location and see him suddenly jam on his brakes and jump out of the car with his camera to photograph an accident on the highway. That night, his film will be seen by the TV viewers of the local news shows.

Professional and semi-professional athletic clubs all over the country use film for training purposes and for post-game critiques. Usually these films are done under contract by local cameramen or TV news people.

GOVERNMENT FILMS

This category represents a huge potential for the young filmmaker. True, many government films are sent out for bid to professional film companies, but again—as with industry—there are organizations in city, state, and federal government that have their own audiovisual departments and their own film staffs. Sometimes these people are merely the supervisors for handling outside contract work, but others actually get involved in the film production for their own departments. This includes scriptwriting, production, editing, post-production—as well as a large amount of work in the slide and slide-film area. Some departments even have laboratory services; others work with complete audiovisual exhibits that tie in with film and slides.

In the chapter devoted to getting a job in this field, I have tried to give a fairly comprehensive picture of the agencies of the federal government that have audiovisual departments. You will be amazed at how large the list is. It is another good example of why we have to think further than the feature, the documentary, and the commercial when we talk of the film field.

AND, OF COURSE . . . Since I am a great believer in the premise that a young filmmaker needs something to show to his prospective employer if he is to beat out the competition, don't forget the field of wedding and bar mitzvah photography . . .

A young Joe Longo on location in the Libyan desert for an early CBS series, "Air Power."

CHAPTER 3

WHAT THE JOB IS ALL ABOUT

Discovering the Twenty-Six-Hour Day

My youngest production assistant, Stephanie, has been with me for two years and she is the reason that this chapter has been inserted in the book. A few weeks ago she came to me for one of our usual afternoon talks, when my blood sugar (and thus, my morale) is low. She told me that it was a wonderful field (and it is) but, "You sure do work hard!" And you do. You do put in long hours.

Right after my talk with Stephanie, I left on location to shoot a film on marketing, and with me I had my usual crew. I realized, about three days out, that this trip was a perfect example of what she was talking about. We loved it. We really did. But look at the following itinerary, typed by our travel service. We traveled to six different cities in five days, five of which were practically impossible to get to, worked twelve to fourteen hours each day, and generally never had dinner much before ten or eleven at night.

ITINERARY FOR: MR. MEL LONDON

		DATE	TIME	VIA
LEAVE	N.Y. LA GUARDIA #1	July 23	8:30 AM	TWA #517
ARRIVE	COLUMBUS		10:03 AM	
LEAVE	COLUMBUS #2	July 23	1:05 PM	AMERICAN #364
ARRIVE	N.Y. LA GUARDIA		2:25 PM	
LEAVE	LA GUARDIA	July 23	6:45 PM	TWA #355
ARRIVE	CHICAGO #3		7:59 PM	
LEAVE	CHICAGO	July 24	4:30 PM	AMERICAN #28
ARRIVE	BOSTON #4		7:38 PM	
LEAVE	BOSTON	July 24	8:45 PM	DELTA #220
ARRIVE	PORTLAND #5		9:13 PM	
LEAVE	PORTLAND	July 25	5:00 PM	AIR NEW ENGLAND #649
ARRIVE	BOSTON #6		5:45 PM	
LEAVE	BOSTON	July 25	6:30 PM	AMERICAN #341
ARRIVE	N.Y. LA GUARDIA		7:23 PM	

CHECK IN AT: LA GUARDIA AIRPORT TIME: 8:00 AM

IMPORTANT NOTICE

Upon arrival at each destination city, please reconfirm your continuing or return flight, or at least 72 hours prior to departure. Failure to do so may result in cancelled reservation. Please recheck departure time, flight number and date. The above schedules may be changed at any time.

IF FOR ANY REASON, YOU HAVE A CHANGE OF PLANS, THE VALUE OF THIS TICKET SHOULD BE APPLIED TOWARDS THE COST OF ANY OTHER TICKET ON ANY OTHER AIRLINE.

So what, you say? It sounds great! Well, it was. But you surely don't get to see much of each city and you run into the quirks of weather, early restaurant closings, and location trips arranged by local people that should take ten minutes but end up with one hour's driving each way.

Here are some of the problems that we faced, per my circles on the itinerary:

Note #1. All planes leave very early or very late. No matter what flight you've booked, you always seem to be getting up before the sun has risen, and most film people are neurotic enough to be up before the alarm goes off—afraid that they'll miss the flight. In this case, the earliest flight we could get to Columbus was 8:30 A.M., but equipment must be checked in at the airport about one hour before that time. Working backwards from there, it was—as always—dark when we awoke.

Note #2. Note that I left Columbus at 1:05 P.M. *that same afternoon* to return to New York. The major shooting was completed in the morning, though we arrived at the location after 11 A.M. However, I had a New York appointment with a new client on July 23, and *not* on July 22 or 24; it was the only day he could make it and there was no argument. So, I returned to New York while my first client and the crew continued the job by doing the cutaways.

Note #3. The appointment took about thirty minutes and I went back to the airport and made the 6:45 P.M. plane to Chicago to meet the crew at the hotel. As a surprise, they had booked one of my favorite restaurants downtown, but a sudden thunderstorm hit and all the roads were washed out temporarily. We finally ate in the hotel dining room, something which is violently against my religion as a filmmaker.

Note #4. Notice that this is a connection. First of all, the trip seemed to consist of cities that were impossible to get to directly if you went from one to the other. This increased the chance of losing some of our equipment—we travel with anywhere from ten to fifteen pieces, plus personal luggage—and also makes the trip more fatiguing. Too, if we missed a connection, all the arrangements made by the client down the line would be wiped out and it would be impossible to complete the schedule in the allotted time.

Note #5. Note the time of arrival after working and traveling all day. When we got to the hotel, after picking up our equipment and getting it into the rented van, the hotel dining room was just closing. We were told that there was a twenty-four-hour pancake house next door, but we decided to try the town and we found a restaurant open until midnight (utterly impossible in most parts of the country). That night, tired as we were, we dined on three-pound lobsters and went to bed with indigestion from eating too much.

Note #6. This one is a beauty! Note that again we had to connect from Portland to New York through Boston. The week we were traveling was the one time that all the parents visit their offspring at summer camp, so Portland was packed solidly. No flights available, everything sold out for weeks. But we were lucky (!), and on leaving we were able to get three cancellations on a small Air New England Beechcraft going directly non-stop to LaGuardia Airport in New York. No connections. No delays. I saw myself fishing that evening at Fire Island. Our plane departed on time and was due to hit LaGuardia at 6:30 P.M. Over Poughkeepsie we were told that New York was encountering severe thunderstorms and that all traffic was backed up as far as the area over which we were flying. Delays into New York might take up to three hours, if we were lucky. Our little ten-seat plane didn't have the fuel for that, so we landed at Poughkeepsie and made telephone calls and drank Coca-Colas at the nearly deserted field. Finally, the pilot decided not to continue and we were sent almost one hundred miles into New York *by taxi*. We arrived at 11 P.M. and I did not go fishing that night.

The weekend intervened and I slept a lot. On Monday morning we started the second part of the trip. We left New York on July 28, did all our filming in Providence and left the same day for a flight to Baltimore, the next day's location.

This is the typical life of a film crew on location. Certainly, we have marvelous trips to Zagreb and Hong Kong, Paris and Nairobi. But the same travel rules apply for those places too, with the addition of as much as twenty-six hours' flying time! Remember, once you get there you usually have to begin the job, whether to survey the location or to begin shooting—even if the trip is twenty-two hours to Manila instead of two hours to Cleveland.

Certainly it would be wonderful to arrive in some lovely city and spend the first twelve hours sleeping, sightseeing, or swimming at the pool, but crew time is where the money is spent and any delay adds thousands of dollars to the budget. Salaries are high and overtime costs can be astronomical when we travel. In our company, what we have tried to do is pay our crews a large all-inclusive flat rate so that we need not worry about the eight-hour days. (If they exist at all.)

If you've gotten this far—and you realize how hard film crews work—and you still say, "So what? It sounds like fun"—then you might want to keep reading.

Let's look at some of the specifics in the job categories. What is it you might be doing?

CHAPTER 4

PRODUCTION

The "Glamour" and "Excitement" of the Film Business

If we were to take a survey of all candidates for potential film jobs, the results would probably show that 97 percent say, "I'd like to do something in production . . ." The job in production seems to have connected with it the "glamour" and "excitement" of the film industry and it seems a reasonable request for an entry-level position. But what is "production"? What is the difference between an assistant director, a production assistant, a production manager, a unit manager, a production coordinator, and any other title that indicates that the person works "in production"?

The best place to begin is to state that all of the titles listed above have similar functions. In one instance a production manager might never leave the office, while handling several film projects in all their multifaceted and complex details. The assistant director might be on location or in the studio and many of the same problems will haunt his working day. The same functions performed by an assistant director for a feature might well be covered by the production manager in a documentary unit. It can get very confusing if we stick to titles. Essentially, they all perform the same function, and all of them are "production people." If they're good at their jobs, they probably have the attributes of a saint, the stamina of a cross-country skier, and the knowledge of an encyclopedia.

A production conference at Snazelle Films, San Francisco.

Not everyone can be a good production person, though production is, by far, the best way to learn the most about the film business. Production people must be capable of making rational and quick decisions, be practical and worldly, know how to do most anything, and be willing to do it with flexible aggressiveness. Most of all, production people must be good with other people. Not all of them are, but the best of them meet that qualification. Some time ago, the magazine of the Directors Guild, *Action,* asked the question, "What is the hardest part of your job as assistant director?" and most of the answers dealt with the problems of working with diverse personalities, maintaining an atmosphere of harmony, communicating with people, and understanding different points of view. After that came the complaints about long hours, budget, and the problems of getting a job.

During my years in the film field, I have fired two production managers while on overseas assignments, both of them because of an inability to get along with people and an innate hostility toward foreign customs. Both had worked for me several years here in the United States and it came as a shock and a surprise when I found that they could not carry their job into another country. Production people are critical to the proper functioning of the entire crew and to the project itself. What knowledge is demanded of a production manager or an assistant director?

THE TELEPHONE AND HOW TO USE IT

If Alexander Graham Bell had not invented the ingenious little device, it would have been invented by a production person eventually. Without the telephone, production people would be lost. Everything—but everything—is set up by phone in the beginning stages of a schedule. Almost everything that follows must be started with a call: reservations, crew, equipment, transportation, permits, information . . . The successful production person is a joy to hear on a telephone conversation, acting as a guide, ambassador, questioner, convincer, executive. Remember, the telephone call is frequently the first contact made on behalf of the entire production. The reaction of the party at the other end may well determine just how far the crew will get in filming some delicate location (such as a hospital operating room). Think about what you might answer if the other person said to you, "No

way! We've had a film crew here before and they ran roughshod over our place." A good production person would eventually get the permission needed.

PLANNING

With the director, the production people must be able to break down the shooting script or treatment and plan the schedule. How many travel days to the locations—by air—by car—by bus? They take into consideration the length of each work day—will there be overtime? How much, and for how many members of the crew? How many shooting days? What about weather? Supposing it rains and exteriors are scheduled for that day—can an interior be shot at a nearby location so that the crew is being fully utilized? Is there an allowance for one day off a week? A seven-day schedule brings huge overtime penalties. Travel days are considered work days. Parenthetically, are there any "laundry" days in the schedule? A laundry day is one full day and night—usually on a weekday—in which the crew can turn in laundry in the morning and get it back that night. But supposing the location is at the Poison Oak Motel in Lower Seepage. Do they do laundry at all? All of this sounds minor, but just listen to the film crew that cannot get laundry done on a two-week trip. Who gets the complaints? Find the person in charge of production.

Studio shooting is still used for many television commercials, both on film and on videotape. Here, Gregg Snazelle, director, and Joe Feke, J. Walter Thompson producer, are shown on the set for a Ford Motor Company commercial.

CREWS

The production manager (or whatever his title) is usually the one who hires the crew for the film—making the original contact, giving dates and locations, setting fees. So he must know *how* to hire the crew, sometimes giving specific and firm dates, at other times giving "first refusal" (having first call on the crew member, should anyone else want him for that period). If this is a union crew, what are the regulations—do they travel First Class or Economy, what is the normal starting time and when does overtime begin? What about pension and welfare? How are travel days counted? Is there a per-diem arrangement or does the producer pick up all expenses for hotel and food? What is the function of each member of the crew and how many can do the job most economically? And again—that lovely word—"compatibility"; for a crew lives very closely together, and, whether in a studio or on location, personal habits and good humor are most important to a smoothly functioning operation.

Most production people make mental note of their favorites, and we find the same crews working over and over again as units, mostly because of compatibility.

TRAVEL

AIRLINES Take a look at the page from the *Official Airline Guide* (following page). It is a typical section from a monthly book that is the size of a telephone directory. Suppose you had to get a crew from New York to Dallas at a certain time. It's probably fairly simple and if you study the page for any length of time you'll soon find the non-stops, the ones that serve lunch or dinner, and whether the plane leaves from LaGuardia, Kennedy, or Newark. But supposing you had to get the crew to Dallas from Oshkosh, Wisconsin (see same page). There are no direct flights—only connections through Chicago and Milwaukee. There are connections to be made from one airline to another, some flights serve meals, some serve nothing at all. Some do not fly on Saturday (and that's probably just when you'll want to go), and the fares are different on various connections. The publisher of the *OAG* publishes an instruction book,* but most of your learning will come from using the *OAG* itself. We have also printed a self-test from the instruction book. (See pp. 20-21, and p. 21 for the answers.)

Production people must learn, especially, about air *fares*—how to devise packages that give them the best deal. Sometimes there are excursion fares, and special round-trip plans, and all of these must reflect in the budget, especially when the crews are large. Furthermore, commercial airlines don't fly into the middle of the canyon called for in the shooting script, so what about charter air companies, and how many planes are needed to take both crew and film equipment (as well as the personal luggage, with all the dirty laundry that has been collected so far)?

Various airline-reservation strategies become second nature—not the least of which is trusting no one and reconfirming (with names of the people on the other end of the line) and then reconfirming again, later. We once arrived at an airline counter (after double reconfirmation!) to find that two of us were booked on the flight, two had been booked for the following day, and two were in the computer on the flight that had gone the day before and thus had been canceled since they, naturally, had not shown up. What did we do? We jumped up and down on the supervisor and he got us on the flight, even though it was fully booked. (The name of the airline will remain unpublished, since they all manage this at one time or another. And they always blame you or "the computer.")

And then there's that problem of excess baggage. A film crew generally travels with no fewer than ten or twenty large pieces of equipment, plus personal luggage, plus hand baggage. Good production people count the number of pieces at least two times, make sure it all goes onto the moving belt, and then pray with the rest of us that it will arrive at the other end, every item accounted for and all of it undamaged. And if it doesn't happen that way, someone has to trace the lost pieces —always the film stock or the camera, never the unimportant electrical cable! And someone has to file the claims for the pieces that were dropped from ten feet onto a concrete floor. That person? Right again—our overworked and beloved production manager (assistant director, unit manager).

On a long trip to South America, we landed in Lima, Peru, on a dark and dreary night (about 1 A.M.) and two pieces of equipment failed to come off the plane and into the terminal. (The film stock and tape recorder this time.) Convinced that the luggage was still on the plane, the production manager tried to get the supervisor to keep it from taking off—and was firmly refused. Not to be put off, he leaped the fence past two armed guards and lay down in front of the wheels of the DC-8. It is something we would normally not recommend, and the ploy is nowhere to be found in the book of Production Management, but in this case the supervisor laughed and the plane was searched. Ideally, the story should end with everyone happy as we located the missing cases. No such luck. The luggage had been off-loaded in Bogotá, Colombia, by mistake and we got them the next afternoon, meanwhile losing one full day on our shooting schedule. But our production manager's attitude was the thing that we find in most good production people, even though his will to live seemed a bit faint.

Finally, production people must be familiar with air cargo and air freight carriers who will deliver film stock back to the laboratories

**Complete Instructions in the Use of the Official Airline Guide* (Reuben H. Donnelly Corp., New York).

Freq. Leave Arrive Flight Class Eq Ml S

To DALLAS/FT. WORTH, TEXAS CDT DFW

D-DFW (DALLAS/FT. WORTH)
L-DAL (LOVE FIELD)

From NEW ORLEANS, LA.-CONT. [illegible]

NEWPORT NEWS, VA. EDT PHF — CONNECTIONS [illegible]

NEW YORK, N.Y. EDT NYC [illegible]

NOME, ALASKA BDT OME — CONNECTIONS [illegible]

NORFOLK, VA. EDT ORF — CONNECTIONS [illegible]

To DALLAS/FT. WORTH, TEXAS CDT DFW

From NORFOLK, VA.-CONT. [illegible]

OAKLAND, CALIF. PDT OAK [illegible]

OKLAHOMA CITY, OKLA. CDT OKC [illegible]

To DALLAS/FT. WORTH, TEXAS CDT DFW

From OKLAHOMA CITY, OKLA.-CONT. [illegible]

OMAHA, NEBR. CDT OMA [illegible]

ONTARIO, CALIF. PDT ONT [illegible]

ORLANDO, FLA. EDT MCO [illegible]

To DALLAS/FT. WORTH, TEXAS CDT DFW

From ORLANDO, FLA.-CONT. [illegible]

OSHKOSH, WIS. CDT OSH — CONNECTIONS [illegible]

OTTAWA, ONTARIO EDT YOW — CONNECTIONS [illegible]

PADUCAH, KY. CDT PAH — CONNECTIONS [illegible]

PALESTINE, TEXAS CDT PSN — COMMUTER AIR CARRIERS [illegible]

PALM SPRINGS, CALIF. PDT PSP — CONNECTIONS [illegible]

PANAMA CITY, FLA. CDT PFN — CONNECTIONS [illegible]

CONT. NEXT PAGE

NORTH AMERICAN EDITION — FOR EXPLANATION OF CONNECTION FARES FORMAT SEE "HOW-TO-USE" SECTION — July 1, 1976 Page 255

SELF-TEST

Here is a self-test to see what you have learned. Use opposite page for schedule information.

A. The first morning non-stop flight from Pittsburgh to Miami on December 23 is ________ Airlines flight number ________ leaving at ________ and arriving at ________. The type of aircraft is a ________. The class/es of service is/are ________. Do both First Class and Coach passengers receive the same type of meal service? ________.

B. What is the one-way fare, including tax, on a Sun Valley Key (Commuter Air Carrier) flight from Salt Lake City to Grand Junction? ________.

C. What is the 7-21 day excursion fare published between Pittsburgh and Miami? ________. Does this include tax? ________.

D. The Military Reservation fare one-way, including tax, between Grand Rapids and Chicago is ________.

E. From what airport does the 7:10 a.m. flight from New York to Philadelphia depart? ________.

F. What is the latest time on Saturday a passenger could depart El Paso, Texas to fly to Cincinnati, Ohio? ________. The connecting city for this flight is ________. From ELP to the connecting city, the passenger would fly on ________ Airlines flight number ________. This flight arrives at ________. Is there any meal service? ________.
From the connecting city to CVG, the passenger uses ________ Airlines flight number ________, departing at ________ and arriving at ________. How many stops does this flight make? ________. Is there any meal service? ________. What is the total fare (including tax) for a Jet Coach passenger on this connection? ________.

G. What is the latest time on a Saturday that a passenger could depart New York's JFK Airport to fly to Philadelphia? ________.

A page from the Official Airline Guide. This book is the production manager's Bible. Above, and pp. 20-21. The publishers of the Official Airline Guide provide this instructional test for the beginner.

H. A passenger wants to fly from Springfield, Ill. to Grand Rapids, Mich., leaving as early in the day as possible. Determine the best possible schedule.

Connecting city ____________.

Springfield to connecting city ________________.
(carrier and flight number)

Connecting city to Grand Rapids________________.
(carrier and flight number)

I. How many miles and in what direction is the Grand Rapids airport from the city? ________. What type of ground transportation is available? ________.

(Answers are on next page)

Freq.	Leave	Arrive	Flight	Class	Eq	Ml	S
To CHICAGO, ILL. CDT CHI							
C-CGX (MEIGS FIELD) O-ORD (O'HARE) M-MDW (MIDWAY)							
From **SPRINGFIELD, ILL.** CDT SPI							
A 25.93 2.07 28.00 56.00							
QX 1 A 25.93 2.07 28.00 56.00							
1 INTRASTATE							
S 27.78 2.22 30.00 60.00							
UX YM 19.00							
OZ YM 22.00							
UX YZ 19.00							
QX•YM 19.00							
• INTRASTATE							
QX•YZ 19.00							
• INTRASTATE							
	6:27a	7:40a O	OZ 920	SB	D9S		1
X67	9:35a	11:00a O	OZ 816	SB	FH7		1
	11:05a	12:15p O	OZ 956	SB	D9S		1
X67	1:00p	2:00p O	OZ 820	SB	FH7		0
67	2:20p	3:45p O	OZ 890	SB	FH7		1
X67	3:05p	4:30p O	OZ 826	SB	FH7		1
X6	4:47p	5:47p O	OZ 842	SB	FH7		0
	5:25p	6:25p O	OZ 848	SB	FH7		0
X6	7:03p	8:30p O	OZ 854	SB	FH7		1
INTRA - STATE							
X67	7:00a	7:45a C	QX 701	A	748		0
X67	9:00a	9:45a C	QX 703	A	748		0
X67	1:45p	2:30p C	QX 705	A	748		0
X67	3:45p	4:30p C	QX 707	A	748		0
X67	5:45p	6:30p C	QX 709	A	748		0
COMMUTER AIR CARRIERS							
X67	7:20a	8:20a C	UX 212	A	DTO		0
67	1:30p	2:30p C	UX 422	A	DTO		0
X67	4:30p	5:30p C	UX 152	A	DTO		0

Freq.	Leave	Arrive	Flight	Class	Eq	Ml	S
To CINCINNATI, OHIO EDT CVG							
From **EL PASO, TEXAS** MDT ELP							
CONNECTIONS							
A 132.41 10.59 143.00 F JT/THRU							
B 126.85 10.15 137.00 F ((SDF))							
C 101.85 8.15 110.00 FnY JT/THRU							
D 98.15 7.85 106.00 Y ((SDF))							
E 90.74 7.26 98.00 Y ((ABQ))((IND))							
F 81.48 6.52 88.00 YN THRU							
6	3:15a	9:15a	AA 206	FnYnB	72S	S	0
(CF@)	5:40a DFW	6:15a	AA 70	FnYnB	707	B	0
X6	3:15a	9:15a	AA 206	FnYnB	72S	S	0
(CF@)	5:40a DFW	6:15a	AA 70	FnYnB	727	B	0
	3:15a	12:01p	AA 206	FnYnB	72S	SB	1
(BD@)	8:54a ORD	10:05a	DL 759	FYB	D9S		0
	7:00a	2:42p	AA 332	FYB	707	B	1
(AC@)	11:54a ORD	12:45p	AA 282	FYB	727	S	0
	7:00a	2:56p	AA 332	FYB	707	B	1
(AC@)	11:54a ORD	1:00p	DL 643	FYB	D9S	S	0
	8:40a	3:55p	CO 204	FYKB	72S	B	0
(ACE@)	11:04a DFW	12:55p	AA 342	FYB	707	L	0
	8:45a	3:55p	AA 98	FYB	72S	B	0
(AC@)	11:10a DFW	12:55p	AA 342	FYB	707	L	0
	12:13p	8:23p	AA 116	FYB	727	L	0
(AC@)	3:59p ORD	6:30p	DL 337	FYB	72S	S	0
6	2:20p	9:20p	AA 128	FYB	D10		0
(AC@)	4:45p DFW	6:20p	AA 394	FYB	727	D	0
X6	2:20p	9:20p	AA 128	FYB	D10		0
(AC@)	4:45p DFW	6:20p	AA 394	FYB	707	D	0
X6	2:50p	11:24p	AA 336	•	707	D	1
(•)	8:01p ORD	9:25p	AA 216	FYB	727		0
AA 336 FYKB-SAT-FYB							

Freq.	Leave	Arrive	Flight	Class	Eq	Ml	S
To GRAND JUNCTION, COLO. MDT GJT							
From **SALT LAKE CITY, UTAH** MDT SLC							
A 27.78 2.22 30.00 60.00							
FS A 36.11 2.89 39.00 78.00							
S 27.78 2.22 30.00 60.00							
FL YM 22.00							
6	1:50p	2:42p	FL 578	S	CV5		0
FL 578 EFFECTIVE DEC 7							
	6:28p	7:20p	FL 515	S	CV5	S	0
CONNECTIONS							
A 77.78 6.22 84.00 CC							
B 73.15 5.85 79.00 CC							
C 62.67 5.01 67.68 S CC-T							
D 60.82 4.87 65.69 CC-T							
E 42.59 3.41 46.00 S ((GUC))							
	7:25a	10:45a	TT 989	SB	DC9	B	0
(C@)	8:30a DEN	10:00a	FL 63	SB	73S		0
	7:35a	10:45a	FL 14	SB	73S	B	0
(E@)	8:40a DEN	10:00a	FL 63	SB	73S		0
	7:40a	10:45a	UA 166	FYB	727	B	0
(AC@)	8:45a DEN	10:00a	FL 63	SB	73S		0
	12:00n	2:39p	FL 62	SB	73S	L	0
(BD@)	1:03p DEN	1:55p	UA 303	FYB	727		0
X6	3:30p	6:47p	TT 987	SB	DC9		0
(C@)	4:35p DEN	5:50p	FL 677	SB	CV5	S	0
X6	5:00p	8:44p	FL 66	SB	73S	S	0
(E@)	6:03p DEN	7:47p	FL 675	SB	CV5		0
6	5:00p	9:04p	FL 66	SB	73S	S	0
(E@)	6:03p DEN	7:47p	FL 875	SB	CV5		1
X6	6:25p	9:27p	WA 492	Y	737	D	0
(C@)	7:30p DEN	8:30p	FL 671	SB	CV5		0
COMMUTER AIR CARRIERS							
	5:30a	7:10a	FS 362	A	PNV		2
X7	12:15p	1:25p	WE 103	A	PRP		0
X7	5:30p	6:40p	WE 170	A	PRP		0
	6:00p	7:40p	FS 366	A	PNV		2

Freq.	Leave	Arrive	Flight	Class	Eq	Ml	S
To GRAND RAPIDS, MICH. EDT GRR							
13.0 MI SE 30 MIN T RA							
CHICAGO, ILL. CDT CHI							
M-MDW, O-ORD, C-CGX							
F 27.78 2.22 30.00 60.00							
S 21.30 1.70 23.00 46.00							
Y 21.30 1.70 23.00 46.00							
YM 17.00							
7	5:55a O	7:38a	UA 572	FYB	737		0
X67	8:00a O	10:09a	NC 911	SB	CV5		1
	8:44a O	10:27a	UA 642	FYB	737		0
	12:00n O	1:46p	UA 650	FYB	737		0
	12:30p O	2:36p	NC 915	SB	CV5		1
	1:15p O	3:00p	UA 770	FYB	737		0
	3:25p O	5:10p	UA 628	FYB	737		0
	4:50p O	6:56p	NC 919	SB	CV5		1
X6	7:20p O	8:57p	NC 106	SB	D9S		0
	7:40p O	9:28p	UA 626	FYB	737		0
	9:30p O	11:07p	NC 927	SB	D9S		0

Freq.	Leave	Arrive	Flight	Class	Eq	Ml	S
To MIAMI, FLA. EDT MIA							
From **PITTSBURGH, PA.** EDT PIT							
P-PIT, A-AGC							
F 108.33 8.67 117.00 234.00							
Y 83.33 6.67 90.00 180.00							
FN 83.33 6.67 90.00 180.00							
YN 65.74 5.26 71.00 142.00							
YM 68.00							
EX/4 Y 7-21 DAY 139.00							
	9:00a P	11:19a	EA 303	FYB	D9S	B	0
EA 303 DISCONTINUED AFTER DEC 2							
	9:00a P	11:19a	EA 303	FYB	72S	B	0
EA 303 EFFECTIVE DEC 3							
	9:10a P	2:04p	EA 731	FYB	D9S	L	3
	9:55a P	12:15p	UA 563	FYB	727	L	0
	12:05p P	3:26p	EA 305	FYB	727	L	1
	5:50p P	9:37p	EA 327	FYB	727	D	1
	6:30p P	8:50p	UA 315	FYB	727	D	0
6	6:55p P	10:07p	EA 309	FYB	72S	D	1
	10:35p P	12:56a	EA 483	FnYnB	D9S	S	0
EA 483 EFFECTIVE DEC16							

Freq.	Leave	Arrive	Flight	Class	Eq	Ml	S
To PHILADELPHIA, PA. EDT PHL							
From **NEW YORK, N.Y.** EDT NYC							
J-JFK, L-LGA, S-WKW, E-EWR							
F 21.30 1.70 23.00 46.00							
NA F 22.22 1.78 24.00 48.00							
NW F 22.22 1.78 24.00 48.00							
A 19.44 1.56 21.00 42.00							
DR A 25.00 2.00 27.00 54.00							
Y 16.67 1.33 18.00 36.00							
NA Y 17.59 1.41 19.00 38.00							
NW Y 17.59 1.41 19.00 38.00							
FN 16.67 1.33 18.00 36.00							
YN 12.96 1.04 14.00 28.00							
YM 14.00							
NA YM 15.00							
NW YM 15.00							
	2:10a E	2:44a P	DL 689	FnYnB	D8S		0
	7:10a L	7:55a P	EA 519	FYB	727		0
	7:50a E	8:30a P	EA 507	FYB	727		0
	9:00a E	9:32a P	DL 257	FYB	72S		0
X6	10:30a E	11:06a P	NW 537	FYB	727		0
	1:45p E	2:22p P	NA 411	FYB	72S		0
	3:07p J	3:53p P	NA 415	FYB	72S		0
X6	4:15p E	4:52p P	NW 223	FYB	727		0
	6:55p E	7:32p P	NA 417	FYB	72S		0
	9:00p E	9:40p P	EA 481	FnYnB	D9S		0
EA 481 EFFECTIVE DEC16							
COMMUTER AIR CARRIERS							
X67	9:00a S	9:30a S	DR 9	A	DTO		0
X67	9:30a J	10:15a P	WQ 161	A	HRN		0
X67	11:00a S	11:30a S	DR 11	A	DTO		0
X67	1:00p S	1:30p S	DR 1	A	DTO		0
X67	2:15p J	3:00p P	WQ 163	A	HRN		0
X67	3:00p S	3:30p S	DR 3	A	DTO		0
	4:45p J	5:30p P	WQ 165	A	HRN		0
X67	5:00p S	5:30p S	DR 5	A	DTO		0
X67	6:15p S	6:45p S	DR 7	A	DTO		0
	7:15p J	8:00p P	WQ 167	A	HRN		0
	9:45p J	10:30p P	WQ 169	A	HRN		0

Answers to previous questions:

A. Eastern 303 9:00 a.m. 11:19 a.m. Boeing 727-200
Jet First Class/Jet Coach/Controlled Inventory-Coach Yes

B. $39.00

C. $139.00 Yes

D. $17.00

E. LGA (La Guardia)

F. 2:20 p.m. DFW (Dallas/Ft. Worth) American 128 4:45 p.m. No
American 394 6:20 p.m. 9:20 p.m. 0 Yes (Dinner) $110.00

G. 9:45 p.m.

H. Chicago OZ 920 UA 642

(The passenger could not use QX 701 which leaves SPI later than OZ 920, which seems to have enough Minimum Connecting Time, because QX 701 arrives at Meigs Field (C) and not O'Hare (O). Additional traveling time is required between airports at the connecting city).

I. 13.0 miles southeast taxi, rental car

69.

The NAOAG is published twice monthly — normally to be effective on the 1st and 15th of each month. Each edition incorporates changes received by the publisher prior to the date printing begins (several weeks prior to the effective date of the book).

The publishers have reserved one page (6), called the "Stop Press" page, for changes received too late to be included within the regular listings. It is extremely important the Guide users examine the "Stop Press" page immediately upon receipt of each new edition. Pencil corrections should be made in the regular listings of the NAOAG. The changes contained on the "Stop Press" page will automatically be incorporated within regular listings in the next printing of the Guide.

from location. Which ones are the most reliable? Which ones are, indeed, even available at the location site? And, should a piece of equipment break down, what is the quickest way to have a new one sent out to the crew?

HOTELS AND RESTAURANTS There are many hotel guides, and there can usually be found a history of travel that helps to choose a specific hotel or motel; there are recommendations —good reports and bad reports. Some hotels are better with film crews than others. (At one time, a chain of deluxe hotels in Europe would not take any film crews, after a bad experience with a group of Hollywood stars.) Most cameramen and their assistants require ground-floor motel accommodations with an outlet to their cars, because the camera and film magazines are brought in each night for cleaning and loading. So production people read the AAA guides, the Mobil guides, and others that are available and they soon learn to read between the lines when accommodations are described.

Some production managers like particular chains. My own production manager books places that have saunas (even if they don't have rooms). Some hotels give commercial rates—and all good production people *demand* confirmations (and reconfirmations, as well as the name of the person confirming the reservation). When a crew "guarantees" a reservation in a hotel it means that they pay whether they show up or not and the room is held through the night for them. But sometimes the hotel or motel has a "guaranteed" reservation and still gives the rooms away. It is one o'clock in the morning and the crew has traveled two hundred miles by car. Someone has to fight it out—of course, the production person.

And—film crews must be fed. Most eating places in the United States are crowded between 12 noon and 1 P.M. and empty after that. But getting a crew in and out of a restaurant in one hour is usually an impossible job. Should the lunch be set up in advance? Should it be catered on location by a local service? What about a picnic lunch and who will deliver it? Would it help if menus were brought to the location and the crew chose the lunch at 10 A.M. to be ready for them at noon? And then, having done all that, suppose the director decides to work one hour overtime, until 1 P.M., and the lunch sits and waits and gets cold or warm, or spoiled? "Don't complain to me. I'm the director. Tell the production manager!"

CARS, VANS, BUSES, BOATS, AND VARIOUS OTHER FOUR-, SIX-, AND EIGHT-WHEEL CONVEYANCES There is Hertz and there is Avis and there are National and Airways and Budget and a hundred others, and for the average sedan it's an easy matter to book a car. (With reconfirmations as usual.) But if we start with the premise that film crews travel with large amounts of luggage (and we have already set that premise), then sedans are not very good. Feature locations with large casts also require "honey wagons" (portable toilets). We need station wagons—or vans—or buses. But station wagons can be hard to work from, and vans and buses are hard to locate. You, as the production person, merely have to guarantee that two large vans will meet your 2 A.M. flight in West Bubblegum (which will arrive two hours late). From that point on, you'd better know how to read a road map so that you can deliver the crew right to the motel on Rural Route 238.

LOCATION SCOUTING

Someone on the production staff has to look at the location before the crew arrives. This is not always a prerequisite, of course, but on any complex shoot it certainly saves time if someone has scouted the place. Too often, a "charming house" turns out to be a run-down shack, and many times the promise of "plenty of power" means that two electrical shavers can be plugged in instead of the usual one and any kind of movie light would blow the circuits for twenty miles down the road. So a good production person knows something about electrical-power requirements. What kind of lighting is to be required to do the job? How many amps are available? What kind of power? And where are the outlets or the main boxes? There are other factors: Is there any noise that might present problems to a sound man? Airports nearby? Reapers in the field? A highway? Schoolyard? And, above all, what is the visual effect of that location on the structure of the film? In other words, is it right? Most production people keep a file of the locations or potential locations that they see while on other jobs. And all of them must know how to get film permits where they're required—from the city, the private owner, the township, the building . . . In New York City it requires one kind of permit; in Peoria you probably would not need a permit to shoot. But a good production manager always asks.

EQUIPMENT AND FACILITIES

If you handle production, either on a free-lance basis or for a company, a part of your job will include the rental and, occasionally, the purchase of equipment. What kind of camera will be needed, and what kind and how many lenses, batteries, magazines, cables? If the camera operator is providing some of the equipment, such as a personally owned camera, what will you need to order to fill it out? What about a backup camera? Lighting? What will be needed for the job and have you decided to ship it ahead, rent it on location, or carry it right with you as personal luggage? Sound? Dollies? Helicopters? And is there a pilot available who is good enough to handle the chopper while a cameraman is working through an open door? What about Tyler mounts—the rig that helps keep the camera steady in a helicopter? Does the cameraman want one, need one, and would it be just as good to use a gyroscopic device, at one tenth the price? Laboratories and film stocks? Hydrofoils and cherry pickers? And, of course, all at the best possible price.

PEOPLE AND ANIMALS

Some jobs use actors, some use "real people" on location. Frequently, and especially in the lower-budget films, production people are expected to know where to find the agents who handle the talent, to know the best place to locate a home economist or a narrator or children, or, as one of our people calls them, "critters"—dogs, cats, cows, and other varied livestock. Most production people keep complete files, never knowing when the next piece of information may be needed for a production.

We heard a story recently about one such case. A production manager on a commercial that was being shot in New York was told to find eight baby elephants and get them to the studio as quickly as possible. There had been a change in script and time was of the essence. He found the animal talent agency through his files, went over at lunchtime and, sure enough, the eight baby elephants were waiting for him. He ran out into the street, hailed eight large Checker taxicabs, put one elephant in each,

The late Jock Leslie-Melville and his wife, Betty, combined a safari company with the production of their travel and animal films. With them is the star of one of their features, the giraffe, Daisy Rothschild.

and the convoy made its way back to the studio in time for the shot. Frankly, I'm not even certain the story is true. But it's typical and it doesn't surprise me at all.

Production ingenuity can be found in other areas. Recently, we were asked to do a film for National Park Service, *Kings Mountain: Turning Point in the South*. Since the location gave very little photographic opportunity—it was merely a national park built on a former battle site—we decided that re-creating some of the battle might be an excellent way to present the story. The idea was good—but the budget was too thin to hire actors. The production manager got on the telephone and began to call historical societies all around the country. In about one week of intensive contacts he discovered that there were actually two groups in existence which were carbon copies of a British unit and a Tennessee Mountain unit that fought the Revolution in the area. Both groups had full costume, both held weekly bivouacs in the area, both were authentic, colorful, and historically accurate—and *both* said they would be more than willing to appear in the film if we would buy new muskets for their armory. As a result, the completed film shows the 63rd Regiment of Foot and John Sevier's Mountain Men in a colorful re-creation of the era. And the production value of the film was far greater than if we had used drawings or abstractions to tell the story.

But, over all, the handling of people is the thing that keeps coming back to me in describing the production job. The good production person "baby-sits" for the crew, takes care of their laundry and their reservations, finds lost and misplaced articles, tips the bellmen, skycaps, taxi drivers, and chambermaids. Diplomacy is a real part of the job, for people must often be convinced that they should allow the film crew inside their homes, in their factories and research labs, and into their offices. Letters of request must be written, so production people become talented letter writers too, for the written word may be the first contact in asking for permission to film. After the job is done, letters of thanks must also be sent—by our overworked production manager, of course. To this we can add, also, the angry letters (and complimentary ones) that go out to hotels or airlines that have given extremely bad (or extremely good) service.

Of course, some productions—particularly documentaries—use "real people": people on the street who happen to be passing, working people in the pursuit of their normal jobs, or just curious watchers as a film crew sets up on a street somewhere. Someone has to ask the stranger, "Sir (or madam), do you mind if we interview you?" or "Sir (or madam), would you mind standing on the parapet of the World Trade Center while we take this little old shot?" Well, some people mind and some people are natural hams. It is an art, nevertheless, to get people to appear in your films, because (1) most people are immediately shy when you ask them to do so, (2) the hams generally turn out to be less than adequate, and (3) even if they do agree to appear in the film, someone has to get a release from them so that you can use the shot in your film. "What is it I'm signing?" they ask, all at once suspicious. There is no one way to do it; every production person finds the easiest path. Here is a sample release form.

POST-PRODUCTION

Following the shooting of the film, it goes through a series of stages. Some production people, particularly those in feature films, are mainly concerned with this area, called post-production. They must know about editors, screening rooms, labs, mixing studios, title and optical houses, special effects, and finishing costs. They are responsible for shepherding the film through to its final completion—the answer print.

OVERSEAS PRODUCTION

Take everything that has gone before in this chapter, add a ten-hour or a twenty-five-hour air trip (with severe jet lag), and then add to that the following areas of knowledge that you must have—and you will have a fair idea of what production people need for their job while on a foreign location:

- Currency exchange
- Languages. Even a few words will help, but a conversational working knowledge can be an incredible asset.
- Brokers and how they are used
- Allowances for cargo and personal effects for shipment of luggage and equipment
- U.S. Customs
- Foreign Customs
- Bonding of equipment
- Registration forms
- The use of the carnet. An international docu-

DATE:_____________

PRODUCTION:________

Vision Associates Inc.
665 Fifth Avenue
New York, N.Y. 10022
212-935-1830

PERSONAL RELEASE

I, ___________________, for just and sufficient consideration, receipt of which is hereby acknowledged, hereby irrevocably grant to Vision Associates, Inc. your successors and assigns the right to record my likeness and/or voice or film, to edit such film at your discretion, to incorporate the same into a motion picture, tentatively titled:_____________, and to use or authorize the use of such film or any portion thereof in any manner or media at any time or times throughout the world in perpetuity and to use my name, likeness, voice and biographical and other information concerning me in connection therewith, including promotion in all media but not for the endorsement of any product or service.

I hereby release you and anyone using said film or other material and from any and all claims, damages, liabilities, costs and expenses which I now have or may hereafter have by reason of any use thereof.

Signature:____________________

Address :____________________

A typical release form. Written permission is required from anyone who is to be photographed or recorded. Generally, it is the function of the production assistant to get the signature.

ment used in bringing equipment across borders, it is recognized as a standard Customs document by many countries throughout the world.

•Local contacts overseas

KEEPING CURRENT

Since there is so much free time on the job, all good production people manage to keep up with the field through reading everything available: *Backstage*, *Variety*, *American Cinematographer*, equipment catalogs, and every other newspaper and magazine that will keep them up-to-date on the latest technology, news, and film information.

And finally:

THE BUDGET

Though the details of budget are in another section of this book, production people *must* know comparative costs in every one of the areas mentioned in this chapter. You've located those elephants and you've been ingenious in getting them to the studio and you've saved the day, *but* you spent too much money. You discover, to your great dismay, that you really aren't a very good production manager at all!

Look the position of production manager, etc., over carefully. There are really no exaggerations in the above job description. It is one of the most trying jobs in film—and one of the most rewarding, as everything (hopefully) falls into place. And—as my own assistant, Jon

Fauer, once said—it has to be done without becoming:

(a) neurotic
(b) paranoid
(c) exhausted
(d) all of the above

A TYPICAL DAY Reviewing all the details that production people must know, we must admit that certainly they do not come into play all at once. Of course not. In any given day, only thirty or forty of these problems are ever obvious and some days are easy ones with only a few catastrophes befalling the crew. Most important, keep in mind that the average day is *not* eight hours. With all the pre-planning necessary, the reconfirmations, the changes in plans, and the normal shooting schedule to boot, the day can run twelve or fourteen hours without anyone half trying. After a particularly strange and complex shooting schedule, I asked our production manager to outline in diary form just what the day had been. Here is his report:

Tuesday, March 25

The "day" actually begins the previous evening. Crew is flying in from various points. Cameraman and production manager from Miami. Director from New York, client from Atlanta. It will be a miracle if they all meet on schedule in Houston so that they can drive to the hotel together. They don't. The plane from Atlanta is four hours late(!) and some arrangement will have to be made to get the client to the hotel.

Confirmations have been made, checked and double-checked. We arrive at the hotel at 10 P.M. and are asked whether we'd prefer a room overlooking the Interstate or overlooking the railroad tracks. We take the railroad tracks under the false assumption that the trains can only run a couple of times a day. But this is Texas and trains are miles long, and this is the busiest stretch in the state. We go to dinner (The Fox and the Hounds or The Whale and the Quail—all restaurants in the United States are derivations of these names anyhow), and we return at midnight to be greeted by our first long Texas train.

Wednesday, March 26

6 A.M. The crew call. The coffee shop is

CALL SHEET

PROD. NO 132 DATE Sept. 9th — RAIN OR SHINE WEATHER PERMITTING

TITLE "The Savage Bees"

DIRECTOR Bruce Geller

Lee Rafner — ASST. DIRECTOR
Lee Rafner — UNIT MANAGER
SHOOTING CALL

CAST — BITS — TALENT	In Make Up	In Wardrobe	On Set	SET — LOCATION — SCENES
1.M. Parks-Jeff 2.G. Corbett - Jean 4. P. Hecht - Rufus 10.B. Holliday-Stilt	6:30A 8:30A 9:00A 6:30A	Lv. for Lv. for Lv. for Rept. to Loc.	7:30 9:30 10:00	EXT. SUPERDOME, ROAD AT RAMP & DOOR Sc. 172, 175, 176, 177, 178, 181
1.M. Parks - Jeff				INT. CHURN'S CAR AT SUPER-DOME. Sc. 180
4. P. Hecht - Rufus 10.B. Holliday-Stilt				EXT. SUPERDOME RAMP & DOOR Sc. 188
1. M. Parks - Jeff 2. G. Corbett- Jean 4.P. Hecht - Rufus 10.B. Holliday-Stilt				INT. SUPERDOME DOORWAY Sc. 182, 184, 186
1. M. Parks - Jeff 2. G. Corbett-Jean				INT. SUPERDOME FLOOR AREA Sc. 189, 192A, 192E, 195 196
2. G. Corbett - Jean				INT. JEANNIE'S VW INT. SUPERDOME FLOOR AREA Sc. 190, 192B, 192C, 196A

Feature productions present the most complex logistical problems. This is a call sheet from the NBC feature film, The Savage Bees.

closed—we will try to grab breakfast later in the morning. Load equipment. The bellman is not yet awake. We commandeer a four-wheel cart. The hotel is very upset.

6:30 A.M. Arrive on location. It is a bottling plant and though arrangements have been made (and checked and rechecked), it is not yet open. A maintenance man has the key but cannot let us in because he has not been told that we would be there.

7 A.M. We are to film a meeting scheduled at this hour, but we have been let in the doors only three minutes earlier—and after lighting in a record three minutes, we film the meeting and are told not to worry because the next location is "just down the street."

8 A.M. We leave for the location "just down the street."

9 A.M. In Texas, not only are the trains very long, but so are the streets. We have been traveling for one hour, and finally arrive several counties away. Our interviews are supposed to be exterior to save on lighting time, but it is pouring. At that time, someone drops the line we hear everywhere in the world: "You should have been here last week. The sun was shining." Again we move indoors. This time in a crowded supermarket. And again we light in a record three minutes, even though the only outlets are on the food freezer and in the men's room. The interviews are successful.

11 A.M. Our client had told us the week before that we were to go to Chicago from Houston—and as long as we were flying over Dallas, it might be nice to stop there to "get a couple of shots." Our plane to Dallas is scheduled for 12:30. We still have some on-camera interviews to do, but we convince our client that to make the plane we simply must leave right now. Our escort (who has lived in Houston all his life) knows a "shortcut" to the airport, but according to our map it is twelve miles further. We do not argue. He has lived in Houston all his life. Of course he is wrong. Even shortcuts are long in Texas.

12:15 P.M. We check into the airport with our twenty-four pieces of luggage and equipment and we have five minutes in which to buy plastic sandwiches and canned soft drinks.

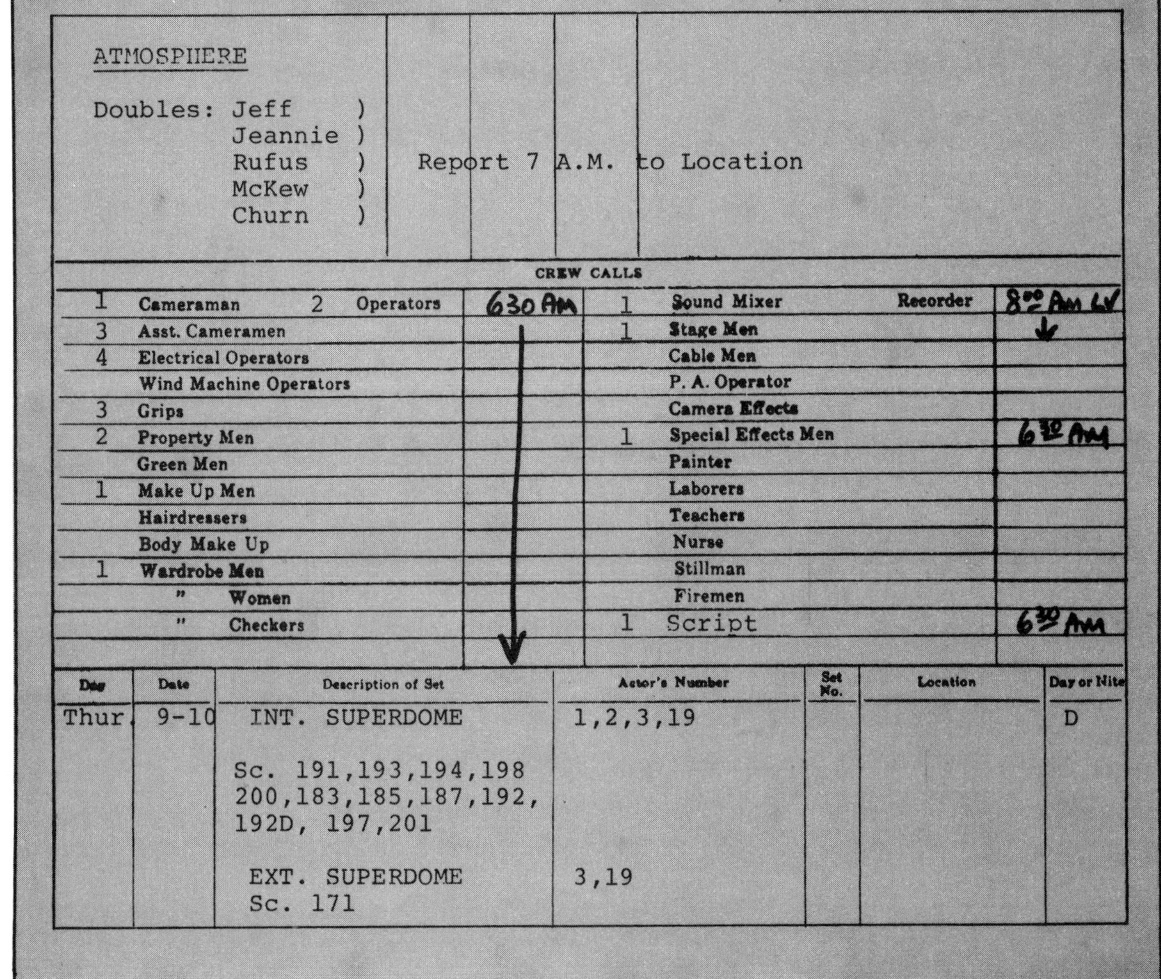

ATMOSPHERE

Doubles: Jeff) Jeannie) Rufus) McKew) Churn) Report 7 A.M. to Location

CREW CALLS

1	Cameraman 2 Operators	630 AM	1	Sound Mixer Recorder	8:00 AM LV
3	Asst. Cameramen		1	Stage Men	
4	Electrical Operators			Cable Men	
	Wind Machine Operators			P. A. Operator	
3	Grips			Camera Effects	
2	Property Men		1	Special Effects Men	6:30 AM
	Green Men			Painter	
1	Make Up Men			Laborers	
	Hairdressers			Teachers	
	Body Make Up			Nurse	
1	Wardrobe Men			Stillman	
	" Women			Firemen	
	" Checkers		1	Script	6:30 AM

Day	Date	Description of Set	Actor's Number	Set No.	Location	Day or Nite
Thur.	9-10	INT. SUPERDOME Sc. 191,193,194,198 200,183,185,187,192, 192D, 197,201	1,2,3,19			D
		EXT. SUPERDOME Sc. 171	3,19			

12:30 P.M. We take off. I am sitting next to an Ecuadorian couple who cross themselves at least ten times on takeoff. It seems to work. The plane lifts off.

1:30 P.M. Dallas. We arrive in a fantastic hailstorm. The hail is the size of camphor balls. As we load the station wagon, the hail turns into a torrential downpour. On the way to the location, the crew is hungry (the crew is always hungry) and we stop for a quick bite at The Fox and the Hounds (Dallas branch).

2:30 P.M. We film in Dallas.

7:30 P.M. We are at the airport again, waiting for our flight to Chicago, which is delayed one hour because of snow over Lake Michigan.

11 P.M. We arrive in Chicago. The crew checks into the O'Hare Hilton, while the production manager gets the station wagon. En route to the parking lot to pick up the wagon, the driver of the Avis shuttle bus is arrested by the airport police for speeding.

11:30 P.M. In the parking garage, with the equipment inside the wagon, the production manager removes the plastic handles from the door locks to make theft more difficult. He locks the wagon, then notices his jacket still inside. Unfortunately, the key to the wagon, which worked in the ignition, will not work in any of the door locks. And Avis has given us only one key.

Midnight. Call Avis. They promise to leave a key with the hotel bellman.

It is now:

Thursday, March 27

12:30 A.M. Call and reconfirm next day's flights, hotels, and cars. Go downstairs for some dinner.

1:15 A.M. Go to sleep.

6 A.M. Get up to check if Avis key is at bellman's desk. By Murphy's Law—which states that if something can go wrong it will—the key is not there. Call Avis. Yes sir, we know all about it. However, the night manager forgot to tell us which hotel you're in. The key will be right over.

And so begins another day.

Now that we've made the job appear so attractive, and now that you realize that your only salvation is a sense of humor, perhaps you also have more respect for the poor downtrodden of our industry who make the wheels turn and who oil the machinery of potential disaster.

The entry into production can also be made in several ways. Some people do it by becoming production assistants, busily picking up the pieces left behind by the senior production people. Bit by bit, they learn the production job—by making hotel and air reservations, placing calls to locations and getting permits, constantly checking the other arrangements that have been made, observing, being near the professionals in all areas of filmmaking and learning day by day. Eventually, they learn every one of the functions described in this chapter.

And there are, in addition, the production secretaries—and we do not mean to overlook them or demean their jobs by putting them at this late page of the chapter. Basically, the production secretary has the normal secretarial skills with the addition of a fairly good understanding of the production process and the working hours of a turn-of-the-century sweatshop. When everyone else has gone home, she or he is usually back at the office typing the final crew call sheet for the next day. When asked for a photo to use in this book, one of them said, "They only take photos of the stars, they never photograph us!"

And finally, at the other end of the spectrum, are those production titles that are certainly not entry jobs in the film business: producers and executive producers. These people, if they have done their jobs properly, also know the things we've outlined in this chapter. But film is a strange business and sometimes the title of "producer" is given to a person who has raised the money for a film but knows no more about production than I do about the structure of the Yugoslav Air Force. We used to define a producer as "anyone who says he is." Sometimes that holds true, but, more often than not, a producer is in over-all charge of the production, usually in the determination of just who gets hired, what the budget is, and how the money shall be spent. Sometimes the producer is also the director and that is the ideal situation—for then it is difficult for the producer to fire the director when the job is going badly.

"I want to get into production."

And I don't blame you. But keep in mind what the job entails. And if you do make it—and you find yourself setting up a location in two feet of mud in the worst, disease-infested slum in Asia, your boots covered with black muck, the heat hovering somewhere near one hundred ten degrees with the humidity of a Turkish bath (and you can't even drink the water)—just remind yourself of the "glamour" and "excitement" of the film business!

CHAPTER 5

WRITING FOR FILM

"Speaking as an Engineer..."

A number of years ago, I used to work with a writer by the name of Sam Moore. Sam was always busy, had a great many clients, and a superb sense of humor. At the endless client committee meetings at which films were discussed, restructured, rewritten, and reconceived, Sam would sit back quietly. When everyone had exhausted the subject, he would lean forward and say, "Speaking as an engineer . . ." and then go on to make his point.

When asked about this, Sam's explanation was simply, "No one listens to a writer, but everyone wants to hear an engineer."

Yes, someone has to face the blank piece of paper with the three lonely words sitting on the carriage of the typewriter: "The scene opens . . ." And someone has to struggle and fight through the ideas and the doubts. Someone has to do the research and know more about the subject than anyone else who is to see the script or outline or treatment. What follows those first three words will eventually become the skeleton of the film. Good films are not created by a committee, neither are they created from blank pieces of paper.

Some directors disagree with the last statement and have tried to structure a film by utilizing actors and their personal experiences in the development of a film story through improvisation. Documentarians have gone on location without any semblance of concept or continuity—certain that it could all be saved when they began to assemble the finished footage. Many, if not most of such films, have been unmitigated disasters, for actors are not writers and improvisation is better left to the acting class. In the area of the documentary, the lack of a written outline creates a need to overshoot by vast amounts, thus making problems in the budget if not in the continuity. It takes a written word; it takes structure and style and pacing; it takes thought and an ear for the way the world speaks and an eye for the way the world lives.

Eddie Adler, President of Writer's Guild East, who works on both features and television's top series. Most writers in the industry have replaced their battered typewriters with word processors. The author is the only exception.

There is a vital need for the writer in the film world today—whether it be for photoplays, documentaries, or commercials. But problems arise for the writer not only in starting out, but *after* the words are on paper. Once the *process* of writing is completed, the words are there for all the world to tear apart, restructure, and re-edit. Then comes the time when the writer must finally lean forward and say, "Speaking as an engineer . . ."

The "stables" of Hollywood writers are long since gone and most feature scripts are written under contract by independents. For the smaller companies, it is uneconomical to keep writers on staff, and, as a result, most feature-film writing today is done on a free-lance basis. The larger producing companies in the field of the *television series* will generally keep several writers on staff for the length of time that the shows appear on the air. An analysis of the people who work at this craft, however, shows us that almost all of them are experienced, with superb reputations acquired over the years.

Occasionally a beginner is "discovered" by accident—there are stories about messengers and secretaries who have had their script ideas accepted. But these are rare. In the area of the television commercial and, more specifically, in advertising agencies, the staff copywriter is, however, still an important functioning member of the group and is generally hired on a salary basis. Another place where a writer might be a member of a permanent staff is, logically, where the writer on the project is also the director or producer, or even a partner or owner of the company. Some educational film companies, government audiovisual departments, and in-house corporate divisions also keep their writers on permanent staff.

Many writers have moved into production after years of experience with the written word. It is still an excellent way to become involved in the very heart of the filmmaking process. Others (the author included) have gone the other way, beginning in production and then eventually writing their own treatments and scripts.

If you look closely at the "story board" illustrated on page 118, you'll notice that the writing is strongly structured and has disciplined continuity. The reasons are simple: this commercial can take only so much time, and the writing and development of the story line is necessarily confined to that time. You have sixty seconds or you have thirty seconds and that is all the time you have. Not one second more or the networks will not accept the finished product. It is an area of specific talent within the advertising agency. The writer in this field generally works closely with others on the creative staff—and the art director will

104 CONTINUED: 104

JEFF
Well -- hello.

JEANNE
Hi.

They embrace.

105 EXT. SHERIFF'S STATION - NIGHT 105

An old Chevrolet pulls up, parks. The lights go off. And Jeff du Rand steps out. In his hand is a paper bag. He slams the door and enters the station.

106 INT. SHERIFF'S STATION - NIGHT 106

The station is deserted. Jeff takes several steps inside, then knocks on the desk, calls.

JEFF
Anybody home?

McKEW
No.

NEW ANGLE

McKew sits, still in his office. Although he has put his feet up and has tilted his hat over his eyes. His voice sounds as if coming from a deep, deep well.

Jeff leans on the doorjamb, examines him.

JEFF
Mister Cheer. Wow...

McKEW
My wife won't talk to me, the
City Council is going to have my
job and what do you want?

JEFF
A cup.

McKew points. Across the main room of the station is a drinking fountain. And a rack of paper cups. Jeff turns, walks to it.

McKEW
(heartsick)
I sent another victim in. Albert
Caziot. Farmer. Good man. He...
I've seen... oh, God.

This typical script page from a feature film also appears on page 92, with the script supervisor's comments.

probably have as much to say about concept as will the writer. The visual story board becomes the final "script" to be presented to the client and eventually produced as the finished film.

There is one other factor that has come into prominence in these past few years: the legal area of commercial scriptwriting. Because of "truth in advertising," the agencies have insisted that all scripts be checked and approved by their legal staffs. As a result, the copywriter must not only think in visual terms, but also in terms of legal nuances. In other words, the sentence, "The best coffee . . ." would never be allowed since there is no way to prove this statement. However, time and again, you'll hear the line on television that tells you it's "A better coffee . . ." The next time you watch your favorite television show, pay some attention to the commercials instead of going out to the kitchen for a ham-and-cheese sandwich. Listen to the words carefully and try to break down the thinking that went into the copy and the picture.

Here are some steps of the types of writing in the film industry:

THE PROPOSAL

At some point in your career, someone will come to you and ask you to write a "proposal." Possibly that person will be a potential client or a foundation looking for a film producer or a corporation trying to determine just which producer will make its film. The document you produce will probably be the most important piece of writing in the long chain of events that leads to the finished motion picture.

Generally, the proposal contains information about your company, your background, a few words about awards (modestly outlined), your current clients and film projects—and, most important, how you *might* handle the film *if* it were awarded to you. Keep in mind that this is a phase in which you have done no research, a time when you barely know the subject, and yet it is a time when the potential client will be making a value judgment of you and your filmmaking abilities—and all from your written word. Certainly, you will eventually show your sample films, and even a superb written proposal can be destroyed by a bad sample; but the first stage is still a critical one, and the proposal takes all your talents as a writer.

If we follow the logical path of the writer's role in the making of a film, it might well be: (1) the sales letter, or the letter in answer to a request by mail or by telephone; (2) the first meeting with the potential client; (3) the proposal. Of course, if you are a free-lance writer and you are hired by the production company to write the film, all of the steps thus far would have been taken care of by one of the executives. Nevertheless, thinking in terms of the filmmaker concept, where one person does several jobs, all of them might be in your domain and you had better know how to handle them. In the feature or television film fields, the assignment would usually come through an agent.

Assuming, then, that the job has been given to your production company or to you as an individual, and a contract has finally been signed, your next steps would be: research (which might be done on location, by telephone, in the library, and in many cases through on-the-spot interviews) and the "treatment."

THE TREATMENT

In various segments of the industry, the writer may be asked to do a "treatment" rather than a script. This might happen in the feature field, but it most often happens with the documentary and the business film. Simply stated, the treatment is a narrative description of what the film will look like. It does not detail the specific shots nor does it indicate exactly what the dialogue or narration will be. It paints word pictures to give the reader a visual idea of the finished product, and the better the word descriptions, the more vivid the images are for the reader. Here's an example from a recent film about the energy crisis and the potential of Western coal:

The opening shots are from a helicopter—swooping low over the desert—through the canyons of Utah—along the brush and across the lone highway that cuts its way through the beautiful country. It is our introduction to the film, but also our introduction to the story of the energy crisis and the story of coal . . .

As the helicopter swoops across a cut in the canyon and we see a power plant—or a coal mine—perhaps the narrator tells us that fossil fuels have never really been gone, and that for twenty years there have been people who have felt that the largest single source of energy in the world is coal. We hear that it is unlimited

in its supply—possibly into the year 2000.

The helicopter continues its flight and the first words of the title appear on the screen . . .

Notice that the treatment is vague and yet fairly specific in what it demands of the filming. The words of the narrator are suggested and the helicopter flight is, at this point, still in the writer's imagination, allowing flexibility when the crew is actually on location.

THE SCRIPT

On page 30 we have printed a script from the television feature *The Savage Bees.* When it comes to dialogue and actors, the form changes somewhat from the treatment concept, and the instructions become more specific. The documentary is generally made from a treatment concept, while the dramatic show is always shot from a script. Both might change during filming, but the writer has given the director a working document and the film production continues from that point. The writer in the field is required to research the project, struggle through the days and weeks of putting words on paper, and then deliver to the production unit a visual concept of a film.

And—you have to like writing. You have to like it a lot. Even after you've "made it" there will be those 1 A.M sessions when you've just begun the third rewrite of the script—the coffee, as always, cold in the Styrofoam cup—and somehow you're not thinking about all that money you're making. The only thing that seems important at the time is doing a good job, pride, and a sense of fulfillment when the words begin to work. Added to this is the area of personal relationships. They come into play when we deal with the writer–producer relationship, the writer–client relationship, and the problems of just making a living as a freelance writer. Particularly in the beginning years, it is most difficult to struggle over a concept for long hours and then find that it is to be torn apart by almost anyone up the production line: the director, or the client, or the art director, or, as we have had happen, the client's spouse—who just happened to be there when we were presenting the treatment. For the writer, these are agonizing and difficult times, and one of the things you will no doubt learn in the field is to handle the situation with tact, diplomacy, aplomb, and genius, while inside you are seething with the protest of frustration. And maybe you will become a director, so that you can hire *yourself* as the writer!

Getting a job as a writer takes pretty much the same qualities as the other crafts require. Good writers work at it—they're tenacious and they actually write! If the last statement seems strange, it is explained quite well by an acquaintance of ours who says, "Too many people want to be writers, but no one wants to sit down and write!"

In one sense, it is a difficult field to crack: for the bigger jobs, you *must* have an agent, yet agents will not handle anyone who is not published! The networks will not even look at a script that is unsolicited or does not come through the channel of a literary agent. It's not that they don't want new ideas—their insurance policies will just not allow them to read the treatments or scripts, and they must be sent back intact. Too many beginners have been quick to sue when "their ideas" were seen on a network television show. In another sense, breaking into the field is fairly simple. Unlike an actor, you don't have to be a "type" to be a writer. You can never be too short or too tall or too black or too pale to fill the role. The important thing, however, is that you have to be *good.*

The best way to break into writing is to *write;* to keep writing—treatments, scripts, your own films in conjunction with other filmmakers. If you want to write comedy, contact the comics who are looking for new material. Even if no one will pay you for your writing, write anyway. There are benefits that need writers, fund-raising organizations, football dinners at your alma mater, speeches, pamphlets—any of them good practice if they get you to a typewriter without making you wait for an "inspiration." The best thing you can show to a potential employer is a sample of your work—ideally on film, but it can also be done on paper. Your entry into the field might even be in the area of radio writing or TV continuity at a small station.

From a purely practical point of view, it might be wise to learn to touch-type. When you know how to type, it takes less time to write a script, though some of our better writers scrawl their illegible way along yellow sheets of paper and their work turns out beautifully —with someone else typing the finished product. But typing can speed your work along considerably.

Learn to take notes. Not every interview or research conversation can be tape-recorded (and even then, someone has to type the transcript when you've completed the interview), and some people do not want to be put on tape while they speak. Learn to take the important notes and then transfer them to your treatment or your script at a later time.

And—most of all—learn to write visually. Learn to paint pictures with your words, to make people "see" your film as they read. Take a subject, write a treatment. If it's good, it can be a sample for a prospective employer.

The filmmaker today must also be able to write in other areas. Film is, after all, a business—whether or not we like to admit it—and the talents of the writer can help even in the day-to-day routine of administration. In addition, your beginning days in the industry are going to be taken up with the mundane and routine things that go into just getting a job. Your writing talents can certainly help.

LETTERS The film business is filled with letters. They are, after all, a primary means of communication, and if they are delivered by the postal service with any kind of efficiency, they constitute a reasonably priced method of getting information from one person to another. Of course, that assumes that the recipient reads the letter past the first sentence.

Though letters are being discussed under this chapter about writers, keep in mind that everyone in the field writes them. The production manager, the director, the producer, the business executives all write letters of request, of thanks, of proposal. If they are to get the attention you think they deserve, they must be succinct, articulate, and strong. In writing for a grant under which you will produce your film, your letter would come under the most intense scrutiny, as would your proposal outlining just what the film is expected to be. Frequently, the letter of proposal is more attractive than the finished film, but those are the chances that a foundation has to take.

SCRIPT TABLE		
Approximate Number of Pages	Running Time	Average Number & Length of Acts
30	½ hour teleplay	2 Acts — 15 pages each
60	1 hour teleplay	4 Acts — 15 pages each
90	90 minute teleplay	6 Acts — 15 pages each
110	2 hour teleplay	6 Acts — 18 pages each
125 to 150	2 hour feature screenplay	No act divisions

A chart from an excellent guide for the beginner, Professional Writer's Teleplay/Screenplay Format, by Jerome Coopersmith.

Certainly letter writing has none of the glamour of scriptwriting, but we hope you have already accepted the fact that much of the film industry is far from glamorous.

CONTRACTS The lawyers will shudder, but most filmmakers must generally write their own contracts, to be checked later on by counsel. Certainly, the major feature productions are covered by a battery of lawyers, but the average film company is small and the film specifications change from job to job. Some years ago, we wrote a seven-page contract and sent it to the corporation for whom we were to produce a film. Ten weeks later(!) their lawyers sent the contract back and it was expanded to thirty-six pages! Though we might better cover contracts in the business section of this book (Chapter 12), keep in mind that you should be conversant with them and you might very well have to write at least the first drafts.

There is no book that will make you a writer. You can learn form, certainly, and you can learn technical terms, such as "close-up" or "dolly in," but putting words one after the other and making sense out of them requires an innate talent that you either have or lack. Practice, however, helps. Any kind of writing improves your craft, and in the early days of your career no writing job should be too small for you or too undignified to tackle. Whether you are writing spots for a local television sponsor or scripts for a major network show, you will be practicing your craft in the best way possible—*by writing.*

Most important of all, don't give up too easily. Many years ago, I wrote variety and quiz shows for radio and television. I became known in that area and I was busy most of the time. But I was unhappy. After all, I wanted to do dramatic shows. I wanted the feel of writing dialogue and moving people through the "life" of a half-hour script. My agent said, "But you're a variety writer." Bit by bit, on my own insistence, by knocking on doors and writing script after script, I finally began to sell to the dramatic shows on television. Two years later, my agent got a request for a writer on a variety show at an astronomical weekly salary, and she gave it to another writer. Angrily, I telephoned her and asked why she hadn't considered me. She answered firmly, "But you're a dramatic writer!"

My grandmother never said that life would be fair!

Herbert Raditschnig of Salzburg, Austria, with the ingenious rigging he devised for photography on the ski slopes.

CHAPTER 6

CINEMATOGRAPHY

Shooting Above the Garbage

If sound people are the "ears" of the film industry, then certainly cinematographers are its "eyes." Cinematography is, next to production, probably the most sought-after entry job—and one of the most crowded. Without doubt, it is also one of the most rewarding crafts in the film medium, for in terms of tangible gratification—the picture on the screen—it has no equal. One day after the shooting, the dailies (a print made of the previous day's film) are screened and the results are on view for everyone to see (Of course, there are occasions when the cameraperson wants to crawl out of the room.)

No one on the set or on location has quite the power over the image as does the cinematographer. Though the director is in control, only one person has an eye to the viewfinder, only one person really controls what is being recorded in close-up at an emotional point in the film. At that moment, solely the cinematographer is interpreting for the audience.

But cinematography is, also, one of the most frustrating and nerve-wracking jobs in film. First of all, no one seems to travel quite as much as the people who operate the cameras. With the world as "studio," a telephone call can take the cinematographer to a three-week location in Bali, followed by four weeks in the swamps of Louisiana. "That's great," you exclaim. "Look at all that travel!" True, but just try to develop personal relationships when you're gone all that time, try to keep a marriage intact or raise kids or have some kind of rapport with another person. One well-known cameraman would only date airline flight attendants, because they understood what it meant to be called on a trip at the last moment and, from a more practical viewpoint, they were able to travel at a discount to join him on location.

Because of the very nature of the role, the responsibilities are awesome. How many cinematographers have awakened in a cold sweat in the middle of the night, wondering if they forgot to put on the correct filter when the shooting moved from interior to exterior. Could the sequence have been lighted better? And now that it's all done, will the laboratory put a scratch down the middle of the negative? But, in spite of all this—and quite understandably—it is a sought-after and much-respected job among professionals.

Because of the popularity of photography among the general public, because of the facility of owning a camera and taking "home movies," because of the maturing of entire generations of audiences on Hollywood films, as well as because of the "glamour" (that word again) of the cameraperson, the constant publicity about photography, and the improvement of photographic techniques over the past twenty-five years, the field of cinematography is certainly one of the most crowded on the professional level. But it is also one of the best entries into the film business—for the very nature of the art provides even the beginner with samples of his work. And, if you are willing to work at it, willing to practice and improve, willing to throw out thousands of feet of expensive film just to get a hundred good feet of sample footage, then perhaps you should pursue it.

Good cinematographers will go anywhere for an angle. Jon Fauer descends into the depths of a manhole for the film *More Than Meets the Eye*, produced for the Southern Company.

For the beginning cinematographer, technical books are on the market—some good, some very bad by last reports from my own staff. There are ways described to improve your eye, the way you see things through the lens, the way you become selective in what you shoot and how you shoot it. You'll need to learn much technical information and practice constantly to develop a creative eye.

Though the world of feature film, commercials, and television is strongly structured with union jobs, most beginners learn their craft as non-union camera people. Throughout the industry are hundreds of small, non-union productions, and it is here that all beginners get their start. Most important, whether union or non-union, the profession requires the same elements of technical know-how and creativity from all cinematographers. For the easiest understanding of the available jobs (and knowing that all beginners will start out shooting films without regard to category) here is the

structure of the cinematographic field as it appears in the industry:

CAMERA ASSISTANT

This is often the first step toward becoming a cameraperson, though many assistants prefer to remain in that category and never want to take full responsibility for the photography. This is probably most true in Europe and in California, where some assistants remain in their jobs throughout their entire careers.

The good assistant is highly valuable to the camera operator and shares much of the responsibility for the quality of the work. He must know how to dismantle and reassemble, load and reload three to four 16mm cameras and three to four 35mm cameras. On location, the assistant usually puts in a full day and then goes back to the room to clean the cameras, reload the magazines, set up for the next day. Sometimes this goes on until midnight. The assistant is also responsible for keeping logs and records, labeling the film cans when they've been exposed, following focus for the camera operator, changing lenses, reloading magazines in a changing bag—and generally being the good "right arm" of the camera operator.

There is tension, pressure, responsibility. And there are moments of panic. There are times when the assistant is constantly on the run; some camera operators treat their assistants as lackeys or valets, others work with their assistants as a team in a smoothly running operation. When the sequence is completed, it is the assistant who is responsible for opening the lens to check the gate in order to see if any foreign matter (pieces of dirt, hair, shaved edges of film) has ruined the scene. In a documentary, when a critical event is taking place and the operator is down to the last magazine, fast running out, it is the assistant, sweaty hands in the black hot changing bag, who suddenly realizes that the film roll has slipped out of its core and he has only seconds to make it right.

A feature-film camera crew on location in Louisiana for The Savage Bees, produced by Landsburg/Kirshner Productions for NBC.

NEWSREEL CAMERAMAN

This is not necessarily a limited specialty, for commercial cameramen and Class-A operators (below) can also do newsreel work. But it is a field all its own, with its own special kind of talent and the basic prerequisite of being able to shoot quickly, in often difficult situations—paying more attention to the subject and the fact that what is happening may disappear in a few minutes than to getting an "artistic" shot. Political figures go through crowds quickly; the push and shove are tremendous; other networks and newsreel people are there to get their own shots; and frequently the crowd is hostile to film crews, particularly when the news event will not reflect too well on the persons photographed. Seldom is the tripod used in such work and the "documentary" style would probably be a better description of the kind of camera work done by newsreel people. There exist, of course, the stories of newsreel cameramen who managed to shoot disasters such as the Hindenburg explosion by just being there and having the foresight to turn the camera on. But there are also stories of camera people arriving at a news event too late to film the story, which has been scooped up by the other TV stations. The job requires constant running: a newsreel cameraman for a network is constantly being moved from place to place, always following events.

The frustrations, as in any craft, are many. Too often, the cameraman puts in a twelve-hour day chasing a story, the heavy camera on a shoulder pad, breath and energy giving way quickly, the film finally delivered—and the nightly news show presents thirty seconds of the story while the rest of the exposed film is relegated to a vault in the deep recesses of the editing room.

Sometimes, in the midst of tension and violence and tragedy, humor surfaces. One of our favorite cameramen began his career in newsreel work and the training he received has served him well in his work as a documentarian (he is fast, he is observant, and he is flexible). He remembers one of his first assignments as a novice newsreel cameraman, in which he was sent to film the riots in Watts. The rumors had been flowing fast and thick: any newsreel car caught in the area would probably be burned or destroyed in some way —and along with the car would go the newsreel crew. Cameramen were being shot at, a soundman was beaten quite badly, and all in all, it was not one of the healthiest places in the world for the press corps. Our hero arrived in the area in a closed car; he was to meet a reporter on a street corner. But the signs were down; there was no way to tell direction; the corner gas station was afire; smoke filled the streets. He pulled over, windows rolled up, and shouted at a local resident, "Is this Watts?" The man could not hear, and came close to the car. The cameraman rolled down the window a bit and shouted again, "Is *this* Watts?" With a small grin, the man leaned closer and shouted back, "Well, it sure ain't Marlboro country!"

Michael Livesey, one of the best of documentary cinematographers.

COMMERCIAL CAMERAMAN

Basically, this category is that of a Class-A cameraman who specializes in the field of the television commercial; and on the East Coast about 75 percent of the union members work in this area. The commercial cameraman can also do documentary work, or photography for features, but generally this specialization is geared to the particular needs of the TV spot. After a while, these people become known to the advertising agencies as specialists of product, people, or location photography and we hear too many agency producers exclaim, "Oh, he's great with beer!" It's certainly unfair to categorize someone, even in this age of narrow specialization, but reputations are made this way and though the cinematographer may also be a great documentarian, in the world of the commercial he often ends up as a genius in the narrow spectrum of product photography.

CLASS-A OPERATOR AND CLASS-A DIRECTOR OF PHOTOGRAPHY

These two categories began in the feature field many years ago, when the standard camera was the Mitchell BNC Reflex, with its huge blimp and all the associated equipment that went with it. There are still Mitchell BNCs in use, and now we have the special Panavision and Panaflex wide-screen cameras, but just as often the much-lighter Arriflex is used on the job, particularly for hand-held shots or for getting fluidity in a sequence. In the feature film,

the director of photography is in charge of the entire camera crew: the lighting of the set, all movement of the camera, the framing of the shot, and the planning of the photography worked out in conjunction with the director. Once the setup is completed, the director of photography (D.P.) generally does not handle the actual camera work himself. This part of the job is done by the camera operator, and, in an ideal situation, the D.P. trusts his operator totally, for it is the latter who has his eye glued to the camera during the entire take, while the D.P. generally stays in the background and supervises. For some directors of photography, this is a frustration; for others it is a pleasure.

Cinematographers like Haskell Wexler made their reputations by hand-holding the 35mm camera, specially rigged to facilitate the fluidity of movement with jumpiness. However, with the invention of the Steadicam Camera Stabilizing System, a whole new generation of films shot "off the tripod" has changed the look of the feature film. Possibly the most famous of these is *Rocky*.

In the picture *Body and Soul* (1947), starring John Garfield, James Wong Howe got into a boxing ring on roller skates, carrying an Arriflex, so that the audience would feel like part of the action.

The prime example of a combination D.P.–operator–director is Claude Lelouch, who not only handles the camera, but supervises editing and is in total control of all production. In this case, his camera operator ends up as a focus puller and all-around assistant. With all of Lelouch's feature credits, one of his most astoundingly beautiful films was a short subject about Turkey, for which he handled all photography.

Garrett Brown, with his ingenious film/video camera stabilizing system, the Steadicam®. The development changed the look of film and Brown, along with Cinema Products Corporation, was given a special Academy Award for his work.

Stanley Kubrick, though not technically a cinematographer, also handles his own Arriflex to cover the action he wants to highlight, such as the dueling scene in *Barry Lyndon* and the gang rape in *A Clockwork Orange*.

Of course, these are people at the top of the list. They control their own productions, their own destinies. They are much sought-after, famous in their own right—they can demand what they want from a crew and from the film itself. For ordinary camera people the frustrations can be severe through the learning years. However, there are times when the director or the client or the agency has envisioned a totally impossible shot and turns to the cinematographer for salvation. On other occasions, it is the camera operator who develops the shot, has the camera set for the take, turns to the director—who looks through the viewfinder and then says, "I don't like it!" Still other directors actually set the camera position from which they want the scene shot, thus eliminating the need for another (and possibly better) viewpoint. In all of these cases, the natural instinct of the cinematographer is to stick to his convictions, but the trick is to know when to accede—and when a graceful compromise can be worked out. This is another case where personalities come into play, as they do throughout the film industry.

PREPARATION AND TRAINING

No formal survey has been made to discover

where camera people come from, but you would probably find that most of them working today originally began in one of three areas:

•The film schools. This would include primarily the younger cinematographers.

•Ex–Army Signal Corps. These people are generally older, and were trained in combat photography and in the production of training films and army newsreels.

•Camera supply houses. There is no better way to get technical training than constantly to break down and repair every kind of camera available. Two of our best cameramen began their careers by spending their evenings and Saturdays at camera-rental houses learning how to repair equipment.

Of course, there are the exceptions, and perhaps your career will begin in a way unusual enough to warrant a story in a future book. The late James Wong Howe, one of the pioneers of cinematography—an ex–prize fighter working as a delivery boy for a commercial photographer—was wandering through Los Angeles when he saw a Mack Sennett comedy being shot. He went up to the cameraman and asked for a job, was sent to see the boss at Jesse Lasky Studios, and was turned down because he was too small. However, he was persistent, and finally he was hired—to pick up film scraps on the cutting-room floor. He went on to become slate boy for Cecil B. De Mille, then camera assistant to Alvin Wyckoff—until in 1922 he was asked by De Mille to take some portrait shots of the silent film star Mary Miles Minter. Except for the

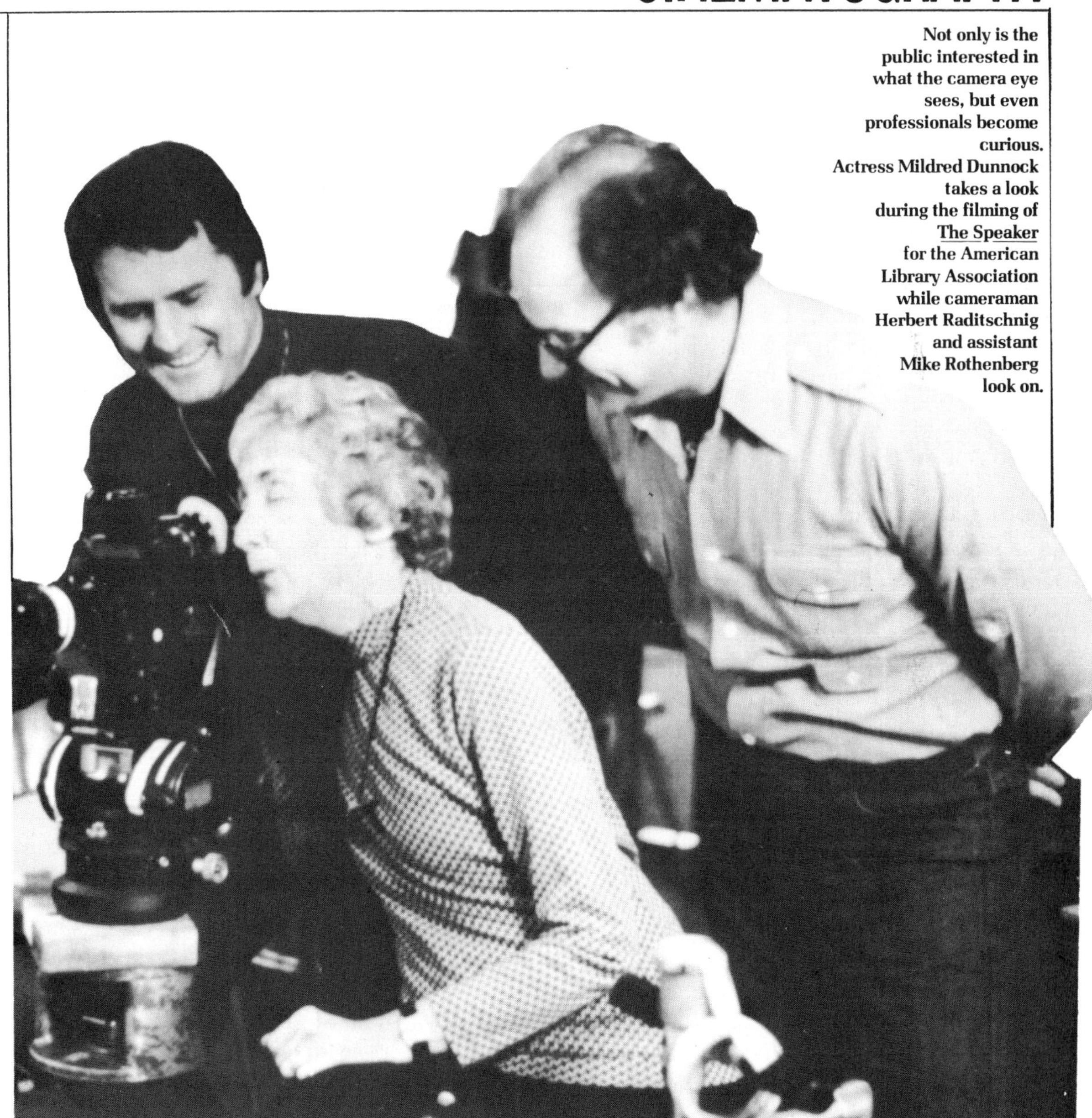

Not only is the public interested in what the camera eye sees, but even professionals become curious. Actress Mildred Dunnock takes a look during the filming of The Speaker for the American Library Association while cameraman Herbert Raditschnig and assistant Mike Rothenberg look on.

fact that Mary Minter had blue eyes, James Wong Howe might have gone into obscurity. In those days, the film stock made blue eyes disappear or become almost expressionless. Howe constructed a frame of black velvet, cut a hole in it for the camera, and shot through the hole. The light reflecting off the velvet made Miss Minter's eyes look darker and Howe's career as a photographer was launched.

Now, we realize that in today's world anyone walking up to a contemporary director on location and asking for a job as a cinematographer would probably be asked by the police to please leave quietly. Let's look at some more practical ways in which you might practice and eventually work your way into the field:

BOOKS, MAGAZINES, ARTICLES, AND MUSEUMS Keep up with the cinematography field, for it changes constantly. Standard camera lenses are replaced by new design, ingenious engineering feats move the camera and its associated equipment ahead, and suddenly everyone is talking of a new development, of a new stride forward. Most of the cinematographers we know still keep up with equipment manuals, *American Cinematographer, Film News, Film Comment,* and even magazines devoted to the art of still photography. Take a look at the books about photography, the books that show the collections of still photographs shot by the known and the unknown. What did Steichen have that you don't have—or that you *do* have, but is as yet undiscovered?

Try to go to every photographic exhibition and art museum that you can get to. By studying painting, you can also develop an appreciation of form, color, and composition. What about the lighting in Caravaggio's paintings? How might you re-create it on film if you were asked to do so? As art has changed, so has photography. The abstraction that once sent people shrieking from the museum (think of the reactions to Pollack, Duchamp, Picasso) has now been accepted not only in the art world but in the world of film. The extreme close-up, the unusual viewpoint, the personal way of looking at an object, the dramatically lit subject are all things that make film a changing and challenging art.

This is a 35mm camera on location in the Superdome in New Orleans for The Savage Bees. In the 16mm field, the camera crews can be fairly small, but feature production with 35mm and 70mm cameras requires a larger staff and more complex backup equipment.

DEVELOPING THE EYE Cinematography is, luckily, a craft in which practice helps considerably. The constant use of the camera—any camera—trains the eye and the mind and shows you how to put a frame around life on the other side of the lens. The more you shoot, the better you should become. Exposures improve, the selectivity process is refined, the dexterity in the handling of equipment begins to make the camera an extension of the body.

Most cinematographers began by working with a still camera, perhaps one given as a gift for a birthday, and gradually bought more and more complex pieces of equipment. Then came the home laboratory, with acid etching the kitchen sink into oblivion; learning how to crop and frame and print; and learning what the different film stocks would give them. It is still a good way to begin.

From that beginning, the simple 8mm motion picture camera is a good step forward, then on to Super 8 with sound, and finally, to 16mm film. The costs of the latter are terribly expensive for the beginner, and many students get their "short ends" from professional film companies. ("Short ends" are pieces of film remaining when only part of the roll has been shot.) The beginners can use these for their own film projects or for practice. Of course, the eventual progression would take you to 35mm Negative film, but the costs would be astronomical for the beginner, and even the average documentary or television unit shoots in 16mm today. With the new liquid gate* blowup process, this can be enlarged to 35mm for eventual theatrical screening. Basically, only the feature film and TV commercials still use 35mm as a standard stock, but even here there has been an occasional successful film shot in 16mm and blown up to 35mm (*Smithereens, Lianna, Chan is Missing, Angelo My Love, Welcome Back to the Five and Dime*).

Whatever your camera—still, 8mm, or a first gleaming 16mm instrument—develop your eye through practice and by learning to *see*. Notice how light affects the world around you, both inside and out. Watch the changing light throughout one day as it affects a single object: a building, the beach, a grove of trees . . . Try to duplicate for your camera the changes from lamplight to candlelight. See subjects that are backlit and those that have only an edge of light across their faces. Try to put a frame around a segment of the world. Block out what you don't want to see and then tell us through your camera what it is you want us to look at. You are the final judge. The top, the bottom, the sides of the frame outside your viewfinder are blocked from our view by personal choice. Nothing else matters. And it really works. The practice begins to show results.

VISION ASSOCIATES 665 Fifth Ave. New York NY 10022 phone 212-935-1830

400 feet exposed MAG. #3

Prod'n. 641 "A TOUCH OF LOVE" Roll # 7

CAMERA REPORT STICK UPPER PART TO EXPOSED FILM CAN. TEAR OFF AND RETAIN BOTTOM.

Prod'n. 641 "A TOUCH OF LOVE" MAG. #3 Roll # 7

Date 1/26/77 Dir. LONDON Cam. FAUER Snd.

SOUND NO.	SCENE TAKE NOTES
29	FATHER BURPING BABY
MOS	CUT-A-WAYS OF BABY AND HAND
30	MOTHER SPONGE-BATHING BABY
31	CUs MOTHER - SPONGE BATH OF BABY
	(NOTE: SOUND RAN OUT DURING #31)
MOS	CUs BABY
32	CU CUTAWAYS OF MOTHER (END SLATED)
MOS	BABY ALONE IN CRIB

A typical camera report for a documentary film.

Some years ago we were filming a travel documentary on the shores of the Caspian Sea. With us constantly was the trusty government supervisor, there to see that we did not shoot anything that would be embarrassing, political, or filthy. We came upon a most unusual village—the fields crowded with dirty cows, the land a morass of swampy water, the hillocks covered with the residue of two hundred villagers with no place to throw their trash. But crowning the hill was a group of the most exquisite thatched-roof huts glistening against a bright blue sky. The cameraman set up the tripod and began to look through the lens of the camera—and, at the same time, the Government spy, seeing the entire scene before him, exclaimed, "You can't shoot that!" The cameraman led him gently to the eyepiece

*As the film passes through the enlarger, the liquid "lens" improves the resolution and hides the physical defects present on the original 16mm stock.

and showed him the shot. There, in all their glory, were the thatched-roof huts with the filth of the village framed out. It was a classic scene from any travel film. The cameraman explained to the smiling official, "We're shooting above the garbage!"

THE TRIPOD Though this is perhaps better left to a technical book about film, it might be wise to give one word of warning to the beginner. The camera came off the tripod years ago, when it seemed necessary to take it off and when equipment became lighter. It was called "hand-held" then, and in the normal metamorphosis of terminology it became the cornerstone of cinéma vérité. It has now returned to its former definition as "hand-held." Most of such filming is downright terrible, and the shaky camera is no excuse for thinking that therefore you have captured "life in the raw." Learn to use a tripod first. Learn to frame your shots with the extra comfort of a stable camera and *then*, if you like, learn to use a body brace and a hand-held camera. Even our most professional cinematographers find that they are frequently torn between tripod and hand-held. I have seen many screenings in which the cameraman mutters, "I should have used a tripod," and, conversely, after a particularly rigid series of sequences, the muttering becomes, "I should have taken the camera off the damned tripod and moved in!" But at least they know the difference.

THE OUTLINE We have discussed the value of treatments and scripts in an earlier chapter, but for the beginning cinematographer it is a warning worth giving twice: Try to have an outline of what it is you are going to shoot. In the professional-film field, the ratio of footage shot to footage used is about 10 to 1, and even up to 30 to 1 (29 of the 30 gets thrown away). Of 12,000 feet exposed, for example, 11,600 will go on to the cutting-room floor. It is one of the things that makes filmmaking so expensive and, for the beginner, an impossible economic pinch.

Most beginners make the opposite mistake because film is so expensive; the finger comes off the camera trigger *too early*. The ratio of shooting in colleges is closer to 1½ to 1 than 30 to 1! This is understandable, but one of the first things we teach our younger camera people is to keep shooting until they are certain that everything is covered.

But cinematography is not an entirely wasteful field. Alfred Hitchcock is reputed to have shot about 3 to 1 because everything was so well

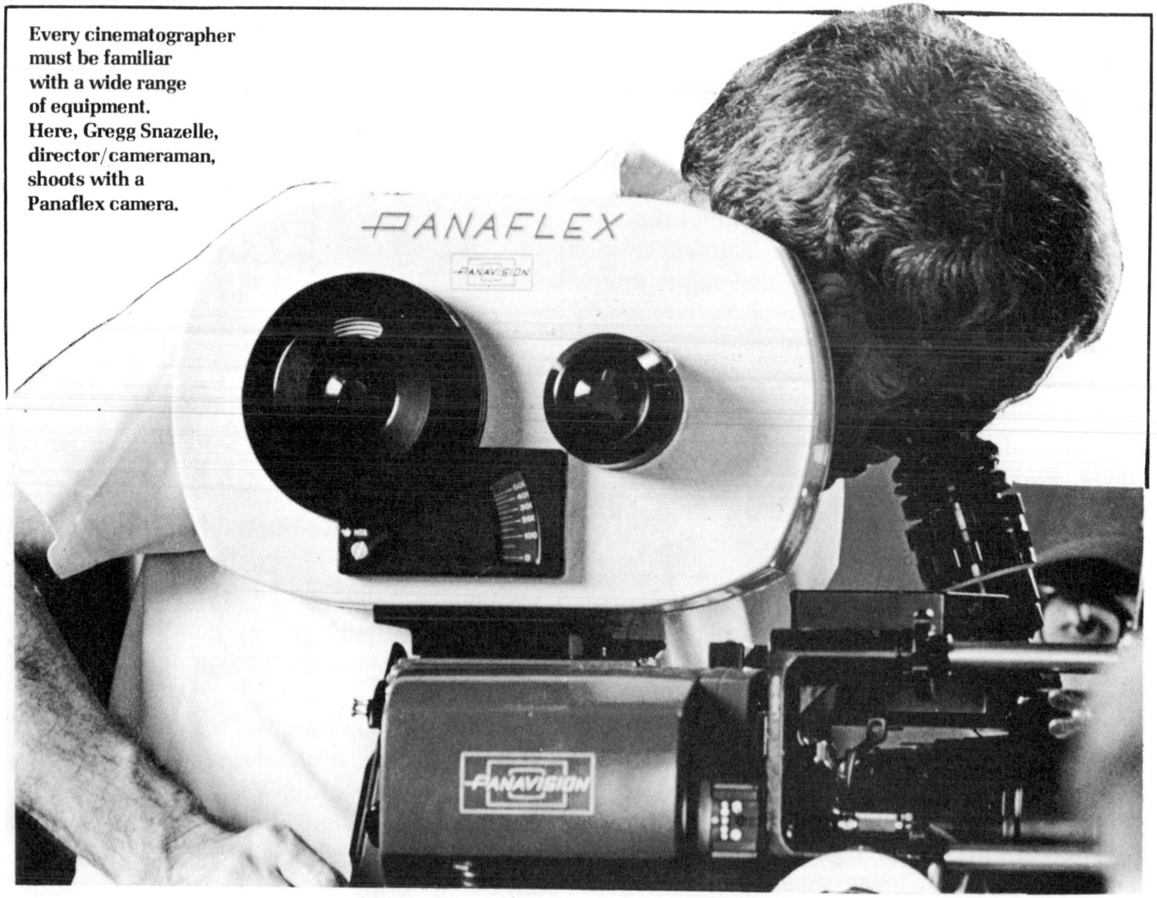

Every cinematographer must be familiar with a wide range of equipment. Here, Gregg Snazelle, director/cameraman, shoots with a Panaflex camera.

planned in advance. If Hitchcock could do it, so can you. Plan your shots, plan your outline, your continuity—as much of the finished film—before you even begin to expose one single foot of expensive film stock.

YOUR FILM SAMPLES Perhaps one of the most important assets in choosing cinematography as your career is the fact that you will eventually have a work sample to show your prospective employers. There is no better way for a cameraperson to get a job. The screen is the employment office and the interview. If the work is bad, there's no sense in going any further. If it's superb, then the producer can begin to look for the other factors that count: personality, speed, reputation.

Be selective. As you gain experience, you can begin to assemble only your best work, culling extraneous material from your reel. Some producers like to see clips from various films; others (such as the author) prefer to see one completed work, beginning to end. Sessions with producers will be difficult, at the very least, but they are quite necessary. You will be viewing your film for the two hundredth time, the producer for the first. When the voice comes out of the darkness and asks, "Did you shoot all of this?" you won't quite know whether it's good or bad when you whisper, "Yes."

STARTING OUT Possibly you will "hang out" at a camera-rental place—learning the technical aspects of the equipment, getting to know the people who drop in, and those who work there. Eventually you will take your test for the union, fully confident that you can break down and put together eight different kinds of cameras. Possibly you will act as a non-union electrician on a job that pays nothing while you observe the way the camera crew operates and you ask questions. On occasion, you may be asked to observe; or you may ask a question and be invited to see a film crew on location. Somewhere there will be the first glimmerings of a beginning, and somewhere you will start, all the while practicing and reading and learning about the craft.

My friend, cameraman Joe Longo, tells a story that I think says everything there is to say about cinematography—and about film in general:

I remember once, I was asked to do a film—it was a local film—and when I inquired about my crew they told me not to worry since they had the entire graduating class of the film school of the local university to help me. They would do anything I wanted them to do. Well, I had no idea how it would turn out, but I had to be fair about it and I said "O.K. Fine. We'll try it."

We went ahead, and from the very beginning I began to notice something. Everyone arrived at the location and got out of the cars. One guy had an expensive stopwatch on a leather thong around his neck. Another guy had a clipboard. Another one had a funny special hat to keep the sun out of his eyes. Somebody else took off his shoes and changed into Adidas sneakers—and still another was putting on a Gucci belt.

All this time, the camera was still in the case—and the case and the film were still in the car. I realized that if we were ever going to get this production off the ground, the first thing that had to happen was that we had to get the darned camera out of the case! The entire crew was so concerned with the glamour of the business that they assumed that someone else was going to do the menial work!

Well, it's all hard work—and somebody has to roll up his sleeves and push the dolly and someone has to sweep the floor before the take, and someone has to handle the slate.

So you'd like to have a career in cinematography?

Why not begin by taking the camera out of the case!

The Tyler Mount is generally used for helicopter photography in order to steady the camera and eliminate the bumps caused by air turbulence.

Editor Thelma Shoonmaker, of Snazelle Films, at the KEM 8-plate editing machine. New generations of flatbeds by Steenbeck, Moviola, and KEM have made the film editing process more flexible and innovative.

CHAPTER 7

THE EDITOR

"Don't Worry About Mistakes. You Can Always Save It in the Editing Room."

We have come to the reluctant conclusion that we will forever have to live with the reviewer of motion pictures. Whether in the feature field or in the narrow, lesser known realm of the independent film, as well as in the television documentary and even in commercials, the written word of approbation, criticism, or downright venom can help or hinder a career. For, long after many films and their artists have been consigned to the archives or have met a deserved fate of nonrecognition ("Whatever happened to . . . ?") the printed words of Arthur Knight, Judith Crist, Vincent Canby, and John Simon—if favorable—will still be pasted in the yellowing pages of filmmakers' scrapbooks and may still be used as credit material in the quest for new and better film jobs.

Too often, however, the work and genius of many people in the field goes unrecognized and unrewarded in the reviews printed in newspapers, magazines, and trade journals across the country. The director is certainly a personality in the making of the film. The camera work is obvious. The music may even be a critical factor. But, too often, because of ignorance or sloppiness, the reviewer gives credit where credit is certainly *not* due. Speak to the editor of a film and ask about the reaction to a rave film review that says, ". . . the excitement is enhanced by the *fast-paced photography.*" At this point, the editors throw up their hands and cry quietly among the faces on the cutting-room floor. How on earth would we get "fast-paced photography" (a non sequitur if there ever was one) if it were not for the film editor?

From the point of view of the producer and of one who has worked closely with editors over many years, editing certainly must be one of the most rewarding and, at the same time, one of the most frustrating jobs in the film field. The script was written a long time ago. The film was produced in Bangladesh and Bali. The production crew has been on location for two months, having all sorts of adventures, agog with the serendipity of new people and new places. They return, tired and with jet lag and complaining about how hard they worked and how difficult it was to get what they wanted. The editor sits in a darkened and quiet room in the middle of some anonymous building, and, into the lap of this uncomplaining genius, the production manager drops sixty hours of unconnected footage, the voice and sound tracks still not tied in in any way to the picture, none of the photography matching the original treatment—and a voice echoes hollowly as the door closes, "Make me a picture!"

Of course, the editor is not left entirely alone. The director does not really abdicate responsibility at this point for the feature film; and all motion pictures—including the commercial, the TV documentary, and the business

film—still have their many checkpoints, with agency producers, clients, committees, and the director all having their moments of re-creative glory. For the editor, who must attend these "bloodbaths," a great amount of patience, diplomacy, and fortitude are needed as the film is cut to shreds. Most editors are convinced that they are eligible for sainthood when checkpoint sessions are completed.

In today's film world, the good editor is no longer the one who merely "pastes" the film together. Even in the feature, where the script is generally adhered to in the shooting, and where it then also serves as a "road map" to the eventual editing, the mark of the editor is very much in evidence. A good editor brings to the film an ability to feel a story by the use of pictures, a superb eye for the selection of just the right shots, and a host of other talents, some of them innate and others acquired through years of experience. Pacing, timing, even structure, are in the realm of the editor, and the top people in the field, such as Dede Allen and Ralph Rosenblum are in demand because they add a fresh, creative eye and a talent for continuity to film. Some directors still demand almost total cut-by-cut control, and in fact, David Lean *edited* and directed *A Passage to India* in order to achieve his personal vision of what the film should look like, its rhythm, and its visual impact.

In the commercial, the editor is bound by a story board and a tight time frame, whether sixty seconds or thirty seconds. Frequently, though, the shooting does not go according to plan and sequences run over or under, photography is not what was expected (better or worse), and the editor is, in the final analysis, responsible for the pacing of the spot. The TV spot editor always seems to have people looking over his shoulder and reviewing the work in its various stages, but we did mention that the craft took patience and fortitude as well as skill.

Vision Associates, Inc.

REEL 1
SHEET 1

CUE SHEET

Prod. No. 543 Title To Make The Most of Today

NARR	DIAL 'A'	MUSIC		NARR	DIAL 'A'	MUSIC
9½ (B)	9½ (B	9½ (B)				
				191	up	
		12½ FI				
	31 FI			220	DOWN	
41						
		69 F.O.		292½	up	
68						
	70 DIAL					
				305½	DOWN	
88	DOWN			324½	up	
98	up					340½
				341½	341½	
120½	DOWN					
150½	up			365		
159	DOWN					

An editor's cue sheet prepared for a mixing session. The tracks and music are on separate reels and all will be blended to make one sound track for the picture.

Perhaps it is in the documentary that the editor has the greatest freedom. The film is generally shot to an outline or a written treatment, for no one really knows what will happen on location or what unusual event will take place just as the crew arrives. Back to the cutting room comes the uncut footage on large reels, perhaps logged by description or camera reports (but frequently not), thousands of feet of film to be looked at scene by scene, frame by frame, reel by endless reel. At this point, the editor has no preconception, though the director probably does, and the detachment necessary for this kind of job takes a particular kind of personality. The editor now becomes a diplomat, confidant, and artist.

Perhaps the director and crew, while on location, have gotten a particular shot with great difficulty and they are madly in love with the idea of how hard they worked to achieve that objective. In order to film the sequence, they have had to climb a mountain, haul the camera equipment up by cable and climbing equipment, drop part of the crew by helicopter, and then wait three days for the sun to set just behind the temple on the opposite mountain. Considering the work, the agony, the effort and the sheer logistics, they breathlessly tell the editor that it must be the most beautiful series of photographs known to mankind and that it will, indeed, make the film an Academy Award winner. Finally, the film comes out of the laboratory, the editor looks through the reel, and the monumental sequence really looks like any old sunset; they could have saved themselves the trouble of climbing the mountain. The editor, the only fairly objective person at that point in the film process, now must find a way to tell the director that it was not the editor who climbed the mountain—and that the shot is really not worth putting into the film. What words would you choose if you were the editor?

Aside from the necessity for an editor to have a deep personal and professional rapport with the director, and in addition to the creative aspects of the craft, there are several abilities that cannot be overemphasized:

ORGANIZATION

If you were to take a look at the raw footage as it comes into the editing room, you too would put this requirement at the top of your list. All editors organize differently, but all of them *organize*. Some editors, after the film comes back from the lab, laboriously catalogue the shots, one by individual one—description, reel number, and code number (the sequential numbers printed on each foot of film to allow for matching the work print to the original, later on). The time spent in these early stages will save hours later, when someone says, "Don't we have another scene that might replace this one?" Some editors break down the film into small rolls by scene or sequence, with labels on each roll, and each sequence in its own large box. Others break down their selected takes and hang them on pins in editing barrels, each pin labeled with the subject. Whatever their method, they all must be able to find what they want at a later date. It is awe-inspiring to watch a good editor find an additional ten frames of a scene that was cut three weeks before.

At least 50 percent of the editing process is organization—and the larger the project and the more footage involved, the more essential it is for the editor to be able to find selected shots quickly.

The editor may, in addition, have to research the subject of the film he is to edit, for each film is a process of self-education about a new subject, and the finished film will either have a shallow surface or a depth of understanding. The editor is as responsible for this as any member of the film team.

MANUAL DEXTERITY

I could never be an editor. After more than twenty-five years in the business, my manual dexterity is still where it was when I tried to pick up the tiny parts of ship models and succeeded only in cementing my first two fingers together. Even today, I am amazed at the dexterity displayed by the editor as he splices the tape with ease in a split second, moving on to the next cut, the next splice. The rhythms in an editing room are marvelous to watch: the threading of the Steenbeck or Moviola (editing machines), the handling of the film, the splicing, resplicing, structuring of sequences, and then, with incredible facility, the breaking down and restructuring for a second and a third time.

A SELECTIVE EYE

The editor must have "a good eye," like the cinematographer and director. Though "dailies" are usually screened by everyone concerned with the selection, the editor is the one who is finally alone in the room with the footage. He must be able to understand what the cinematographer and director had in mind.

A GOOD EAR

There is good sound and there definitely is bad sound. The editor's selection process includes not only the visual aspect of the film, but also sound "takes." An editor needs "a good ear"—the ability to hear sound as it changes tone, as voices vary, as inflections change the meaning of a word or a sentence. Some of the best editors in the documentary field—Ted Kanter, Suzanne Jasper, Sara Stein, and Peter Rosenbaum—are all adept at taking hundreds of pages of taped interview material and making a logical, sensible, exciting sound track for a picture.

Since visual editing is a fairly well-known phase of the industry, what follows is an example of *sound* editing for a documentary film we produced for NBC, *In Mister Lincoln's Footsteps.* The original pages are transcripts from an interview with a Lincoln historian in northern Kentucky. The numbers refer to the edge markings that identify the track at any given point. First, read the entire transcript (next page) from beginning to end.

The problem for the editor, Peter Rosenbaum, was to condense the story into a concise, interesting paragraph while retaining the thrust, the meaning, and the continuity. If you now go back and follow his cutting from number to number, the story unfolds as a totally rewritten "narration." And this is how it appeared in the film:

So at age 19 he took his first trip down the Ohio and then the Mississippi River to New

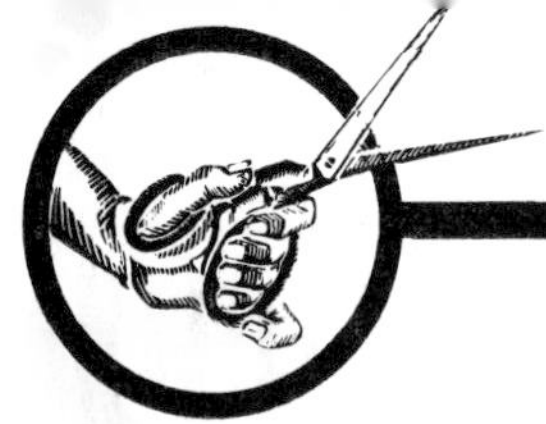

Orleans on a flatboat. He was a crew member. A cousin by the name of Hanks and a friend by the name of Johnson went with him and they took produce and that sort of stuff and went all the way to New Orleans. It must've been pretty rugged. It took about 5 months to go from here down to New Orleans. It's hard to believe, I mean Daniel Boone was still alive and this sort of thing, it was the tail end of the fabulous era of frontiersmanship. We had a great cotillion of river pirates up and down the rivers those days and I guess fast buck artists; they seemed to take advantage of young Mr. Lincoln and some of his friends, and they whomped him pretty good as the story goes, and the next year of course he grew, as many teenagers and he was a pretty good rough and tumble fighter . . . Not many people remember that, and he just slipped around and trapped a bunch of the pirates, and according to how the story goes, beat the daylights out of them. So Mr. Lincoln believed in paying his debts.

LABORATORIES

In the large cities, such as New York, Los Angeles, and Chicago, are many laboratories competing for the business given out by film companies. Though the total price per developed and printed foot may seem small, the huge amounts of footage delivered for each job can run into large amounts of money. Though one lab is a few pennies cheaper than another, the

Lincoln 3-7

she would be his wife. And she thought about it a few minutes I suppose and she said, no, I don't think I can, Tom, because I have too much indebtedness. And he said, well don't worry about that; we'll take care of your bills. And the story goes that he paid the bills, or the bills were paid that she had incurred and the next day they were married and they started making plans and preparations to move ...to move her and her family and goods into Indiana. C1004

WILD SOUND - BUTTER CHURNING REEL I W.T. AC0000

A1760–1817

WILD TRACK, flatboats, Bob Riley.

A1826

Bob, I think...let's, you know, start from the beginning. Now what did...and when you speak, if you'd speak in total sentences cause my questions are cut out... what did Abraham Lincoln have to do with flatboats?

B. Riley: Well flatboats were well developed by the Lincoln era, and of course he was born in 1809. By the time he was 19 his family had gone through a lot of difficulties and that was about the time that the young men struck out on their own. So at age 19 he took his first trip down the Ohio and then the Mississippi River to New Orleans. [how?] On a flatboat. He was a crew member. The second year, in his 20th year, and there's some discussion whether it was his 20th, 21st year, like there is in all Lincoln stories, but he took off himself running the program. And a cousin by the name of Hanks and a friend by the name of Johnson went with him. And so two different years there's a record where he actually was a crew member or ran the flatboat and they took produce and that sort of stuff and

1920

Lincoln 3-8

went all the way to New Orleans and...

What was it like in those days?

A1924

Riley: It must've been pretty rugged. It took about 5 months to go from here down to New Orleans. TO P3-9 ..the record time was set at ST. Louis to New Orleans was 4 months even. A1935

And the river? Was it a safe river or not?

Riley: Well the river was generally outside of the spring floods, we down to... 2½ 3 foot depth. It was fraught with many sand bars and the biggest troubles they had was sandbars and of course river pirates. Not many people understand it but FROM 3-9 we had a great cotillion of river pirates up and down the rivers in those days and I guess fast buck artists and, you know   they took advantage TO 3-9 of these people, and particularly the homesteaders who weren't well adapted. This method of transportation was really developed in the A 1983 late 17 hundreds and people brought household goods and things like that down the Ohio and they populated most of the river communities, particularly Henderson and Owensboro and that. This was called yellow banks here, and it was called red banks in the Henderson area. 2012

Now on this...Lincoln himself...didn't Lincoln have a run in with some pirates...

Riley: Well, they tell the story that, not on his two long trips to New Orleans but that he got on his experience as a deck hand, so called a ferry deck hand, was around the falls of the Ohio which is now Louisville. And they'd bring a flatboat in upstream and then they would have to portage the stuff or carry it by back around what we call Louisville now and get on the second   and the first time

A 2063

Lincoln 3-9

FROM 3-8
A 2069

they seemed to take advantage of young Mr. Lincoln and some of his friends. He probably was 17 or 18 and they whomped him pretty good as the story goes and the next year of course he grew, as many teen agers did and he was rather well prepared they say and he was a pretty good rough and tumble fighter...not many people remember that but you know, most frontiersmen if they still were in the 1830's.. FROM 3-8 it's hard to believe, I mean Daniel Boone was still alive and this sort of thing, it was the tail end of the fabulous era of frontiersmenship TO 3-8 and he just slipped around and trapped a bunch of the pirates and according to the story goes beat the daylights out of them. I suspect he had a little help here and there. But they got even with them and as what the narrators say that they recognized some of the ruffians from previous encounters. So Mr. Lincoln believed in paying his debts. A2155

Now about today. What's about these races here. What's the reason for them   could you just start by saying well today we've kept, you know, something like that...

Riley: Yeah, the races today, so called races because they're floating on the current, there will be a little rowing here and there to steer and to get some speed and stay out of the way of the power boats but the...it's a throwback to the bicentennial days of the 1890s and so forth. A2201 The flatboats of course, really, the race itself started because we started talking about John James Audubon who came down about 1808 and populated the area, and of course was very famous in this area and lived in Henderson for a number of years and so we jokingly said that well if Audubon could come down the river in a

The original transcripts from the location recordings for In Mister Lincoln's Footsteps. By restructuring the sentences, the editor created a totally new narration (see text).

more expensive supplier may be the best one to use. The editor must be aware of laboratory facilities, prices, quality, and delivery. Also, when a new film stock is developed by a film manufacturer, the editors and producers watch carefully as the laboratories work with this new stock. One particular stock I've had experience with had a tendency to pick up dirt, which showed as white spots on the film; the emulsion was thinner and needed care in handling of the original; optical effects were difficult to achieve. Some labs managed to deliver good work, but some struggled in vain—and producers tore their remaining hair out by the roots. The editors watched the development carefully and they were the ones who gave good advice and counsel, knowing that each time the new stock was used it would be the editor who had to see it through the lab and on to completion.

The problem of delivery is, furthermore, a critical one for commercial producers and television documentaries, but it is also a factor for feature films that have screening dates. The editor is generally the one who works with the laboratory to see that the dates are met.

A FEEL FOR MUSIC AND RHYTHM

Whether the film is to have an original music score or a library score (see Chapter 8), the editor must have an innate sense of music and rhythm. Composers find it easier to work with a film that has been well edited, for the pacing and timing are generally rhythmic and well structured. In addition, the editor frequently cuts a film, then *recuts* it when the music track is completed; animation is frequently designed and edited to the finished score. Some editors not only cut the picture, but also the music track, in order to give the film a unity and a sense of pace.

AN ABILITY TO DESIGN OPTICALS, TITLES, AND CREDITS

Some editors lay out their own optical effects (split screens, superimpositions*) and handle title design for the films on which they are working. Other productions utilize art directors and graphic designers for the job. In either instance, the editor must know how to get the job accomplished; which optical house is best for the specific project; where the typefaces are available for the titles and credits and how to get them on to the screen. Just as a sense of composition is necessary in the editor's work with photographic content, so is a sense of design important in the finishing of the film through opticals, titles, and credits.

THE ABILITY TO "FINISH" A FILM

When the editor cuts the film, each element is done on a separate roll: the picture, dialogue tracks, narration track, music tracks, sound-effect tracks, loops (tracks that have a constant effect repeated over and over, such as wind or birds or the hum of a crowd)—all of them separate and distinct and easily changed. Then, at some point, the producer or client or agency says, "O.K.," and the film goes into its finishing stages. It is here that the editor's technical knowledge is terribly important, for much of the finishing is done alone, without supervision, with deadlines and pressure mounting to see the finished product.

The editor must know how to select a mixing studio, where all the tracks are blended into one "mixed" track, with the proper balance of sound to music, and all of them helping to strengthen the picture. Again the "ear" comes into play. The balance of the track is as much the editor's choice as the mixer's.

The editor generally works with or chooses a negative matcher (someone who matches the original to the work print). All original film is maintained uncut until the film is finally approved, and then is matched to the material with which the editor has been working—the workprint. And finally, the laboratory again; and the follow-through to the "answer print"—the first print that utilizes the mixed track and the cut original. If the color is not quite right, the editor must know it. If the track is out of synchronization or the sound is bad, the editor must fix it up.

Editing, everyone will tell you, is an extremely competitive craft. The unions do not actively seek new members because many of their members are out of work at any given time. Yet people manage to get jobs and new editors appear every year—some of them very good and quite talented. One of the advantages of choosing this career is that, once again, there is something for you to show if you de-

*The split screen shows two or more images on the screen at one time with the screen divided into two or four or eight segments. Superimposing merely describes printing one scene *over* another.

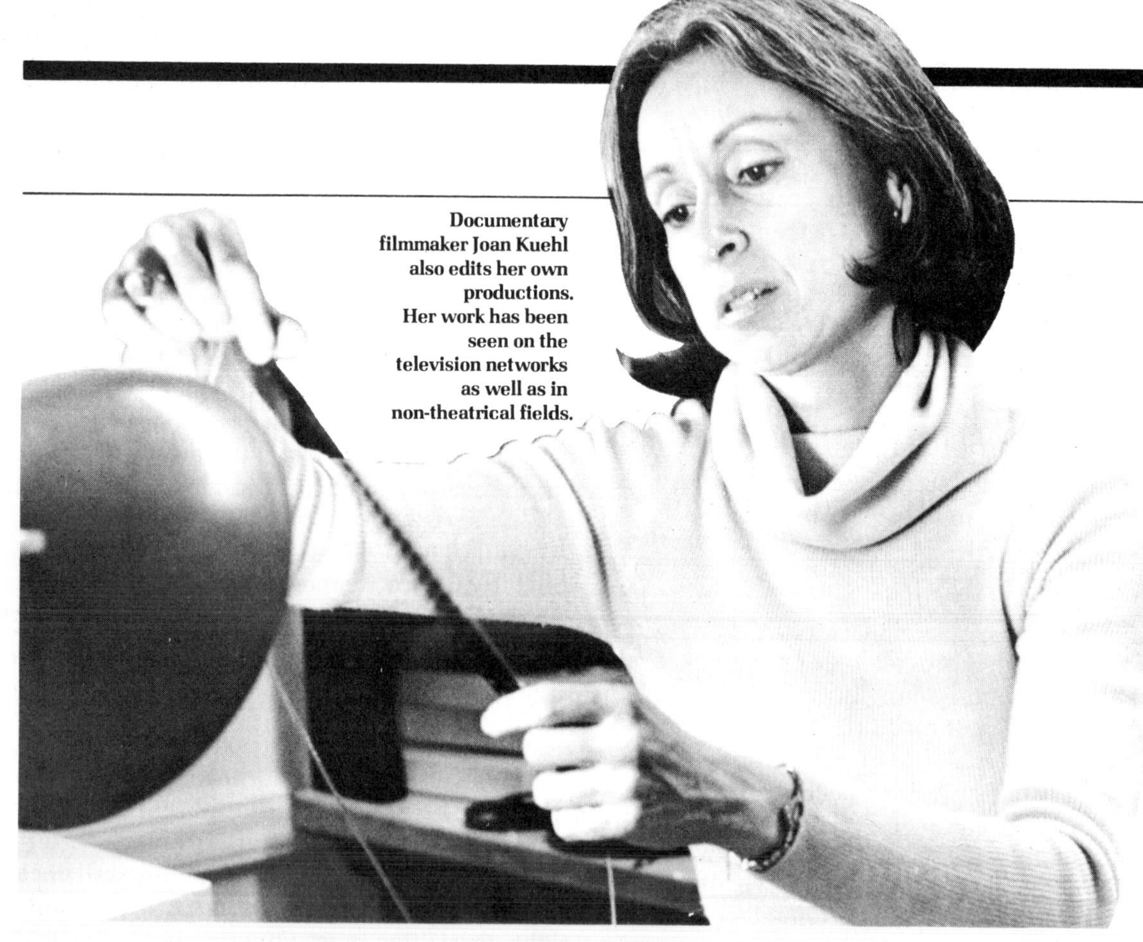

Documentary filmmaker Joan Kuehl also edits her own productions. Her work has been seen on the television networks as well as in non-theatrical fields.

cide early enough that editing is your choice. School films, independent films, even your first small professional projects are all potential samples for your job hunt. If you have edited a film, the results will show on the screen, much as they will for the cinematographer.

The three major job categories in editing are: editor, assistant editor, editing room assistant. The editor makes all the decisions. The assistant is generally responsible for synchronizing the sound to the picture when the dailies come in, finding material that has been catalogued, helping in the process of organization, and splicing. The "learning phase" of the craft is covered by the editing room assistant, who might make trips to the lab, help in rewinding of film, and clean up the scraps on the cutting-room floor.

On occasion, we come across other categories in the editing field: sound editor, motion picture librarian, and assistant librarian. The categories are almost self-explanatory in their titles. If the editing room is located at a network, for example, the librarian is solely responsible for filing, cataloguing, arranging, and selecting footage for the film editors who work on the news shows and special events. Both categories provide excellent entry positions into the field, with the added advantage of close proximity to working editors.

But there is no rule of thumb for entering this specialty and then rising to whatever heights your talents will take you. Editing is technical, but it is also creative—and the editors who can add a strong visual element to a film will find their way to the producers who recognize that talent.

There will be frustrations, as with everything else. There will be the lonely days (and nights) in the closed editing room, the air conditioning for the building turned off because of the late hour, the coffee in the paper cup cold, the film barrel full, the cut reel not full enough, the mind filled with thoughts of, "Why didn't they think of this while they were shooting the film? It would have saved me hours!" If someone could answer you in that dimly lit, tiny cubicle, the voice might tell you words of wisdom that some editor sagely uttered: "Editing is like flowers at a wedding . . . absolutely necessary but never thought of until last."

The next morning, red-eyed and weary, the editor greets the director, who has just come from a good night's sleep. The editor is convinced, having worked so hard and so long, that the film is in great shape, the sequences are fantastically paced, and that this must certainly be the best cut ever given to a motion picture in history. After all, if one has worked so hard to achieve this, the results must be obvious to anyone. The director looks in silence, turns to the editor, and says that it needs a lot of work—the pacing is off, and the structure doesn't seem to work. "Let's start from the beginning and go through it again. A few more days and nights should do it."

The editor has just climbed the mountain.

CHAPTER 8

MUSIC

"Lamar Loveless Is the Best Durn Fiddler in These Parts"

Unless the intent is to produce a period piece—therefore using the costumes, decoration, and ambience of a particular time and place—three things will "date" a film more quickly than anything else.

The first, of course, is fashion. Women's clothes, for example, change each season and every few years the hemlines go up or down, silhouettes vary from generation to generation, and the observant moviegoer notices quickly that the film was obviously made at another time. The students in a college classroom of the forties, whether male or female, would certainly not look the same as those attending school today. In some films, this makes absolutely no difference at all: the film may be designed to play for a short time and then disappear, to reappear years later as a "period piece." However, if the film is to have a longer screen life—perhaps as a travel film, for example—timelessness plays a part in its design and fashions must be very much considered.

The second factor that quickly dates a film is the use of automobiles.

The third is music.

Music, like fashion, comes into style quickly and seems to go into oblivion just as quickly. In an era where disc jockeys consider a song written two years ago an "oldie," what chance did sixties rock have to survive its era without appearing dated? When electronic music became the vogue, filmmakers flocked to use it and soon everything sounded as if the same composer had been let loose on the Moog synthesizer. For almost two years, no film score was complete without the use of electronic music. Certainly, it was a breakthrough, and it is still being used—but with moderation. The synthesizer provides a vast range of electronic sounds, some re-creating standard instruments, others that are sheer and unusual invention. By combining many of these sounds, a new kind of music has been made available to the motion picture.

Some time ago we screened some of our earlier films. Along with the laughter and self-consciousness that always goes with seeing early works, we noticed that the photography of people like Richard Bagley and Bernie Hirschenson was nevertheless still exquisite, the editing exceptional for its time, and the music—well, if we could have changed the music scores, the films would still have had a totally contemporary feeling.

Some filmmakers have overcome the problem of "dating" by utilizing classical pieces in otherwise contemporary films: Bach, Mozart, Corelli . . . Sometimes it seems strained, at other times it works beautifully. Terrence Malick, in his lovely film *Badlands,* used a Carl Orff oratorio during the fire sequence and the juxtaposition resulted in one of the most original uses of music in feature films. In the early fifties, a charming travel film about Italy was produced by Kit Davison for Alitalia Airlines: *Variations on an Italian Theme.* The country, of course, is beautiful and much of it has not changed over two thousand years. The music chosen was Vivaldi's *Four Seasons* and the film is still playing today because of its absolute timelessness.

Certainly, budget plays a large part in the choice of music, and most young filmmakers, strapped for cash, try to utilize only a few instruments. As a result, we have probably seen upwards of 750 student films scored for solo guitar or flute.

For the filmmaker interested in music, there is still great flexibility and opportunity in the field, though the competition (as in every other phase of film) is horrendous. The prerequisites may seem strange to you as you read them, for in many cases a knowledge of music is not even necessary! But before all the budding Francis Lais and Max Steiners and Quincy Joneses raise their eyebrows, let us go on.

There are basically three methods of providing music for films: location music, original score, library score.

LOCATION MUSIC

The first is easiest to explain in that it is merely the music recorded on location at an event and then later used on the sound track. Of course, the music of *Woodstock* would be in this category, for it was an integral part of the story and had to be recorded on location. When an event is taking place, a recording of the "real" sound is certainly much more effective than filming silent footage and then trying to find music to fit, later on. Location music also lends "presence" to the track.

The category of location music is sometimes concerned with finding the indigenous music of a people in order to lend an aura of believa-

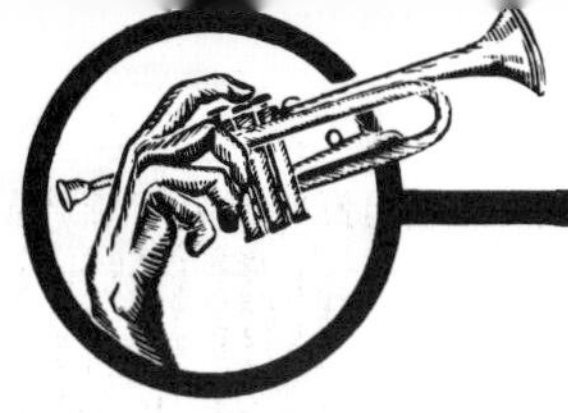

bility and authenticity to the photography on the screen. With only a tape recorder, any filmmaker can find some music of the locale and record it for possible future editing into the finished film.

Some time ago, during the filming of a series on Americana, our assistant director thought it might be a good idea to find some fiddle music to go with a sequence to be shot in the hills of Kentucky. My first instinct was to override the suggestion because we had a very tight schedule, the weather had been playing havoc with our travel arrangements, and I felt that we would eventually find a fiddler or a piece of recorded music back in New York. "But not like a fiddler you'd find here," the stubborn A.D. insisted. I decided that perhaps he was right.

We were working in the rural areas of the state and we began to inquire about a fiddler. Finally, we found an old man in a country store and asked him if he could give us the name of the greatest fiddler in Kentucky. Without hesitating a moment, he said, "Lamar Loveless is the best durn fiddler in these parts—up near Whitehead."

Whitehead was eighty miles from where we were—and our next location was over one hundred miles in the *opposite* direction. Again I gave my opinion, but the crew seemed determined that nothing would help this film like the "best durn fiddler in these parts"—and, in any case, they would just drive faster to get to the next location. We set off for Whitehead. The crew was jubilant. Audiences would breathlessly exclaim, "Who's the fiddler on that sound track?"

In the town square of Whitehead, near the courthouse, among the hangers-on and the whittlers making toothpicks out of logs, we began our quest to find the legendary Lamar Loveless. We asked an old gentleman if he knew where we could find Lamar. Another whittler looked up and murmured, "Best durned fiddler in these parts!" The first gentleman kept whittling, his Caterpillar tractor peak hat pulled over his face, and then looked up slowly. "That's goin' to be a mite difficult. Ol' Lamar's been dead nearly forty year." And, as he went back to his whittling, the shattered crew heard him mutter, "Sure could play the fiddle, though!"

Location music is not always possible and certainly for many, if not most, films it just would not work. The music is either not available (where would you find it in a steel factory?) or it is simply not the best way to provide the score for the film. In terms of this book's purpose, location music provides few openings for the beginner in film music and certainly no glowing future as a film composer or music editor.

The other two avenues in the craft of film music are certainly more important and considerably more complex.

ORIGINAL SCORE MUSIC

Film is a visual medium, of course—with factors that help the images: voices, sound effects, and music. But these three are subservient to the film itself and each of them must enhance the visual imagery without getting in the way of the film.

Malcolm Dodds began his career as a serious classical composer, but found a better way to make a living in the field of commercial film. He also did the vocal arrangements for the Broadway show, Sophisticated Ladies.

As a result, there are composers, many of them quite talented or even touched by greatness, who cannot write music for film. Writing for concert is one thing—for the music takes the lead, and is the only factor that has to be considered. In writing for film, it is the structure of the editing, the mood of the individual sequence, and the pacing of the film itself that controls the music that is to be written for it. Nowhere is there a chance for the abstract composition, unrelated to theme, for the *picture* must lead the composer into the eventual phrases that will be written. Think of a storm—or an idyllic meadow—or a duel—or a blast furnace in a steel mill—or a canning machine. There would be many ways to handle the composition of music for those images, but the picture comes first. The composer finds the moods of the film and then writes to those moods. Even in the field of the commercial jingle, the composer is bound by certain parameters: what story must be told, what the story-board structure is and the mood of the spot, and whether or not the words have been written first.

Malcolm Dodds, one of the more successful writers of music for television, puts it this way: *A good arranger or composer in utilitarian music—TV, the stage or films—must be able to weave all styles and forms into whatever the particular assignment requires. I suppose that I would say that the two most important attributes a composer in these fields can have are discipline and the ability to sublimate ego. You have to know all the rudiments of music in order to achieve the discipline—and you can never let your ego overcome the assignment given to you. In other words, you're writing a*

The Malcolm Dodds arrangement for the short subject Look Up, America, produced by Vision Associates for Coca-Cola and distributed by United Artists. © 1974-1975 Shada Music, Inc. All rights reserved.

commercial or movie theme and you find it's absolutely delicious—sounds great and you want it to go on—almost like a painter wishing he had a four-foot canvas instead of a four-inch canvas. You've got to learn to restrict yourself to the demands and to force into sixty or thirty seconds something that Brahms and Beethoven might have expanded to twenty-five minutes. We don't have the luxury of time.

Discipline? Of course. Sublimation of ego? With difficulty, perhaps. And there are still other factors that come into play if you are to write original music for film:

BUDGETS You must know—probably in advance—just what the budget for the music will be. Since cost is a factor in every production, the music budget is a part of it and many would-be composers are asked the question, "What will it cost?" even before they can figure the specific items or screen the film. Union rules, if they apply, must be considered, as well as rates for musicians, copying fees, recording fees, arranging, transfer of original tape to larger magnetic tape for cutting and mixing, studio time—and, hopefully, a small profit for you as the composer for writing the score. The amount of time it takes you to compose, record, and mix the eight- or sixteen-track tape will reflect itself in the final budget for the music track. The more adept you are, the shorter the time from start to finish, the more the chances of making a profit on the job.

TIMING In concert, it is a simple matter to play "The Minute Waltz" in a minute and ten seconds. No one is counting, we hope. However, in film, the music is generally composed to the edited film, where rhythms remain constant within sequences and the music must be accurate. (Purists will point out, accurately, that *some* music is written first to story board—as in animation—and then the picture is done to the track.)

Because of the nature of film, though, the film composer works to *footages* rather than to time on a clock, though one eventually translates into the other. For example, 36 feet in 16mm film would be one minute. The minute can then be broken down into 18 feet for thirty seconds, and so forth. In smaller increments, the composer figures 24 frames for one second, 12 frames for half a second, 6 frames for a quarter-second. (In 35mm, 90 feet represents one minute, while frame counts remain the same—i.e., 24 frames per second.)

One of our favorite composers cannot add, and, at a recent work session for a seven-minute film, his outline seemed awfully long to us. "It works out," he insisted, "it's exactly on time." We went over it—section by section—and then added the seconds. Proudly, he turned to us and smiled. "See, it adds up: seven hundred seconds—*seven minutes!*" At a time like that, the choice is to laugh or to cry, for the recording session was scheduled the next day and the composer had divided 700 by 100 instead of by 60. The track was actually eleven and a half minutes long. It had to be cut down in a matter of hours. And it was.

The composer is not only creating to images, but is bound by edited rhythms, by footages on the track, and, of course, by time. You begin to see why composing for film is quite different from a future in Carnegie Hall. At the recording session, a "click track" is provided, through headsets, for whoever is to set the rhythm of the music—usually the composer and the drummer. The click track might well be called a "film metronome," and if the music needs a beat at each 12 frames in order to cut to the film, a click will be heard every half-second. When the music is recorded and then laid against the film, the picture and track can then be synchronized.

RECORDING The field of recording is a necessary part of the composer's storehouse of knowledge. He must know what studios are available, the best recording engineers in his area of the country, how the mixers work, the flexibility available with multitrack recordings, the potential for overdubbing, and how to mix the finished track. It is much easier to mix and balance the completed sequence than to re-record with all the costs involved for studio time, musicians, and singers.

In the world of original film music, the role of the recording engineer is critical, for he controls much more of the completed sound than does the composer or conductor. In the concert hall, the total sound is a unity and the audience hears an end result that is pre-mixed by the very fact that the orchestra is hopefully playing together. Not so in the recording studio. With the advent of eight-track and sixteen-track recordings, the engineer has become the good right arm of the conductor.

The music session builds a track layer by layer. Because of the problems of budget and because there is greater control of sound when we separate the tracks and then mix later on, the conductor generally schedules the musicians and singers by time of day. They arrive at different hours because they are paid for "a session," a period that ranges in time from two to three hours' duration. For the conductor to utilize the instruments most effectively, the singers should not be sitting around waiting for the rhythm section to finish its work.

Each group (or "choir") is taken individually and the engineer decides which instruments will go on the same track, for if there are twelve instruments and only eight tracks, we must find some way to combine instruments, all of them later to be mixed into one master track that contains the whole piece of music, properly balanced. One of the most astounding things to greet the eye of the uninitiated at a recording session is that all the musicians, at first glance, would seem to hate one another—or at the very least have some dread disease that might be spread by close contact. The drummer sits behind a large wooden baffle, headset on his ears listening to the click track. The guitarist is in another part of the studio, the bass player back against the wall, facing sideways and seemingly not a part of the group, while the conductor faces the engineer, who is isolated behind a double plate glass and is sitting with his mixing console and tape machines like someone out of *2001*. As they play, each instrument or choir will be put on its own track. As a result of this recording technique, the conductor (through a music contractor) might plan the recording day as follows:

9 A.M. Start of session, with rhythm section—possibly drums, piano, bass guitar. Since all musicians hate to get up early, the 9 A.M. session will probably begin closer to 10.

11 A.M. Add color with woodwinds, flute, violins, harmonica.

1 P.M. Lunch on paper plates of soggy hamburgers, pickles, warm Cokes, greasy French fried potatoes sent up by the local Ptomaine Tavern. This is usually eaten on the run while listening to the last take and does not count for "time out."

1:30 P.M. Add Moog synthesizer to one of the tracks. All of the musicians who are added through the day wear headsets so they may get the proper beat of what has gone before.

3 P.M. Add voices of singers.

When all of this has been completed and the musicians have departed, the sound engineer and the conductor begin to mix the tracks, all eight or all sixteen of them. It is an incredible sight to watch and hear. All kinds of things

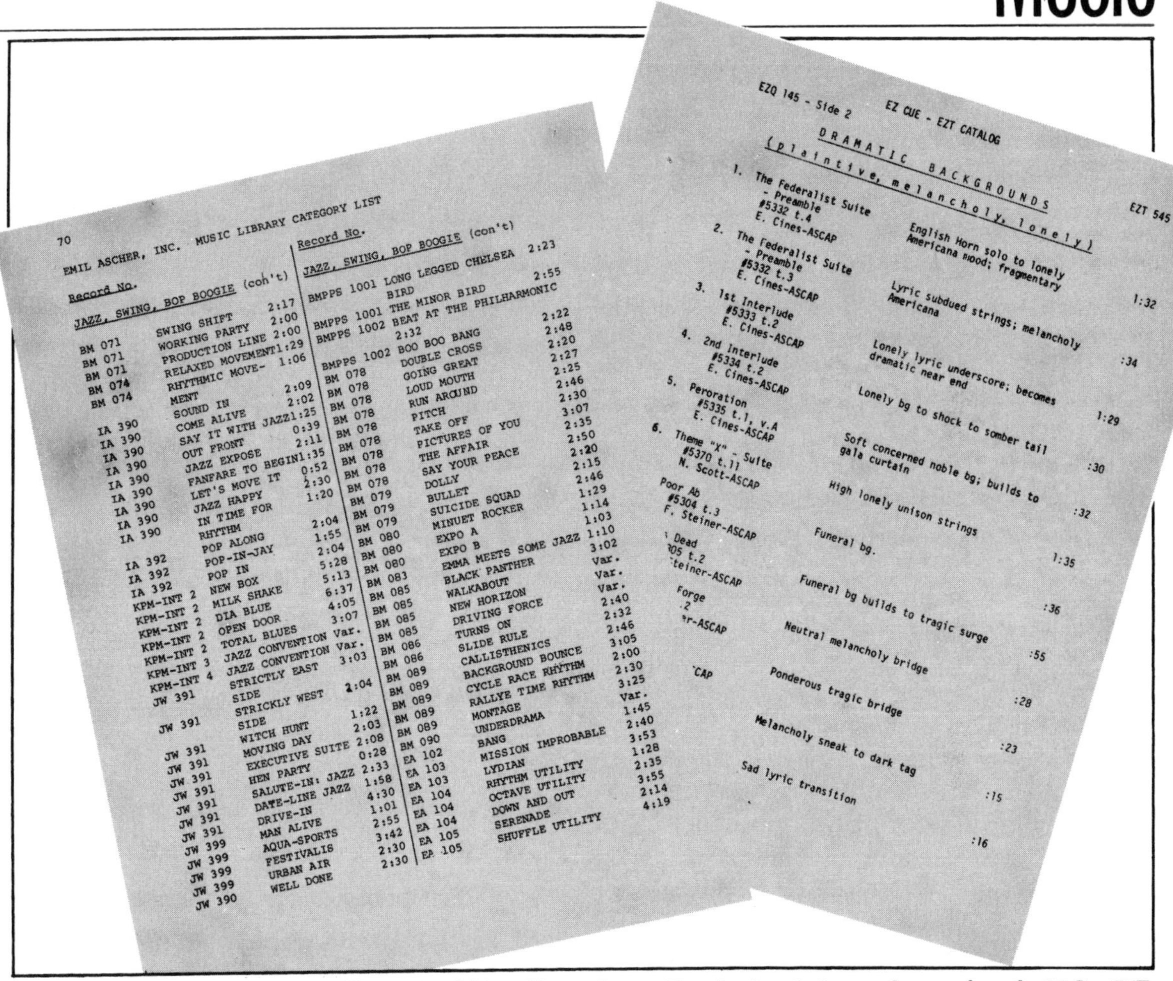

70

EMIL ASCHER, INC. MUSIC LIBRARY CATEGORY LIST

Record No.

JAZZ, SWING, BOP BOOGIE (con't)

BM 071 SWING SHIFT 2:17
BM 071 WORKING PARTY 2:00
BM 071 PRODUCTION LINE 2:00
BM 074 RELAXED MOVEMENT1:29
BM 074 RHYTHMIC MOVE- 1:06
MENT
IA 390 SOUND IN 2:09
IA 390 COME ALIVE 2:02
IA 390 SAY IT WITH JAZZ1:25
IA 390 OUT FRONT 0:39
IA 390 JAZZ EXPOSE 2:11
IA 390 FANFARE TO BEGIN1:35
IA 390 LET'S MOVE IT 0:52
IA 390 JAZZ HAPPY 2:30
IA 390 IN TIME FOR 1:20
RHYTHM
IA 392 POP ALONG 2:04
IA 392 POP-IN-JAY 1:55
IA 392 POP IN 2:04
KPM-INT 2 NEW BOX 5:28
KPM-INT 2 MILK SHAKE 5:13
KPM-INT 2 DIA BLUE 6:37
KPM-INT 2 OPEN DOOR 4:05
KPM-INT 2 TOTAL BLUES 3:07
KPM-INT 3 JAZZ CONVENTION Var.
KPM-INT 4 JAZZ CONVENTION Var.
JW 391 STRICTLY EAST 3:03
SIDE
JW 391 STRICKLY WEST 2:04
SIDE
JW 391 WITCH HUNT 1:22
JW 391 MOVING DAY 2:03
JW 391 EXECUTIVE SUITE 2:08
JW 391 HEN PARTY 0:28
JW 391 SALUTE-IN: JAZZ 2:33
JW 391 DATE-LINE JAZZ 1:58
JW 391 DRIVE-IN 4:30
JW 399 MAN ALIVE 1:01
JW 399 AQUA-SPORTS 2:55
JW 399 FESTIVALIS 3:42
JW 399 URBAN AIR 2:30
JW 390 WELL DONE 2:30

Record No.

JAZZ, SWING, BOP BOOGIE (con't)

BMPPS 1001 LONG LEGGED CHELSEA 2:23
BIRD
BMPPS 1001 THE MINOR BIRD 2:55
BMPPS 1002 BEAT AT THE PHILHARMONIC
2:32
BMPPS 1002 BOO BOO BANG 2:22
BM 078 DOUBLE CROSS 2:48
BM 078 GOING GREAT 2:20
BM 078 LOUD MOUTH 2:27
BM 078 RUN AROUND 2:25
BM 078 PITCH 2:46
BM 078 TAKE OFF 2:30
BM 078 PICTURES OF YOU 3:07
BM 078 THE AFFAIR 2:35
BM 078 SAY YOUR PEACE 2:50
BM 079 DOLLY 2:20
BM 079 BULLET 2:15
BM 079 SUICIDE SQUAD 2:46
BM 080 MINUET ROCKER 1:29
BM 080 EXPO A 1:14
BM 080 EXPO B 1:03
BM 083 EMMA MEETS SOME JAZZ 1:10
BM 085 BLACK PANTHER 3:02
BM 085 WALKABOUT Var.
BM 085 NEW HORIZON Var.
BM 085 DRIVING FORCE Var.
BM 086 TURNS ON 2:40
BM 086 SLIDE RULE 2:32
BM 089 CALLISTHENICS 2:46
BM 089 BACKGROUND BOUNCE 3:05
BM 089 CYCLE RACE RHYTHM 2:00
BM 089 RALLYE TIME RHYTHM 2:30
BM 089 MONTAGE 3:25
BM 090 UNDERDRAMA Var.
EA 102 BANG 1:45
EA 103 MISSION IMPROBABLE 2:40
EA 103 LYDIAN 3:53
EA 104 RHYTHM UTILITY 1:28
EA 104 OCTAVE UTILITY 2:35
EA 104 DOWN AND OUT 3:55
EA 105 SERENADE 2:14
EA 105 SHUFFLE UTILITY 4:19

EZQ 145 - Side 2 EZ CUE - EZT CATALOG EZT 545 B

DRAMATIC BACKGROUNDS

(plaintive, melancholy, lonely)

1. The Federalist Suite - Preamble #5332 t.4 E. Cines-ASCAP — English Horn solo to lonely Americana mood; fragmentary — 1:32
2. The Federalist Suite - Preamble #5332 t.3 E. Cines-ASCAP — Lyric subdued strings; melancholy Americana — :34
3. 1st Interlude #5333 t.2 E. Cines-ASCAP — Lonely lyric underscore; becomes dramatic near end — 1:29
4. 2nd Interlude #5334 t.2 E. Cines-ASCAP — Lonely bg to shock to somber tail — :30
5. Peroration #5335 t.1, v.A E. Cines-ASCAP — Soft concerned noble bg; builds to gala curtain — :32
6. Theme "X" - Suite #5370 t.11 N. Scott-ASCAP — High lonely unison strings — 1:35

Poor Ab #5304 t.3 F. Steiner-ASCAP — Funeral bg. — :36

Dead
05 t.2
teiner-ASCAP — Funeral bg builds to tragic surge — :55

Forge
.2
r-ASCAP — Neutral melancholy bridge — :28

CAP — Ponderous tragic bridge — :23

Melancholy sneak to dark tag — :15

Sad lyric transition — :16

Typical music selections in the stock libraries available to film producers. Note the descriptions on the page from the EZ Cue-EZT Catalog.

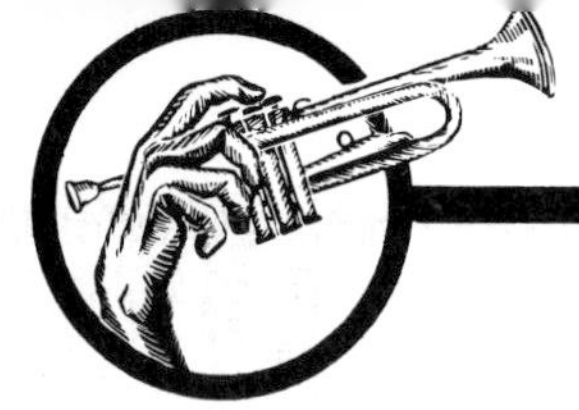

can happen in the music mix: echo can be added to one or more of the instruments, sections of the music can be cut if necessary, and different selections can be blended so that there is no gap between them and they sound as if they were recorded in one continuous session. With a flick of the dial, the engineer and conductor can determine which choir should be higher—and a penny whistle can be made to sound louder than a French horn, the sigh of a singer louder than the beat of a drum. Where the voices must cut through the music, not only can the engineer make them sound louder, but he can also add treble to make them drive through the other instruments. And, out of it all, comes the finished track, soon to be added to the film.

So . . . you will have to know music and certainly the more you know about timing and recording and budgets, the better off you will be. As you progress, keep in mind that the composer, like the amateur cinematographer, also works in an area where the samples are there to show and to hear. The work you've already done, be it a finished film or a recording on tape, is always available to prove what you can do. You will always be questioned about budget: How much did that track cost? How many instruments did you use? How much will the producer have to pay for a similar track? But most important to your potential career is the fact that original music is still used in only a small part of the film field. The feature film and the commercial are almost the only films to use an original score. Many producers and clients would rather use the money for other parts of the filmmaking process, when, among greater priorities, there is the problem of selecting a composer and then several weeks later not liking what has come out of his creativity and time. Most film producers are *not* trained musically and are still a bit afraid of using an original score in their films. And always—ever always—the cost can be 10 percent or more of the film, and many producers cannot justify this.

Nevertheless, there are people in the field making their living in original film music. Beginners might well learn the film music field by working for others who have made their mark—by copying scores, assisting someone who contracts musicians for recording sessions, and then attending those sessions and observing how it's done. And above all, get into the imagery of film. Look at the pictures—understand the feelings, what moods the director and writer and editor are trying to communicate—and practice your music writing by letting the film take that lead. One day, they'll hopefully produce a recording of the score from one of *your* motion pictures.

LIBRARY SCORES AND THE MUSIC EDITOR

Earlier, the statement was made that there are parts of the film-music field where being a musician or a composer is not absolutely necessary. This is true when film music is "edited" from library scores: music composed for various moods and countless situations and then provided as a large library of music to the film industry. Most film music is selected this way. For the most part, because of stringent union regulations in the United States almost all of this music is composed and recorded in Europe. Each time a piece of music is used in a film, modest amounts are paid for its eventual use on television, in theaters, or in non-theatrical productions and the composer collects a small royalty for that use.

These libraries are large and varied. KPM (Keith Prowse, Ltd.) and Brouton, both British firms, have almost 500 hours of music available in various categories and different styles. In addition, there are small, but very good libraries that offer music that fills specific needs. Two of them, both based in the United States, are Network and Omni. Taken in total, you could probably find *twenty-thousand selections* available for use.

The budget advantages are obvious, for even with the time charges for editing music (which is done on magnetic film stock transferred from originals, much as sound editing) and even with the payment of license rights, the costs are a fraction of those of creating original music. The disadvantages are also obvious. If you use a piece of music in your film, there is nothing to keep another producer from using the *same* piece of music, so that each of you will have "Storm at Sea .38 seconds" in your sequence of a roaring ocean washing up on the shores of Cape Cod. Too, library music seems to get dated more quickly, possibly because it is written for general purposes and there is so much of it. Sometimes, though, this can be overcome by the talents of a good music editor.

Since any music library has thousands of selections, and given the fact that film music can be cut to rhythms, images, and moods, some of the best film-music editors have no real background in composition or in playing a musical instrument. With a good sense of rhythm, an innate feeling for image, and a superb memory for all the music available in the library, a music editor can score a film and do it quite successfully. In fact, a background in musicology and music appreciation is more valuable to the music editor than standard music training in reading a score or practicing the clarinet six hours a day. Certainly the latter can help, but are not entirely necessary. For, if you are aware of the dictates of the film mood and it immediately brings a musical feeling to you, and you can then turn to the catalogue or to memory and find a piece of music that seems to be right, music editing might well be better for you than original composition.

Once the music is selected from the library, it is not just put into place and "Voilà!" it fits. The selection may have certain usable segments, while other segments just do not work. The time of the piece may be over or under the length of the sequence. The working material is magnetic film stock, 35mm or 16mm, and the music editor takes the entire selection and then edits selected sections to fit the film. Here is where the sense of rhythm comes into play: the juxtaposition of film with music and the manual dexterity to instantaneously select a place to cut, splice, and then replay a piece of music so that it fits the picture.

One of our best music editors (who is also a composer) runs a company that provides music to film producers. When he was a small child, he remembers being out in the country, and whenever he would see a particular scene—a herd of cows, a stream, a storm—he'd compose music to it in his head. It is not a large jump into film from that point.

The entry jobs in the field are very much the same as for an editor, except that the first attempts should be in the areas where film-music libraries and editing services exist. Most of the work is done in Hollywood and New York, but the field has expanded to include almost all the cities where producers are providing services: Washington, Chicago, Detroit, Dallas, and Atlanta.

For this author, music has been an area of greatest frustration, just as manual dexterity has eluded me through years of building model ships. I look with awe at the film composer and at the music editor and I marvel at the creative dexterity with which everyone works together at a recording session. As a little boy, I always wanted to play the drums. Unfortunately, living in the crowded conditions of a New York apartment, my mother thought it would not be wise and her logic was, "You'll disturb the children in the school across the street!" And so, because of the darned children in the school (who would not have been there when I practiced anyway!), I never got my drums. Years later, on a film job in East Africa, we traveled out of Mombasa, Kenya, to film a courtship dance done by the young people of the Giriama tribe. I was ecstatic, for the live location music of the drums would be the high point of the track. The tribe was waiting for us, row upon row of drums manned by absolutely magnificent people—and the dance began, the cameras rolled, and the sound was recorded on the spot. The little boy in me came back and the sound of the drums I never played made their mark on the tape. And suddenly the drums stopped. Through the jungle came two police officers carrying riding crops, their hats stuck under their epaulets—and we were told in no uncertain terms that we were to stop the drums. It seems that the sound was bothering the students in a school down the road.

The console at a mixing studio.

Composer Gershon Kingsley describes the combination of Moog synthesizer and tape as "the first perfect marriage in creating a personal sound for the motion picture." "Imagine," he says, "no more orchestras and temperamental musicians!"

CHAPTER 9

SOUND

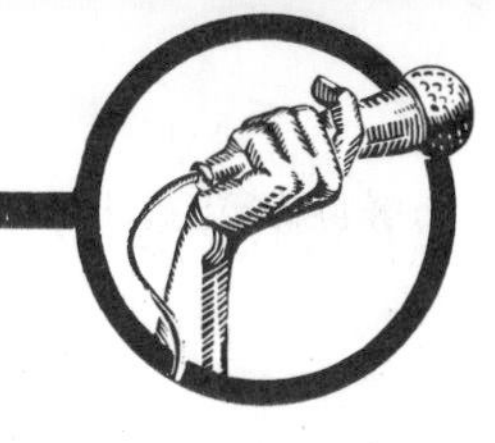

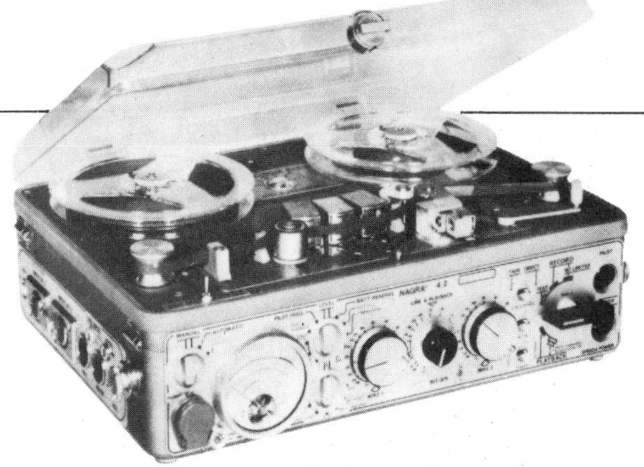

"Help Stamp Out MOS"

A European director was once brought out to Hollywood to work in a large studio. His English was, of course, heavily accented. At one point in the proceedings, the director was asked if the next scene was to be silent or with sound. He answered, *"Mit out sprechen."* And, on the slate, as a gag, the letters MOS were chalked—to imply Mit Out Speaking, or Mit Out Sound. They've been with us in the film industry ever since. Whenever a crew is to do a silent shot, the same MOS is slated even today.

Of course, for every day of silent photography, a sound person is not working on a crew. The more sound, the more work for these unsung heroes. The more silent footage (MOS), the more jobless days. So, if ever you see a car with a bumper sticker that shouted the words of the subtitle of this chapter (and who of us is to say that the sticker does not exist?), you would probably be right in determining that the driver was a sound person in the film industry.

The field of sound recording is, perhaps, one of the most misunderstood crafts in the film industry. In Hollywood's early days, when equipment was bulky and cumbersome, the sound crew consisted of four people. Today, it is structured as a three-person crew on most feature productions:

Production Mixer—the chief of the crew. He equalizes the sound level as it comes through the mixer and records the track.

Boom Operator. He handles the long "fishpole" with a microphone connected to it, or operates the large perambulator boom that can be moved from one section of the set to another.

Sound Assistant (Cable Man). He works for the boom operator by setting up the equipment, running the cable from the set to the mixer, and wiring actors or narrators with the wireless radio microphone when cable would interfere with movement.

Added to this crew, the old Hollywood had a fourth person: the recordist. Whereas the mixer was right on the set, the recordist was generally outside in a truck, or in a separate room, where his function was to operate a 35mm or 16mm magnetic recorder. Still earlier, the recording system was optical (a sound track put directly on film stock) and the recordist was also the operator of this machine.

But the big studios are long gone, for the most part. Location filming began to take their place. Equipment became lighter—and the boom operators and recordists of the fifties became the mixers of the sixties. The sound person began to work in smaller crews and, bit by bit, we began to see only *one* sound person attached to a film crew—and that person now does everything! Where the jobs were once divided, the good sound person is now expert in many parts of the field. And if the job looks "easy" (a statement that upsets any sound person), then it's just that the job is being done correctly; it *looks* simple, but when we analyze the things a good sound person has to know, we begin to respect that ease even more.

WHAT THE SOUND PERSON NEEDS TO KNOW

MICROPHONES AND THEIR CHARACTERISTICS There is no all-purpose microphone and at least twenty different types of professional mikes are available for use in any given situation. The sound person has to know the advantages and the characteristics of the wireless mike, shotgun, boom, condenser, dynamic, and lavalier.

TAPE RECORDERS AND THEIR CHARACTERISTICS As in all electronic fields, tape recorders change from year to year, and even a single brand name (such as Nagra) might have several models on the market at any given time. But it goes even further—for a good sound person should know something about the circuitry of these recorders as well as the structure and engineering specifications of all the other equipment used on the job.

Not too long ago, we were in the deepest canyons in Utah, ready to do a sound take which could only be recorded on that particular day. We were moving on the next morning and we were about 150 miles from civilization and any spare equipment. And the recorder broke down. The sound man and the production manager opened the recorder and placed a telephone call to the Nagra distributors in New York City. With instructions

coming by telephone from the East Coast and the two men probing at the recorder two thousand miles away, the repair was made and the sound take accomplished—a bit late, but accomplished nonetheless. At times like that, no one dares think of what the consequences would be if we could not have fixed the recorder in that remote canyon. We just assumed we would somehow make it work.

LIGHTING Whenever lights are used—either on a set or to "fill" some dark shadows, the sound person must be aware that the sound boom may cast a shadow somewhere behind the camera or across the face of an actor or narrator. Therefore, the movement of the boom is planned to coincide with the lighting plan and the camera movements.

As a natural adjunct, the sound person should also be familiar with:

LENSES The size of the shot also determines just where the microphone can be placed without interfering with the picture. If the lens to be used is for a close-up, the mike might be a bit closer to the person who is to speak. If the plan is for a long shot, the mike has to be out of the picture and yet be able to pick up the speech. It is not too terrible to hear someone shout, "The mike is in the shot—move it back!" It is much worse, certainly, to be screening dailies and to hear someone mutter, "The shot is gorgeous, but is that a mike in the top of the picture?" As a result, most sound people work closely with the cinematographer.

There are times, though, where pre-planning is not possible—especially in documentary situations, where something is happening and will happen only once and the shot must be gotten and the sound recorded. At times like this, the sound person must be able to notice quickly just which lens the cinematographer is using and plan the microphone move accordingly. Of course, in television news film the mike *always* shows as it is shoved into the face of some political figure or some mass murderer. But that, of course, is deliberate since the channel number gives the station free publicity and the mike adds an air of on-the-spot news.

And there is more—much more. The sound person must know:

•Where the microphones must be placed for best sound quality.

The light Nagra tape recorder makes on-location recording a simple matter. Here, Don Matthews tapes an interview with an executive of the Evans-Black Company.

In a documentary or newsfilm with one person, it's fairly easy, but with a meeting of ten it becomes more complex, for anyone may want to speak at any moment and the sound must be recorded with the highest quality.

•Equalization of sounds while recording.

Different voices attain different levels; the sound of a clock ticking should not be as loud as that of a stamping machine. Sound levels must be balanced for a natural effect.

•How to avoid the extraneous noises of the "outside world" while recording.

Wind noises, trees rustling, distant traffic all present problems for sound people. Sometimes they are solved by facing the principals in another direction, sometimes by wind baffles, sometimes by just waiting until the noise is gone. Frequently, the crew will turn to a sound person and look questioningly as some extraneous noise seems to interfere with the take. And, just as frequently, if the sound person has done the job well, the "OK" sign is flashed, meaning that the sound has not been disturbing at all.

Of course, the most frustrating sound to any film crew is the passing of a jet plane or a helicopter right in the middle of a sound take. The roar shatters the silence, the take is canceled and then redone. Sometimes film crews seem to feel that *every* location is near a highway or an air base and that there is no real way to avoid the interruption. Well, you just wait and then do it again.

We were sent to Heidelberg by one of our clients to do a series of film interviews with Albert Speer, the man who ran Adolf Hitler's armaments machine and who had just been released from Spandau Prison. His book had

Idyllic settings are sometimes perfect for the cameraman, but airplanes and chirping birds can make the sound job a nightmare. This was the case when the author produced a series of film interviews with Albert Speer, one of Adolf Hitler's ministers.

been published that spring and there was great interest in Speer, culminating in probably five or six different film crews being sent to put his words on film.

We took one day to survey the house and the grounds that surrounded it and finally decided that we would shoot the interviews outdoors on his lawn rather than setting lights inside the house. The weather was superb, the setting ideal, and we made our decision after both camera and sound technicians had declared the area perfect. The only background noise was the chirping noise of German birds.

The next morning, as expected, the sun was warm and inviting and we settled down on the lawn to do our interviews. No sooner had we begun, than the first jet roared overhead and then disappeared to the west. We stopped the cameras and the tape recorder and then began again when the plane passed beyond the horizon. Take two began and another jet whistled through the sky. Looks were exchanged and frustration began to set in. Finally, after six planes had shrieked overhead, someone made a phone call and it turned out that a storm was raging over Frankfurt airport and the planes were being put in a holding pattern over Heidelberg—directly over the lawn of Albert Speer!

More and more, the sound person is becoming a "one-man band," for as equipment has become more compact through electronic miniaturization, we more frequently see the sound person, loaded down to the gunwales, handling the entire job alone—the Nagra slung over one shoulder, the microphone boom clutched in one hand, and with more equipment slung over the other shoulder: multiple wireless mike receivers, electronic slating systems, hand-held shotgun microphones, a second set of headphones for the director or script clerk to listen to the track as it's being recorded, and lots more cable. Many sound people are beginning to carry backpacks in order to take all the equipment with them. For as cameras get lighter, and cinematographers move more quickly, the sound person must follow more closely behind.

A good sound person on location is constantly moving. When synchronized sound is not called for, you will usually find him recording "wild" sound: the sounds and presence of the area being filmed, whether the bird calls of the forest or the rhythmic chatter of manufacturing machines. He carries his equipment, the microphone held out in front of him like a delicate probe, always listening, always alert to the sounds that will add another element to the film. Not content to swear at airplanes when they're unwelcome in the film, the sound person who works at airports with film crews generally walks around recording the sound of jet planes taking off—just to keep busy, and just to give the director and the editor another degree of realism for the finished production.

In addition to knowing all the aspects of sound recording, from original to quarter-inch tape, through transfer to magnetic tape, and then to optical track, the sound person must be flexible and talented enough to take a different approach for each kind of film.

In the commercial, each word must sound exactly right. The message is generally carried by those words and the agency and clients don't care that an actor might be turning his back, or that his voice is coming from across the room. Perspective goes out the window. The sound may be unreal, but it's certainly clear.

The documentary has a reputation of having mediocre sound and mediocre pictures, but this is just not true. Properly done, documentary sound quality can be just as strong, clear, and effective as the track on a feature film. Again, this depends upon the ability of the sound person. In the documentary, we are really shooting the "rehearsal"—things will happen one time only and perhaps never again. Someone will say something brilliant or funny or important and there is no chance to get it again. Where does the microphone go? And will the subject move just when the words are being said? Since "real people" (versus actors) are generally better and more articulate only on their *first few takes,* the pressure builds on the sound person to get it the first time. If a meeting is being photographed and time limitations have prevented the placing of a series of microphones, which person at that meeting will speak next is a problem. How will the microphone cover him without the equipment (or the sound person) getting into the shot?

In the feature (unlike the commercial), the sound person is most concerned with reality: the balance of perspective to the action on the screen. Someone coming in the door across the room will sound different from a person who is in the foreground of the shot. Here the sound man is a part of a complicated and ingeniously coordinated plan to put on the screen the most realistic effect. But there have been some changes and innovations here, too. In Robert Altman's films, for example, the sound is recorded on several tracks, very much as in the music sessions described in the previous chapter. Finally, in the mixing studio, Altman balances his tracks to give the audience the feeling that they might get in a live situation. In other words, at a party the voices might be almost unintelligible, leaving the audience to pick out the important speeches. Some feel that this kind of confusion has ushered in a new era of realism. Others feel that this realism has ushered in a new era of confusion!

STUDIO RECORDING AND THE MIXER

Some sound is recorded in especially equipped studios where the control is better and where the actor or narrator can sit in an enclosed soundproof booth while the recording engineer controls the levels at a console. This is, in fact, the way all radio recordings are done. It carries over into film when voice tracks are made to a specific script. Foreign language tracks, as well as documentary and television narration, are recorded in this manner and the sound person here is generally an engineer or technician by training.

In the mix, however, the sound engineer's job becomes more complicated and the consoles are fairly complex. As in the music mix (see previous chapter), the tracks are all separate and individual elements, sometimes on 35mm magnetic tape, sometimes on 16mm. The picture is still not connected in any way to the sound and it is projected as an individual element, locked into synchronization with all the tracks that will be mixed at that session. Narration, dialogue, effects, and music are all on separate tracks and some of them may even have two or more tracks of their own. For example, music might be on two individual tracks so that the mixer can blend the end of one selection into the beginning of another. The cue sheet on page 46 is typical of one prepared for a mix (the numbers represent footage). After a discussion with the editor and director about potential problems in the tracks and the effects desired, the lights dim and the mix begins.

With everything locked together so that synchronization is maintained, the tracks move through the playback machines while the picture is projected on a screen, under which the footage numbers flash their progress. Everything is now being put onto one individual track. The mixer controls the levels of each track so that a proper balance is maintained

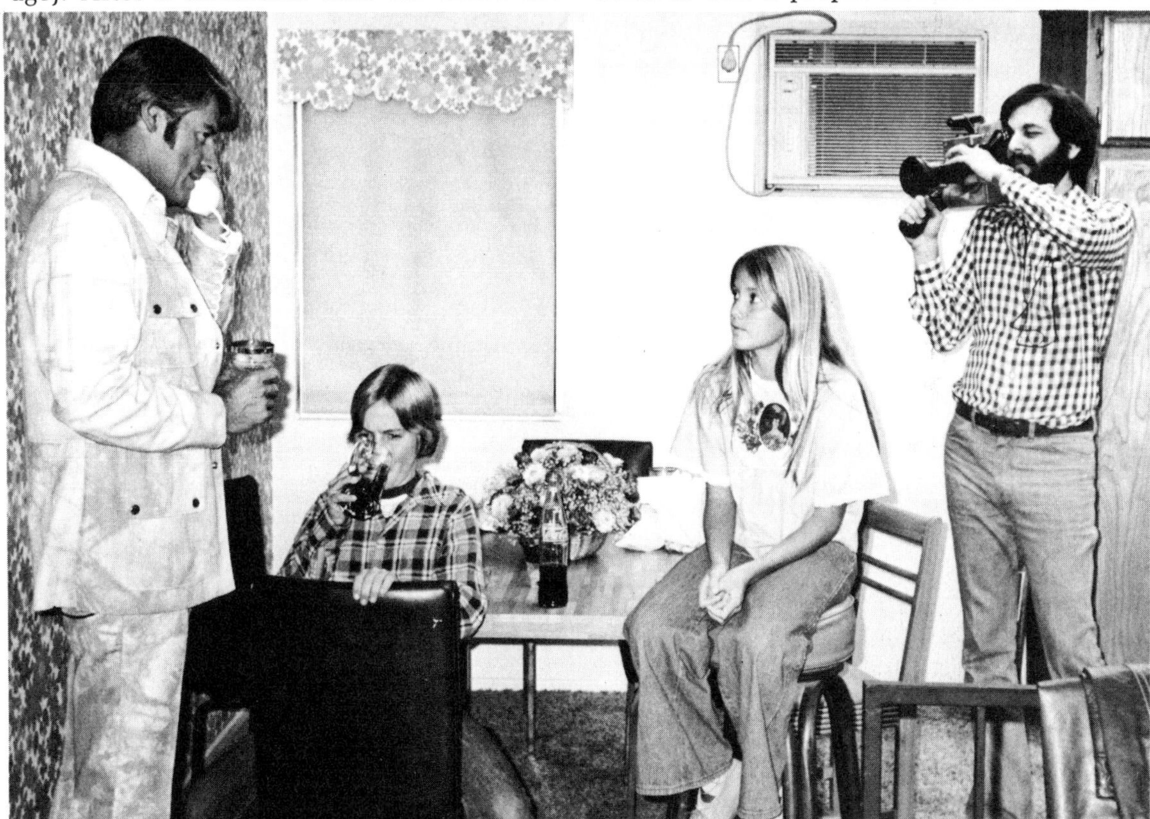

The use of the wireless microphone makes the job of the cameraman easier and allows for greater mobility on the part of the actors. The director/cameraman is Chuck Braverman.

and so that the music does not override the voice, nor does the sound of a bird appear to be louder than an actor's voice. Equalizing is also done at the mix: the tone and level of the tracks, and the bass or treble quality, can all be balanced. Watching the footage counter under the screen, the mixer (with only two hands) controls ten to fifteen dials, switches, and levers all at once, moving one sound up, another down.

There was a time when mixers could not stop and start if a mistake was made. The reel (ten minutes at a time) was rehearsed and then mixed and, as the last minute came up, the tension in the mixing studio became more apparent—somehow everyone stopped breathing—for a mistake even in the last ten seconds meant that the whole thing had to be started again. Mixers such as Dick Vorisek made their reputations by going through twelve and fifteen track mixes without a mistake and with perfect sound balance on the finished track. Today, the equipment allows us to stop, start, back up, and remix a section. The atmosphere in a mixing studio is, as a result, a bit more relaxed than it used to be.

The first time you watch a mix with more than three or four tracks, you will probably come away with the feeling that the mixer is a combination guru, fencing master, and psychologist.

The biggest compliment a sound person can get is that it looks easy. Good sound is complicated and good sound makes the difference between professionalism and just plain recording—so it's not just a matter of picking up the family SONY and going out into the world of noises to record for posterity.

VISION ASSOC. PROD #641 1/26/77

CAM. ROLL 6 SOUND (28) END BEEP
CAM. ROLL 7 SOUND (29) (30) (31)
(32) (33) (34) (35)
CAM. ROLL 8 SOUND (36) (37) (38)

V.O. TRACK - DENNIS & LESLIE (WILD)
WILD TRACK - EFFECTS / ROOM TONE

NAGRA 60 HZ CRYSTAL SYNCH (7½)
SOUND ROLL #5 -8 REF. ON HEAD

TIME CHART	RECORDING BOTH DIRECTIONS							
	150 ft. (45.7 m)	300 ft. (91.4 m)	600 ft. (182.8 m)	900 ft. (274.3 m)	1200 ft. (365.7 m)	1800 ft. (548.6 m)	2400 ft. (731.5 m)	3600 ft. (1097.2 m)
1⅞ IPS	30 min.	1 hr.	2 hrs.	3 hrs.	4 hrs.	6 hrs.	8 hrs.	12 hrs.
3¾ IPS	15 min.	30 min.	60 min.	1½ hrs.	2 hrs.	3 hrs.	4 hrs.	6 hrs.
7½ IPS	7½ min.	15 min.	30 min.	45 min.	1 hr.	1½ hrs.	2 hrs.	3 hrs.

NOTICE: The following is made in lieu of all warranties, express or implied: Seller's and manufacturer's only obligation shall be to replace such quantity of the product proved to be defective. Seller and manufacturer shall not be liable for any injury, loss or damage, direct or consequential, arising out of the use of or the inability to use the product. Before using, user shall determine the suitability of the product for his intended use and user assumes all risk and liability whatsoever in connection therewith. The foregoing may not be changed except by an agreement signed by officers of seller and manufacturer.

THE TERMS "SCOTCH", AND THE PLAID DESIGN ARE REGISTERED TRADEMARKS OF MINNESOTA MINING AND MANUFACTURING COMPANY, ST. PAUL, MINNESOTA 55101.

Magnetic Audio/Video Products Division 3M
3M CENTER • SAINT PAUL. MINNESOTA 55101

Sound notes on the back of the tape box. The camera report on page 41 refers to the same sound numbers, with a description of the scene. Theoretically, these cross-references make the job of the editor easier.

Some sound people have backgrounds of engineering—electrical or radio or television—with a superb knowledge of just how the equipment operates, how to repair it, and how to invent new and better equipment. Most of the other sound people I know just happened to be around, asking questions, learning how to operate the Nagra in their spare time, analyzing their own recording techniques, and then being there when someone said to them, "Would you mind holding the mike boom during this shot?" Occasionally a crew will have to split up, with one sound person doing the major recording while a second person is sent off to record some "presence." If you know how to operate the equipment, you might just be the one to do it. If you have done nothing to become familiar with sound, the opportunity might well pass you by.

One of our editors learned sound in his spare time, and if he ever left his job in the editing room, he would be well qualified to begin work in the field of sound recording. I have even learned to use the Nagra, for many occasions have presented themselves where a recording had to be made and no sound person was available.

The literature exists. The equipment can be mastered if only you take the time and have the interest. Watch the sound people at work—particularly when they make the job look easy. It is a craft where the beginner can really learn by doing, by practicing, by asking questions, by carrying cable for a sound person just to be close by when the recorder is turned on. Slow, low-budget, non-union productions welcome help in any craft—and sound is a specialty that deserves to be given more attention in the art of film production.

Sound producer Stephen Halbert making some final adjustments prior to a mixing session.

Furthermore, of course, sound people travel as much as any other filmmaker, and sound people have their share of adventure. Each one can tell tall tales of locations that gave them more than their taste of the unusual or the bizarre. We once assigned a sound man and cameraman to a hot-air balloon sequence, to be shot near the shores of Lake Michigan. The day was balmy, no wind at all, the right kind of summer weather for hot-air ballooning. The first sequences were easy and went well. They filled the balloon with hot air, and the sound man was right there to record the steady hiss. Then the slow ascent into the blue sky, the air-to-ground radio crackling for a local broadcast. Gently, softly, the balloon rose, and when it was about two hundred feet off the ground—the spectators waving at it from below—a twenty-five-mile-an-hour wind came up. And the balloon took off toward Lake Michigan. The balloonist tried to slow it down, drop it in for a landing somewhere, but below were trees and highways and not a single level spot for miles around. And the lake came roaring on up ahead. The camera kept rolling and the sound man kept recording. Finally, to prevent being blown into the lake, the balloonist dropped down, hit the edge of a factory roof, cracking the basket on the way down; and everyone was tumbled into the parking lot, bruised, shaken, but mostly unhurt—about twenty feet from the lake.

Two days later, awed and impressed, we watched the footage in the editing room and we screened the dailies. Everything was there: the commands of the captain, the radio blaring, the sounds of danger, and the excitement of the crash—in living color and full sound right to the very end. Grateful that the crew had not been badly hurt, we asked the sound man how he could possibly have rolled through the entire thing. Still shaken by seeing the accident again, he said, "We just thought that in case anything serious happened, you'd have a good record for the insurance company!"

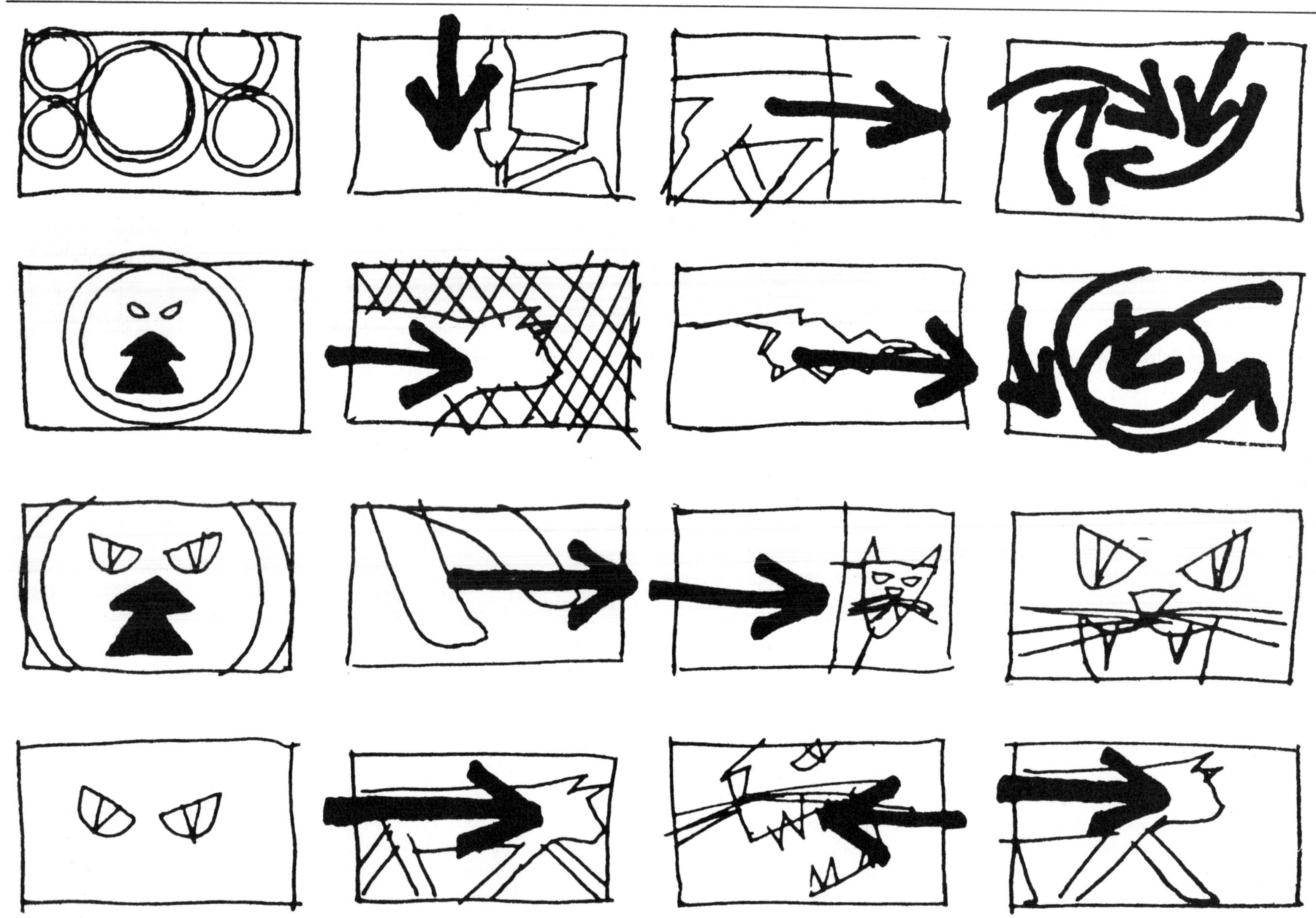

One of the foremost innovators in motion picture graphics has been Saul Bass. This is his original story board of the title treatment for the film, Walk on the Wild Side.

CHAPTER 10

COMPUTER GRAPHICS, ANIMATION AND ART

"Mickey Mouse, Meet Star Wars"

When I was a young boy, my grandmother used to give me a dime for an afternoon at the movies. At the Blenheim we saw three feature films and four serials, including *Flash Gordon, Tarzan in the Pit of Snakes*, and *Buck Rogers in the 25th Century*. By late afternoon they gave away free bicycles to lucky ticket holders, played Bingo, Keeno, and Banko—and then completed the day with cartoons. Sometimes there were ten or twelve animated subjects in a row: Mickey Mouse, Donald Duck, and a few independently made violently cutie-pie cartoons that were the forerunners of today's realistically violent Saturday morning TV fare. By seven that night, our mothers had the police out looking for us, while we were happily wending our weary way homeward, the ten cents all spent.

Slowly, the animated cartoon, along with the live short subject and the serials, began to disappear from the movie theaters. The name of the game became "turnover." Today, for five dollars you get your eighty-seven minute feature plus several minutes in which to change the audience for the next show. Complex animated title treatments (such as those used in the delightful *Pink Panther* series) have also given way, for the most part, to simple white letters on black backgrounds, sometimes with a slow crawl upwards, that let the audience walk out of the theatre while the names of the people who made the film fade into oblivion unnoticed and unread. Whatever animation we do see these days is generally relegated to early morning television, some commercials, and a few business and medical films.

Animator/designer/graphic artist/filmmaker Carmen D'Avino at work in his studio in New York.

And, in the past few years, a new darling has begun to replace the old style standard animation: the ubiquitous computer.

For those of us who have been around for a long time, it has been the most amazing evolution: from the very first cartoon, *Gertie the Dinosaur* (no, not *Mickey Mouse!*), through the Disney world of *Fantasia* and *Pinocchio*, into the fifties, sixties and seventies with the Hubleys, Saul Bass and Ralph Bakshi—and finally, in the eighties, into the most extreme change in the world of graphics and animation, when features, commercials, and television began to utilize computer graphics as a dynamic (albeit expensive) way of communicating their message.

In both the field of the motion picture and its sister craft, video tape, the world of computer graphics has spawned a whole new industry, and with it a completely new realm of job opportunities for talented and well-trained young people who are just entering the communications industry.

Over the years, animation techniques for features and commercials became fairly well standardized, with a time span of about three years to complete a feature animated film. In what we call "cel animation" each frame of the picture must be drawn separately and each stage of the action must be hand-colored, and then shot frame by individual frame. For a full-length animated feature, there can be as many as *two hundred thousand* separate drawings!

In the thirties, Disney employed thousands of people to do the menial, yet delicate jobs of animation, such as painting backgrounds for *Snow White*. One of his employees, the late John Hubley, was to change the face of animation considerably when he left Disney to join UPA (United Productions of America), where he and his wife, Faith, produced some of the most innovative animated films for that time, including the classic short subject, *Moonbird*. Whereas earlier animation forms had been concerned with fairly realistic characters, the Hubleys allowed the free flow of shapes to fill the screen while the improvised track spoke in terms of mood and abstractions. In *Moonbird*, they used the voices of their two children, Mark and Ray, to create the hunt for an imaginary bird in a film that captured the wonder of a child's world. Animation began to loosen up, to become a new and exciting film-art form.

Animation and graphics began to play a role in title design and production credits. Where the early credit listings were simple white letters on a black or grey background, innovators such as Saul Bass began to change the art of title design for the entire industry. Bass commented at the time, "My position is that the minute the first frame of film appears on the screen, the picture begins, and something should be happening that is of interest and useful to its total presentation.

Therefore, the title functions as an introduction and, as such, it can function as a summarizer of the point of view and essential content of the film."

At that point, the title treatment became a part of the excitement of the film itself—*Man with the Golden Arm, Psycho,* and *Grand Prix* became style leaders, and we began to expect unusual titles for our films. It was a rare film that did not have some exquisite graphic opening (sometimes followed by ninety minutes of ennui). Animator/producter Ralph Bakshi took the art one step further with *Fritz the Cat* (the first X-rated animated feature) and *Heavy Traffic,* in which he used a combination of animation techniques and live photography.

As the industry moved into the seventies, animation houses could be found not only in New York and Los Angeles, where about 90 per cent of the theatrical, commercial, and industrial work was done, but also in half the other states of the nation, including Nebraska, Colorado, Texas, Iowa, Missouri, Florida and Kentucky. And though title treatments began to move back to simple white letters on black backgrounds, hundreds of independent animators were (and still are) working in the field in their own innovative techniques, and this will be discussed later in this chapter.

In the late sixties and early seventies, a new and innovative group of graphic artist/animators/electronic geniuses began to enter the film and video fields: the designers of computer graphics. If we consider as industry revolutions the advent of sound, faster film stocks, color, lighter equipment that made location shooting available to even the smallest film crew, then certainly we must also include the development and growth of computer graphics in that listing.

It is not a function of this book, however, to criticize or to critically analyze the impact of computer graphics in terms of aesthetics. Some filmmakers have fallen in love with the results (as have all the advertising agencies in the country), while others have complained that it has made almost everything look like everything else—each and every battle scene in science fiction features and every television commercial and music video an exact clone of every other presentation. However, there is one thing that all of us can agree upon: it has opened up new opportunities and new job categories for a range of talented young people who are trying to break into the industry. And, it is *jobs* that this book is all about.

To explain the opportunities that are available in the field of graphics, animation, and art, it might be well to begin with the standard techniques that have existed since *Gertie the Dinosaur,* and then move on to today and the future.

JOB CATEGORIES IN "CEL"-TYPE ANIMATION

Most jobs are of the free-lance rather than the staff category, and as the film progresses from an idea to a frame of motion picture film, a great many people control production along the way. Depending upon experience, it is quite possible to move from one job to another and this is a craft in which there are many apprentice jobs, since these are usually the most repetitious. But they represent a great learning opportunity and a chance to make contacts in the field.

Director. Generally an experienced animator who controls the entire production from a creative point of view.

Animator. In theatrical productions, the animator is the "star" of the picture, creating characters, rough-sketching action, and making the film "live" on the screen. If a particular scene requires a character to move through twelve

As far back as his title treatment for *The Man with the Golden Arm*, Saul Bass was experimenting with the use of abstract design. It was to be the forerunner of today's computer graphics.

frames of action (a half-second), the animator might design and draw frames one, six and twelve in order to lay out basic action (for example, the movement of an arm from waist to head). Usually, the animator has at least fifteen years' experience in the field.

Animator II and Assistant Animator. Both work under the guidance of the animator. They clean up rough sketches and the Animator II is generally an up-and-coming artist who is just one step away from the top job.

In-Betweener. If the animator has designed frames one, six and twelve, someone has to draw the frames that will make up the entire sequence. The in-betweener designs frames 2, 3, 4, and 5 as well as 7, 8, 9, 10, and 11.

Inker. From the animator's fine pencil drawings, the inker now draws ink outlines and then traces them onto "cels" (transparent Celluloid sheets). On some productions, this job has been replaced by the innovation of yet another machine: the photocopier.

Photocopying Machine Operator and Assistants. This is a much easier way to put the animator's drawings on to cels. Now they are merely placed on the photocopier and a cel is made ready for the next step in the process.

Painter, or Opaquer. Following a standard model sheet for the production, the painter or opaquer fills in the flesh tones for the characters: the hair color, eye color, clothing.

Background Artist and Assistant. These craftspeople are responsible, naturally, for the sky, trees, oceans, cities, and cliffs, etc., for the characters to run across or fall down, chase along, fight or make love on.

Two other crafts are involved in animated filmmaking, though not in this particular order, for they actually precede the work done by the animator:

Layout Assistant. Lays out the scenes before the animator does the drawing.

Storyman and Story Sketcher. Simply, they write the story in a scene by scene explanation and might also provide rough sketches of the action.

Finally, thousands and thousands of finished cels come off the line ready for photography and three other people take over:

Junior Checker (Paint & Ink). Checks the ink and painting before the animation goes in front of the camera.

Senior Checker. Supervises the junior checker and is the pre-planner.

Animation Cameraman. Shoots the finished animation, cel by cel, so that the characters move at 24 frames per second when they're projected.

To keep the production moving and to supervise the entire job, the Production Coordinator is in charge. Most important of all for the entry-level applicant, there are apprentice categories for most of the levels.

JOB CATEGORIES IN COMPUTER GRAPHICS

Almost the first thing that strikes someone like me about the field of computer graphics is that everyone at the top of the field is so young! Jeff Kleiser, now president of Digital Effects in New York is in his mid-thirties, and many on his growing staff are much, much younger than that. Possibly, the best advice that computer graphics designers can give is that beginners have to separate the video games of their youth from the *tools* that are now used in special effects, graphic design, and sophisticated computer generation. On the other hand, the field is so young (even though the earliest computer-generated films were produced by struggling independents as far back as the 1930's) that a whole new film/video

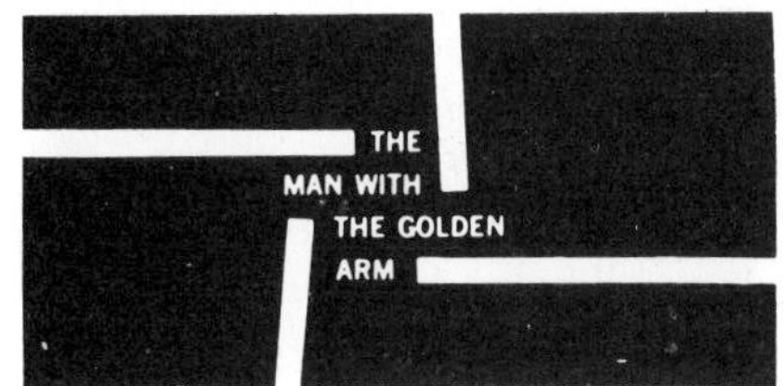

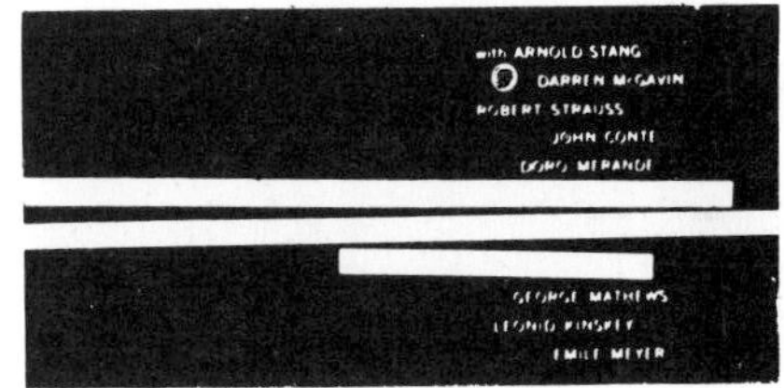

world is opening for this generation of communications students. But, before you jump in to grab the Pac-Man joy stick, you'd better take into account some things that you'll need before anyone will even consider you for the next job opening:

Mathematics. Your background should include a solid base of mathematics. My computer-genius friend, Judson Rosebush, once reminded me that even DaVinci was a master mathematician and history has always shown a close relationship between mathematics and art.

Computer Training. Either in a university or as a member of a corporation, you should have a firm background in computers, including the ability of speaking several computer "languages." You also should know the internal structure of various computers.

Art and Graphics. The more design experience you can show, the more training you can get in art and graphics, the better your chances of breaking in.

A Good Sample. This is a subject that comes up over and over again, both in animation and in live production. If you have spent four years in computer school and you don't have a good solid sample of your work to show on film or video tape, you have probably wasted your time. Competition is so keen that the job applicant with a short, original, innovative sample of computer graphics is far, far ahead of the others.

Once you finally get into the field, here are some of the job categories that you might consider for your future:

Director. As in all other areas of our field, the director is the top person in terms of meeting with clients, supervising the animator, and controlling the entire production process.

A typical example of cel animation: the figures in the middle frame are placed on the background (top) to form the finished piece of art (bottom).

Software Specialist. Designs the graphics and experiments with new images on the various computer systems.

Animator. Using the software designed by the software specialist, the animator writes the software programs and generates the graphic images for the particular job. Generally, this category absolutely demands a background in animation, art and graphic design.

Operator. The Jack-or-Jill-of-all-trades who does anything and everything to assist everyone else, including going for coffee, making trips to the lab, etc. It's a great place to learn, especially if they'll let you use the computers at night on your own time!

OTHER KINDS OF ANIMATION

The film business has a lovely quality: it is amorphous, structured like an amoeba, with constantly changing parameters and no rigid rules, open to innovation in most areas and totally impossible to define and categorize. Although I have outlined the formal organization of both cel animation and computer graphics, I must point out that there are other, independent artists and animators who have transferred their particular genius on to motion picture film and tape.

People like Len Lye, Norman McLaren, and Carmen D'Avino, Bob Blechman, Saul Steinberg, and Saul Bass have all helped to break the chains of Disney and Mickey Mouse (however valuable they were to the budding art of film animation). And even here, the "handwriting" has been noted,

"Key Frames" from the computer generated opening for NBC Nighly News produced by Digital Effects.

for it was the Disney organization that produced *Tron*, almost entirely through the use of computer graphics. (It probably had "Uncle Walt" turning in his grave, and not only because it was financially unsuccessful.) It *is* possible to be innovative in this field—and it is possible to work alone and even to produce an income so that your work might continue.

Independent producers and the producers of commercials and educational television shows are always on the lookout for new techniques. The Public Service television show *Sesame Street*, and individuals such as Edith Zornow of the Children's Television Workshop have given encouragement to a great many animators and graphic film/video artists and provided them with showcases for their work. There are, indeed, various paths that can be followed, their range only limited by the imagination of the people who design them and the producers who are looking for something new.

Object Animation. This is the area in which a product or an object is made to move across the screen or perform some acrobatic feat. Watchbands, cereals, almost any object can be made to move by itself; but if you thought cel animation was time-consuming, try your hand at making an object move without visible means. Ron McAdow did a whole series of films using animated peanuts!

Clay Animation. As early as my days at the Blenheim, George Pal was producing films that used clay characters that talked and acted. In recent years, artists such as Elliott Noyes, Will Vinton and Bob Gardiner have perfected the craft in their films.

Collage Animation. Simply put, it is the art of cutting out shapes and pasting them up while photographing them frame by frame. Collage animators like Carmen D'Avino, Frank Mouris, and Babette Neuberger have used everything including cutouts from magazines, drawings, abstract shapes and colored paper to design their images. D'Avino, who began as a painter and sculptor, has already been nominated for two Academy Awards and his films (*The Room, Tarantella, Pianissimo*) are known by filmmakers around the world. Most importantly, he has been able to support himself with his film work.

And so, Animation lives! And your special talent, whether you go on to become another John or Faith Hubley or a video artist like Nam June Paik, may well be your entry into the film or video field. Whatever your goal, if you can make a pair of argyle socks walk across the room, I'm sure that a lot of established filmmakers might be quite willing to look at the results!

Joe Cirillo became an actor by being the police officer assigned to a location near a film crew. He has since appeared in nearly a hundred motion pictures.

CHAPTER 11

ACTORS AND MODELS

"Lana Turner Doesn't Go to Schwab's Drug Store Anymore"

She was sitting at the counter in Schwab's Drug Store on The Strip (Sunset Boulevard), wearing a sweater, so they tell, and she was discovered and became a star. Her name was Lana Turner and she was followed by thousands of young hopefuls who sat at the counter at Schwab's and got nothing for their efforts but a check for a hamburger and a Coke.

If ever an area of film has maintained the aura of "glamour" and "excitement," it is the acting field. Recognition, fame, travel, money are all there waiting to be swept up by the newly discovered novice just arrived in the movie capitals of the world: New York, Hollywood, Rome. But if Las Vegas were ever to calculate the odds of "making it" in the film business, acting would be the jackpot and the odds would be astronomical. For more people are trying out for fewer available jobs as actors than in any other phase of the industry.

On a recent local television show, the subject dealt with filmmaking in New York and the panel members were people who were prominent in the industry, in features, documentaries, commercials, television. The studio audience numbered about three hundred, and *more than half* were actors hoping to meet a producer, be discovered, or—at the very least—get some advice on how they might break down the doors to fame and fortune, or to even just making a living in this most difficult of crafts.

The lovely thing about all of this—including this most depressing introduction of any chapter in the book—is that I can discourage no one; the acting schools will continue to flourish, and the newcomer will continue to make the rounds of agents and casting offices, résumés and photos clutched in hot sweaty hands, nervous, frustrated, rejected, but hopeful. After all, didn't Paul Newman, Robert Redford, Ellen Burstyn, and Rosalind Russell all come from drama schools and acting classes?* They certainly did. But be prepared for rejection and be prepared for years of working at something else before you begin to make a living in the acting field. Of course, if you've gotten this far, then there's very little that can discourage you.

The acting profession—of the motion picture industry, rather than the stage—is divided between the two coasts as to type: in California, the job market is in features, commercials, and television programs; New York provides most of its work in commercials, additional jobs opening up occasionally in the business-film field and in slide films. Of course, when a feature production is being shot in New York or when a television dramatic series decides to use big-city locations, then the East Coast actor may find an occasional part in these productions. In either case, keep in mind that the largest part of the money earned by actors is divided among a very small percentage of people who seem to work all the time, while many others cannot find even one small bit part.

One of the busiest actors in the business is a New York City police officer named Joe Cirillo. From a lucky break in just being there, where the action was, he has appeared in nearly one hundred films, including *The Godfather* and *The Pink Panther Strikes Again*. A few years ago, he was assigned to duty at a location in New York where Mike Nichols was directing, and Cirillo became friendly with the crew. One day, Nichols came up to him and asked if he'd like to appear in the film. The *timing* was also lucky: the New York City police had just gotten permission to "moonlight." Cirillo's accumulated experience in acting, plus his police background, eventually landed him a job as a technical adviser to the television series "Kojak." Such is the way careers are launched!

In addition to on-camera jobs, both coasts provide an additional source of work for the "voice-over" production, in which a narrator or actor speaks lines and descriptive narration without ever being seen. People such as Alexander Scourby and Norman Rose have made their reputations as narrators, and are in demand all the time. This technique has begun to die out, as documentaries and business films have started to use the voices of "real people" recorded out on location and then cut in as track (see pp. 47-48 of Chapter 7). Of course, someone once countered with, "You mean actors are not real people?"

Still another acting talent is used in the voice-over field. There is a small, élite group who do "character" voices, and from the early days of Mel Blanc's "What's up, Doc?" to the busiest character-voice actors such as Allen Swift, thousands of commercials have been

---

*And so did many more of the well-known actors. The American Academy of Dramatic Arts lists among its alumni: Edward G. Robinson, Lauren Bacall, Kirk Douglas, Colleen Dewhurst, and Grace Kelly.

produced with these trick voices and yet we seldom if ever see the talent on screen. This is a distinct advantage, since actors who appear on screen in commercials cannot then perform for a competing product. (Of course, with union protection and the payment of residuals for reuse of the spots, even one commercial shooting day can provide a fair-sized income over the years.) But people who do character voices are not bound by those restrictions, since they are not recognizable from one job to the next. We know of one man in Louisville, Kentucky, a marvelously talented actor named Charles Kissinger, who makes his living by impersonating twenty different actors, plus doing an entire range of Southern accents as a part of his repertoire.

One entry door into the acting field is modeling. We generally think of models as the high-fashion men and women who appear on the pages of *Vogue* or *Glamour*—and many of them are. But the field of the television commercial provides yet another opportunity: the commercials produced for products such as cosmetics, packaged goods, automobiles, clothing, etc., all use people who have perhaps only one specific, attractive feature to sell. Hand models, leg models, bathing-suit models, attractive men and women who step in and out of car doors, the fingernails that show off polish, the hair that looks shiny after shampooing, the dashing dinner date in the food commercial—these are all people who have gotten into the film business by using their greatest assets. And who is to quibble? If your hands are the most elegant, glamorous ones the producer has ever seen, why shouldn't they hold this product for an extreme close-up? The pay is good. It is an entrée into the field, for you can easily be studying voice while you make your living showing how the legs are shaved smoothly with "the product," and you can meet a lot of people who are active in the field. After all, most beginners want to be seen. Acting and modeling are synonymous with appearing. Whether you have a speaking role or merely a bit part as an extra who walks a dog in the distant long shot of a city street, or are shampooing your hair while looking very glamorous, being seen is, in effect, being Lana Turner at the counter of Schwab's Drug Store.

THE AGENT

Eventually you will have to acquire an agent. In California, it is almost impossible to function without one. In New York, it is slightly easier, but that is like saying that running eighteen miles is easier than running twenty. Most of the jobs come through agents and, as a result, most casting calls and auditions are attended by actors and models who have been sent by agents. The fairly well-known personality is signed exclusively with one agent or with a talent agency. The lesser-known actor or model free-lances, and is registered with more than one agent. In either case, the actor pays the agent a standard 10 percent of all the money earned on a particular job, including residual payments, if any.

So the job hunt becomes more complicated. Not only are you going to have to find your way in a complex and highly competitive field, but you are going to have to face the fact that you need an agent. The legwork begins here, so be prepared to do a lot of walking and a lot of selling.

The agent's office (except for the hallowed, quiet halls of the largest and most successful agencies) will usually be a hectic, vibrant, neurotic, phone-ringing, busy place. On the last visit to an agent friend of mine, his voice could be heard echoing through the hallways, "I need a chicken—I need someone to play a chicken!" I wondered how you begin to cast a chicken. You will be one of many wanting to get on an agent's list of appointments, and once you succeed in getting the interview with him, the odds are that you might well be forgotten two days later when the search for a chicken is underway—and you played that part in a college review! Your face and your résumé (expanded by you somewhat to make the lack of experience less obvious) will become a part of a huge file of people, all of them categorized as to what they look like and what they can do best. For, after all, if the agent can "win" the audition with his actor, it is to *his* benefit too. And many producers will call several agents in order to fill the same part. How will the agent categorize you?

As much as you would like to think that you can play any role, that you would be as marvelous a Blanche in *A Streetcar Named Desire* as you would be a housewife in a detergent commercial, the eye of the agent (and, later, the casting director or director) will categorize you. Your very unique acting talents may well take second place to your physical appearance. Are you short? Tall? Fat? Thin? Old? Young? Pretty? Plain? Handsome? Of what socio-economic group? Ethnic? Middle-American? The harsh reality is that the agent will then

CYNTHIA HORTON
Actress, Singer
AEA, AFTRA, SAG, AGVA

Service: (212) 246-8484

Height: 5'5"
Weight: 115
Hair: Light Brown
Eyes: Brown

RADIO CITY MUSIC HALL	Christmas Spectacular '82
OFF-OFF BROADWAY	The Double Inconstancy....Sylvia (Meat & Potatoes Theatre)
REVUES	"Potshots," Upstairs at the Duplex, NYC "An Evening With Cole Porter," Summer Pops, MN Orchestra
RESIDENT STOCK	Lunch Hour . . . . .Carrie School for Wives. . . . . .Agnes Tribute . . . . .Sally Romantic Comedy . . . . .Allison
DINNER THEATRE	Tintypes . . . . .Anna Sound of Music . . . . . .Maria Guys and Dolls . . . . . .Adelaide Company . . . . .April
COMMERCIAL	Dean Foods Poppin' Fresh Pies WNCI Radio Montgomery Ward Softsoap Prange Way Dept. Store Knox Lumber Richman Gordman Dept. Store
INDUSTRIAL FILM	"Focus Interview Training: (& numerous others, 3M) "IDS Insurance" (IDS) "ISA Essentials" (IDS) "Managing Growth Relations" (Wilson Learning Corp.) "Age of Lifestyle" (Wilson Learning Corp.) "The Perils of Betty Crocker" (General Mills) "News Flash" (Kimberly-Clark Corporation)
TELEVISION	"Private Sessions" (TV movie)
PRINT	General Mills (test commercials for Granola Clusters, Specialty Potatoes and others) Swiss Miss B. Dalton Bookseller Capri Shampoo
SPECIAL TALENTS AND TRAINING	B.A. in Music, Voice study - 12 years Dance: Jazz, Ballet, Basic Tap Driver's license, own car; Biker, own 10-speed; Typist

On the back of each photograph left at a casting call or audition, the actor includes a brief resume of vital statistics.

use your *type* to get you an audition.

You keep trying, you call on the same agents as much as is humanly possible without making them think that you are the biggest pest who ever lived. You work for very little or for nothing in off-off-off-Broadway experimental plays and invite agents to see your work (and mostly they won't come). You continue to take your acting classes and dance classes and speech classes regularly, with great sacrifice to your regular eating habits—for money will be limited. You sit in coffee shops late at night with other out-of-work actors in a strange and close camaraderie of frustration and fun (about which you will speak to your children, as you tell them about how you were discovered in Schwab's Drug Store). You make the rounds again, starting with the first agent you ever saw (who doesn't remember you). And finally, you get your picture and résumé to enough people that perhaps someone does remember you and you are called for an audition. An audition!

THE AUDITION

They are, at best, awful. At worst, they are indescribable. You are on your way to the audition and, if you are lucky, they will have arranged it by time slots—every fifteen minutes they will be seeing another hopeful for the job. That way, you walk into the office of the casting director or to the forty-seventh floor of the advertising agency and only one or two people will be there waiting, giving you hope and making the palms of your hands perspire just a little less. Of course, they have been casting for two days—one person every fifteen minutes—and you will wonder in panic whether it is better to be the first person interviewed or the last. That is something that has never been resolved, in numerous discussions. The first person, if the audition went well, has made a mark against which everyone else must compete. But, at the end of a long day, he is easily forgotten and a fresh face, walking in last, may wipe out all that has gone before. To make matters worse, one of the applicants may have worked for the producers in a previous film and therefore has an edge—or there may be a friend or lover of his on the casting panel. All of this is totally out of your hands and, at best, the odds against you are huge.

At the very worst (if all of this is not bad enough), some auditions are run by insensitive, gauche, rude, ego-driven casting people, whether directors, producers, or casting directors. Some casting calls are made en masse, for after all, your time is not as valuable as theirs and if you wait in a lobby for an hour or two, what else do you have to do? There will be loud denials from everyone in the production end of our business that this is "not our way." Well it *is* someone's and it does happen. Time and again we have seen the waiting rooms crowded with the hopefuls.

With due credit to producers, directors, and casting directors, on the other hand—how *are* they to see all the people who want to break into the business, and still allow enough time for their day-to-day work in production? The actor will forever cry out about not being able to "get in the door," while the people who actually cast the roles will resent the never-ending river of new talent flowing out to both coasts from the hinterlands of Middle America. Both groups, unfortunately, have a point.

Most agents will suggest that actors or models dress the part for an audition, a bit of advice that seems almost naïve. And yet many actors appear at an audition for a truck driver wearing an Ivy League business suit, white shirt, and tie. If the agent has looked at you for "type," the casting director will be more inclined to do so. The film world deals as much in clichés and predispositions as does any other field and out-of-type casting is the exception rather than the rule. Do you remember magazine photo quizzes that showed you ten people and asked you to choose the one who was the murderer? The toughest-looking thug turned out to be the hair dresser, the meek and mild-mannered poet was the one who killed his mother-in-law by having her drink hemlock in orange juice. Well, casting people generally don't work that way.

JOINING THE UNION

You have an agent who actually wants to send you on auditions. You have practiced your sight reading for hours so that, handed any script and given only two minutes to read it

STANDARD SCREEN ACTORS GUILD EMPLOYMENT CONTRACT FOR TELEVISION COMMERCIALS

Date______, 19___

Between______, Producer, and______, Player.

Producer engages Player and Player agrees to perform services for Producer in television commercials as follows:

Date of Engagement______

Time and Place of Engagement______

For______ (Advertising Agency) and______ (Advertiser)

Address______

PRODUCT______

NO. OF COMMERCIALS______

Commercial ID______

Check if Applicable:
☐ Dealer Commercial(s)
☐ Type A
☐ Type B
☐ Seasonal Commercial(s)
☐ Test Market Commercial(s)
☐ Non-Air Commercial(s)

Employer of record for income tax and unemployment insurance purposes is______

☐ Player does not consent to the use of his services in commercials, made hereunder as dealer commercials payable at dealer commercial rates.

☐ Player does not consent to the use of his services in commercials made hereunder on a simulcast.

CLASSIFICATION: ( ) On Camera ( ) Off Camera

( ) Player
( ) Stunt Player
( ) Puppeteer
( ) Specialty Act

( ) Singer-solo or duo
( ) Group-3-5
( ) Group-6-8
( ) Group-9 or more
( ) Contractor

( ) Singer-Signature-solo or duo
( ) Group-Signature-3-5
( ) Group-Signature-6-8
( ) Group-Signature-9 or more
( ) Pilot

Compensation: Session Fee (On-Camera Player) $______ Session Fee (Off-Camera Player) $______

Check if: Flight Insurance ($10) Payable ☐ $______
Wardrobe to be furnished by Producer ☐ by Player ☐
If furnished by Player, No. of Garments______;
Non-evening wear @ $7.50______;
Evening wear @ $15.00______; Total Wardrobe Fee $______

The standard provisions printed on the reverse side hereof are a part of this contract. If this contract provides for compensation at minimum SAG scale, no addition, changes or alterations may be made in this form other than those which are more favorable to the Player than herein provided.

If this contract provides for compensation above minimum SAG scale, additions may be agreed to between Producer and Player which do not conflict with the provisions of the SAG Commercials Contract; provided that such additional provisions are separately set forth under "Special Provisions" hereof and signed by the Player.

Until Player shall otherwise direct in writing, Player authorizes Producer to make all payments to which Player may be entitled hereunder as follows:

☐ To Player at______ (Address)

☐ To Player c/o______ at______ (Address)

All notices to Player shall be sent to the address designated above for payments and, if Player desires, to one other address as follows:

To______ (Name) at______ (Address)

All notices to Producer shall be addressed as follows:

To Producer at______ (Address)

This contract is subject to all of the terms and conditions of the SAG Commercials Contract.

Producer______ Player______

By______

Player hereby certifies that he is 21 years of age or over. (If under 21 years of age this contract must be signed below by a parent or guardian.)

I, the undersigned, hereby state that I am the______ (Mother, Father, Guardian) of the above named Player and do hereby consent and give my permission to this agreement.

______ (Signature of Parent or Guardian)

Special Provisions:

Player acknowledges that he has read all the terms and conditions in the Special Provisions section above and hereby agrees thereto.

Player______ Social Security Number______

NOTICE TO PLAYER: IMPORTANT PROVISIONS ON BACK. PLEASE READ CAREFULLY.

(W-4 form is attached here.)

87

A standard Screen Actors Guild employment contract.

aloud, you can sound as though you've studied it all night. But you must still face another hurdle. (Another hurdle?) You will have to join the union at some point in your career.

Almost all the best acting jobs in the film business are under the jurisdiction of the Screen Actors Guild (see the employment contract this page). Of course, there are roles to be filled in smaller, non-union productions; but for the commercial, the television film, the feature, and the major business films, membership in SAG is a must.

At first glance the membership requirements are a classic "Catch-22" situation. In order to be eligible for membership in the Screen Actors Guild, you must first have a job offer from a producer in any of the film categories. Fine. But, in order to get the job offer from the producer, you must first be a member of SAG. In actuality, the union is open to a degree and the "Catch-22" *can* be overcome, as many actors have found. One way is to be the "perfect" type for a potential production, thus assuring you a job and automatic union status. More practical suggestions are given below. Certainly, you will always have some difficulty, for there are enough people available in the talent pool to fill almost any casting requirement.

First of all, too, one *major* prerequisite must be considered: you must be able to convince the union that you are, in fact, going to pursue a *career* in acting and that this is not just a thing you'd "like to do." For example: Television has become one of the most important parts of the lives of many Americans. Its commercials appear six and eight and more times to the half-hour and its series are part and parcel of the dinner hour, daytime viewing, and the evening's entertainment. Too often, a viewer decides that "If *they* can do it, why can't *I*?" After all, there are ten thousand "housewife and plumber" commercials on the air each year—"and *I* am a housewife." (Or plumber.) "Why couldn't *I* do some commercials and make all that money they write about in *TV Guide*?" After all, Sandy Duncan, Dustin Hoffman, and Farrah Fawcett-Majors all got their start in television commercials.

Well, unfortunately, merely being convinced that you, too, can do the job is not generally considered enough of a "professional" back-

ACTORS AND MODELS

When the feature film goes on location, the producer generally provides small portable dressing rooms for the actors. Between takes, they can study their lines or rest.

ground for Screen Actors Guild; nor is it looked upon too kindly by the casting directors or the advertising agencies. Fortunately, enough professionals in the field look like housewives and plumbers to fill the casting needs for the next fifty years. And, not too surprisingly, some of the most active people who play housewives and plumbers have never been near a home-cooked meal or a clogged drainpipe in their lives.

What the people in the industry and union *will* consider in terms of professional interest might cover any of the following:

- If you are already a member of any other actor's union, SAG will be more receptive to your application.

Actors Equity (the stage union), AFTRA (American Federation of Television and Radio Artists), and AGVA (American Guild of Variety Artists) are the other prime unions in the entertainment industry.

- A college degree in drama, or appearance in enough summer stock or community theater may convince SAG that you are, in fact, looking for eventual professional status.

But, even if you meet these qualifications, the producer must prove through a casting session that you are absolutely necessary to the production because of type, talent, or specialty. *If the producer makes the request,* based upon those prerequisites, SAG will grant a waiver permitting you to join.

You must make the rounds and you must read the trade papers to find out who is casting and where the auditions are being held. Your photograph and résumé must be given to a thousand producers and agents and casting directors. Continuing your training will help—whether in college or after graduation. Showing how well you can act will be even *more* valuable to you. If beginning filmmakers are a step ahead when they can show their samples, actors are in a much better position to demonstrate what they can do if they can manage to perform in any medium: stage, radio, festivals, street theater . . . Reviews of such performances are invaluable. Also, begin to collect your film or tape work on a sample reel. Or, at the beginning, with no film or tape experience to exhibit, even a rehearsed monologue on tape, to show your skill, is better than no sample at all.

COURSES AND TRAINING THAT HELP

Perhaps one of the best types of courses you can take to help you audition is in the area of sight reading. Sometimes the script or story board is given to you just moments before you are to read for a casting director. The words blur, the sentences seem to run together—do they want the accent on the product name or on the adjective that describes it? The waiting room is full and there's no one to ask, and in a few moments you will walk into the conference room to face six faces all trying to look pleasant while you coolly read to them as if you had been studying all night. The ones who seem to do the best are the actors who can take a script and quickly mark off the pauses, the emphases, the continuity, and then read smoothly and effectively. It can be done, and it can be learned by practice and with a little help from people who really know how to teach this phase of the craft.

It also helps to look at yourself on videotape. Some courses use tape machines to good advantage and students are encouraged to read for the machine and then watch the playback. First time through, you will think you look awful—and possibly you do, but again you will find that practice helps. Keep in mind that many auditions today are, in fact, put on tape for future viewing by the casting people, so you might just as well get used to the infernal machine.

Above all, perhaps—mixed in with the stamina and the enthusiasm for a field that has its rewards when you're working and its awful depressions when you're not—you need to look at the life of an actor realistically. Some years ago, after a long day of shooting with Lorne Greene, one of the kindest and most perceptive of film actors, we sat at dinner and he gave me his view of the acting profession. None of us who were there will ever forget it—and many of you might take note of his advice. The life of an actor, he told us, is divided into five stages:

- The first stage: "Who's Lorne Greene?"
- The second: "Get me Lorne Greene!"
- The third: "Get me someone like Lorne Greene!"
- And the fourth: "Get me a *young* Lorne Greene!"
- The fifth stage: "Who's Lorne Greene?"

The story has come back to me time and time again as young people say to me, "Have you ever worked with anyone famous?" I begin my list by saying, "Oh yes, there was Chester Morris . . ." And by the perplexity on their faces I know exactly what the next question is going to be: "Who's Chester Morris?"

CHAPTER 12

THE UNSUNG HEROES AND HEROINES

Eleven Pillars of the Industry

When young people come up to our offices to be interviewed and the inevitable "I want to be in production" is heard, it begins to occur to me that the word "production" is terribly misunderstood. It is certainly covered in the areas described in Chapter 4. But it is more, much more. What about the people doing makeup, the costumers and designers who give the film its "look" and "style"? What about the hundreds, probably thousands, of people doing their jobs in "production" unsung, unrecognized by the great moviegoing public, many of them creative, many of them doing fascinating and worthwhile jobs. And, what do these interviewees know about the studio mechanics and technicians, and how much information do they have about the business people who also are doing jobs in film? The answer, of course, is "next to nothing." It is not just that the interviewees don't know —possibly they don't care enough to know. And yet, the job opportunities—particularly the *entry* job opportunities—are there, some to greater degree than others.

The last time you went to a movie at the local cinema, what happened at the end of the film when the credits began their long crawl up the screen? The lights probably went on and the exodus began. The film was over, the audience was anxious to get out to parked cars, ice-cream sundaes, drinks, and love. It was "a Truffaut picture" or "a film by Coppola," and that was that. And some of us, standing straight up with our necks stretched to the ultimate limit, were vainly trying to see the credits—*all* of the credits: the mixer and the scenic designers and the gaffers . . . Finally the projector is turned off (by a projectionist who has already seen the film twenty-seven times) and the last few people on the "crawl" are doomed to final oblivion and non-recognition by those of us who really wanted to know who they are.

It took Dick Smith four hours to transform F. Murray Abraham into "Old Salieri" for the film Amadeus. Both Smith and Abraham won Academy Awards for their work on the film.

But, even if the public is unaware of the names of such people, the most important point is that if *you* are to become a functioning member of the industry—possibly eventually as a director (and certainly "in production")— then these job categories and the people who perform them are as important to you as the camera and the tape recorder. Thousands of such

Claudia Weill was a documentary director/cinematographer before becoming a director of feature films. Her first job included picking up laundry and cooking for the crew, as a lowly "gopher."

people in the industry are doing hundreds of important jobs and loving every minute of their working day. If the director, cinematographer, soundperson, editor, and stars are all living in a temple called Film—with their names on the mailbox outside—then that temple is held up by a great many pillars, and it is to them that this chapter is lovingly dedicated.

THE GOPHER

Probably more people have broken into the film business in this job than in any other. The word, if you have not heard it before, is derived from the main function of this lowest member of the crew. The gopher (sometimes "go-fer") does exactly that. "Go fer coffee" is the most common order—generally just one of the many commands that might be obeyed by a messenger, runner, servant, and slave. But what an amazing way to learn the film business!

The gopher is close to the technicians, recognized by the director, befriended (hopefully) by the camera crew—and worked mercilessly by all of them. Any job too menial to be done by the crown princes and princesses is generally assigned to the gopher. In talking to ex-gophers and asking them just what it is they did in the job, the answers are as varied as the imagination will allow.

Claudia Weill, who started her career as a gopher and is now a director of feature films, got her first job because she knew someone who was working on a picture about Haight-Ashbury (*Revolution* – United Artists). She began by driving people to the city – first, picking them up at the airport – delivering dailies to the lab, checking on accommodations, picking up laundry for the director, cooking for the crew on location, and making the beds for everyone in a motel that was less than deluxe. And, to make matters even worse, she did it for *free* – the production manager was doing the friend of her friend a favor!

It turned out to be the best break she could have gotten. The crew, for reasons of efficiency, was broken down into two units. The gopher was enlisted to do other jobs besides making the beds and soon she was scouting locations, helping to cast for the extras ("Go out and find me a hippie girl"), and assisting the sound crew when they were shorthanded. Under their guidance, she learned sound and moved on into other phases of production. Someone else was taken on to make the beds and pick up the director's laundry.

This job is not taught in the film schools. You get it because you are lucky, or you know someone, or you ask around until you find one, or you are clever and you take advantage of the fact that a film crew is working under your window on location, or someone just likes you. You may really have to work for nothing—or the pay will be so small that you will have to support yourself doing another job late at night or on weekends, or by asking your rich grandparents for rent money. And you must be able to work hard and enthusiastically, for the gopher's is the least creative job in the field. It is, on the other hand, the job that gives you the greatest opportunity to observe, to make friends, to be a beginning part of the film field. And one day, when *you* turn to someone else and order, "Go fer coffee!" you will have graduated into glory.

MAKEUP AND HAIR STYLING

The make-up artist is very often the first one on the job, particularly if there is anything really difficult to do. Most of my make-ups take two or three hours. Well, this means that if they want to start shooting at 8:30 or 9 A.M., I've got to be there at 6:30 or six, or even five o'clock in the morning, and I live in the suburbs, so I've got to get up two hours before I'm due. We shoot from 8:30 until 5:30, maybe 6:30, and then I've got to get the actor cleaned up if he's all covered with glue—and it may be necessary for me to go see the dailies—the rushes—which may mean I'm not on my way home until eight o'clock. When I arrive home, I'm exhausted, I gobble down a little food and I fall into bed because I've got to get up at 4 A.M. the next morning. This can go on for weeks.

Dick Smith

What you've just read was written by one of the best in the field, and by a man who has encouraged—and discouraged—many beginners who have wanted to become makeup artists. Dick was the genius who created the hundred-year-old man for Dustin Hoffman's *Little Big Man*, did the makeup and much of the special-effects work for *The Exorcist*, and was the inventor of the device that puffed out Marlon Brando's cheeks in *The Godfather*. He is absolutely the best. His quote at the beginning of this section gives an accurate and perceptive view of a makeup artist's life-style and job demands.

As with many of the crafts in the industry, the art of makeup is a victim of the publicity

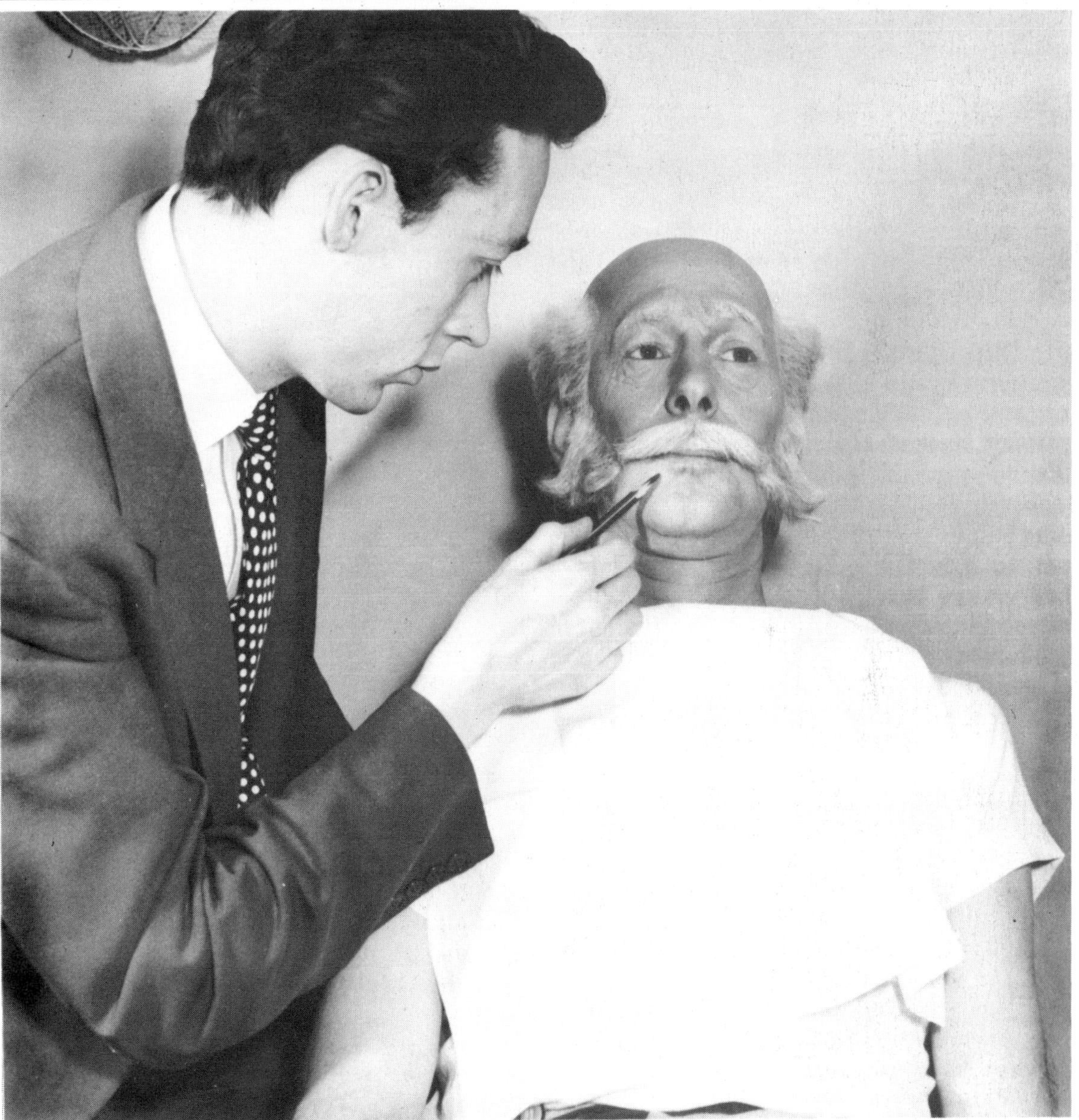

Smith began his career by doing makeup at NBC-TV. This photo was taken in 1948, and the actor was Vaughn Taylor.

MAKE-UP ARTISTS AND HAIR STYLISTS
LOCAL 798
OF THE INTERNATIONAL ALLIANCE OF THEATRICAL STAGE EMPLOYEES
1790 BROADWAY, NEW YORK, N. Y. 10019
(212) 757-9120

EDWARD P CALLAGHAN
BUSINESS MANAGER

THE THEATRICAL MAKE-UP ARTIST AND HAIRSTYLIST

The number of inquiries reaching my desk have made individual answers impossible. This form should provide most, if not all of the information requested.

Theatrical make-up and hairstyling comprises a small segment of the cosmetology industry. This fact explains the limited number of openings and apprenticeships available from time to time. Each major city has a small amount of theatrical production, e.g. film, television, theatre and advertising. New York City and Hollywood are the centers of this industry. Most major film and television studio make-up artists and hairstylists belong to either Local 798, I.A.T.S.E., 1790 Broadway, New York City 10019 in the east, or Local 706, I.A.T.S.E., 11519 Chandler Blvd., North Hollywood, California 91601, in the west. Local 706 is larger than Local 798. Local 798 has approximately 300 members in both crafts in all media; television, film and legitimate theatre.

New members are customarily admitted on an apprenticeship level as the applicants experience is usually gained in an area of cosmetology other than theatrical. To one waiting to "get in" it can seem like an eternity. In times of low employment this is nearly an impossibility and a frustrating experience. A good deal of talent must be coupled with patience and tenacity in order to accomplish this aim.

There are many beauty and drama schools that have make-up courses. Such courses are seldom taught by professional make-up artists and are basic. In the east Local 798 chooses their own apprentices, while out west both the studio (employer) and Local 706 make this selection.

Local 798's apprenticeship course is of 3 years duration. Employment during these 3 years is not guaranteed nor should it be expected, though it usually is provided in varying degrees. Training time is designated not to conflict with the usual work day. In other words an apprentice should not expect employment during this period or feel the union is responsible for his income.

Aspiring members will be interviewed by a seven member screening committee. This committee's prime concern is to compare each person's professional background and select the best of the applicants for the

MAKE-UP ARTISTS AND HAIR STYLISTS
LOCAL 798
OF THE INTERNATIONAL ALLIANCE OF THEATRICAL STAGE EMPLOYEES
1790 BROADWAY, NEW YORK, N. Y. 10019
(212) 757-9120

EDWARD P CALLAGHAN
BUSINESS MANAGER

few occasional openings. Aside from professional background, courses, especially portrait painting and sculpting, are impressive and important for aspiring make-up artists. Examples of your work may be presented. Due to the nature of the work, cleanliness, grooming and personality are very important. American citizenship and an 18 month residency in the state of your application is a requirement of Local 798. Requirement waivers will be considered for outstanding professional make-up artists and hairstylists.

When and if accepted into the apprenticeship program there is an initiation fee and quarterly dues. The apprentice holds a union card and attends monthly membership meetings. It is not unusual in times of low employment for years to pass between the start of apprentice classes.

The work is very glamourous to all except the professional artist. He/she is aware of the long and unusual hours, the loss of family time, the discomforts of strange and/or dangerous locations, and all the other factors that only youth seems to invariably interpret as glamour.

If you still feel you have got the necessary background and talent, come in for an application. Once filled out and returned the long wait will begin. This wait will, if your background is suitable, be climaxed by the interview. Shortly thereafter you will be notified of your acceptance or rejection.

If you are talented, experienced and ambitious come in for an application. If not, please do not waste your time and ours.

The best of luck to you.

Very truly yours,

Ed Callaghan

EDWARD P. CALLAGHAN
Business Manager

EPC/jaf

in newspapers and magazines. The illusion builders in Hollywood deliberately created an industry image that spoke of tinsel and glamour, and perhaps it was not all wrong. Eventually, the public discovered that all those sea battles were done with miniatures in slow motion, and perhaps it was no accident that one of the declines of Hollywood coincided with the revelations of just how "Hollywood magic" was accomplished.

Makeup was and is a part of that "magic." Most beginners who become interested in makeup are fascinated by the monsters, by characters out of horror movies, by the very real genius of people such as John Chambers, who created the makeup for *Planet of the Apes*. For most makeup artists and hair stylists, however, 90 percent of the work is fairly straight: making up an actor to cover five-o'clock shadow, taking some of the circles out from beneath the eyes, touching up with hair spray; it's making up the female lead in the soap opera, every day, Monday through Friday, making her look pretty, putting on false eyelashes, combing her hair. It is a living, certainly, but the beginner must realize that unless you become highly skilled—tops in the field—the above is what most of the work entails. For a few people there is more challenging work. For the beginner, however, there is a need for a dedication to the art. If it is there, you will probably be encouraged by people like Dick Smith. Otherwise, you may find their advice rather negative.

The letter reproduced on this page is probably the most succinct and realistic approach to the field of makeup that I have seen. It is sent to applicants by Ed Callaghan, the business manager of Local 798 in New York. Read it carefully. If it discourages you, then turn to another chapter in the book. If it does not, then perhaps you are one of the few.

For the most part, makeup and hair-styling work in film is divided between New York and Hollywood. Some jobs have opened up in Florida as the Miami area has expanded production and, in addition, there are some artists scattered across the country in cities such as Boston, Chicago, and Philadelphia, but most of the latter usually fill out their free time in other occupations. Some work in the theater, others have their own beauty salons, while keeping themselves available for the occasional location jobs that may come through their area.

Even with discouragement, even with the obstacles that litter the path, some people have made it, hundreds do work in the field, an occasional vacancy occurs, apprenticeship programs do exist, however small they are.

DEDICATION Most makeup artists become interested in the field while still in their teens, usually with a fascination with monster or horror makeup. As a teenager, Rick Baker had a consuming passion for apes—all kinds of apes—gorillas, and chimpanzees, and did makeup and masks that were works of art. These beginnings culminated in one of his most recent jobs: the makeup for the updated version of *King Kong.*

Dick Smith, while still at Yale University, used to practice by transforming himself into classic film monsters: Frankenstein, the Wolfman, Quasimodo, and The Mummy. At that time, he was fairly shy and introverted. But when he put on one of his favorite makeup disguises, that of Mr. Hyde, he would suddenly blossom into the campus maniac, roaming the walks and frightening his classmates while leading the university guards a merry chase.

Essentially, then, the word "dedication" translates itself into the fact that anyone who wants to be a makeup artist must be crazy about the craft.

READING Fortunately, in the field of makeup there are several excellent books available: *Makeup for Theater, Film & Television* by Lee Baygan (1982. Drama Book Publishing, NYC) and *Techniques of Three Dimensional Makeup*, also by Lee Baygan (1982. Watson-Guptil, NYC), devoted mostly to the art of character makeup.

PRACTICE If makeup is fascinating, then the budding artist likes to practice, and should—on himself and on his friends—every spare moment, up to six or eight hours a week.

ARTISTIC TALENT To do makeup it is not, by any means, necessary to be a great artist, though developing a color sense through painting with oils will certainly not hurt. More important, perhaps, is the need to develop a feeling and a facility for *sculpture.*

Sculpture is the key to creating any kind of complicated makeup: a mask, a rubber nose, an odd chin, old-age wrinkles—anything applied to the face to change its quality. For any such "appliance" to be designed, a clay model

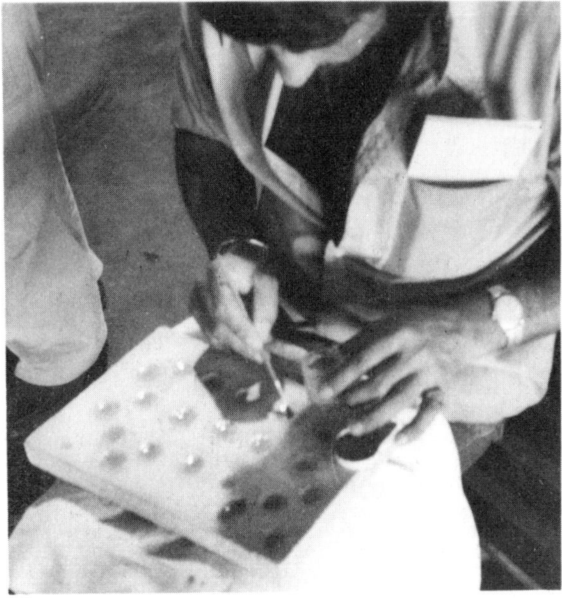

The ingenuity of the makeup artist is constantly tested. Maurice Stein designed "bee stings" for The Savage Bees.

must first be made, and from that the mold for the final rubber piece. A good makeup artist must be able to sculpt human features in great detail, with incredible realism, down to the last pore or tiny wrinkle. This talent can be developed on your own or in a school.

MANUAL DEXTERITY As a makeup artist, you will work with your hands, so any kind of handicraft work requiring manual dexterity will eventually help. This includes the skills needed in building ship or airplane models, carpentry, or even the painting of miniatures.

TECHNICAL SKILLS Since you want to work in a field that requires the formulation and blending of cosmetics, latex, and plastic materials, a knowledge of chemistry can be helpful. The chemistry of the cosmetic industry would, of course, be more valuable than the general courses given in high school or college, and so would a strong background in the chemistry of plastics. Maurice Stein became an expert in the area of plastics, and his "bee stings" in *The Savage Bees* were horrifyingly realistic, each one an individual application made by the makeup artist.

John Chambers is one of the most skilled people in the area of dental appliances and prosthetic devices, and were he not one of the busiest of makeup artists, he would be well equipped to make his way in either of the two fields. Since much of makeup requires these devices, the beginner would be wise to include dental and prosthetics study as something to think about and possibly to pursue as a second profession.

Think of it this way: If you choose makeup or hair styling as a career, and if you accept the fact that you have only a 50–50 chance of even getting into it, the idea of having a second skill becomes more attractive. This is even more important if that second career can, in any way, help you toward your goal as a make-up artist. You stand a better chance of finding steady employment as a dental technician than as a make-up artist, or as a *commercial* hair stylist who also works in film or backstage.

SCENIC DESIGN AND SET DECORATION

It was a windy day in March, and spring had not yet come to the Guadarrama Mountains in Spain. We had left Segovia at about three, trying to make it back to Madrid before dusk, and

Production costs often can be kept low by use of simple but ingenious design. This scene is from Her Office Hero, starring Arnold Stang and produced for the Greater New York Fund with scenic design by Lester Polakov.

while still climbing the forested mountain in our little underpowered SEAT (a Spanish Fiat) car, the snow began to fall and driving became more difficult. With the wind howling around us, we rounded a curve in the rutted road and all of us in the car gasped in sheer horror.

There—crucified to the tall, swaying pines—were human skeletons, yellow-gray against the trunks of the trees. The tattered remains of what must have been clothing fluttered in the snowy wind. They were all around us—perhaps fifty or more, but we didn't stop to count. Eerie explanations flashed through our minds: a hidden battlefield, undiscovered after the Spanish Civil War? A mass murder in the secret reaches of the mountains? Pushing the tiny car to its limit, we tore through the woods and finally came out onto a clearing. A huge wooden fort dominated the hilltop and on it was a sign, proclaiming in big bold letters, A SAMUEL BRONSTON PRODUCTION — THE FALL OF THE ROMAN EMPIRE. We had just driven through a movie set!

If nothing else, the story proves that designing for film is, for the most part, an art of realism. On the stage, of course, the proscenium is the framework within which designers and decorators work — sometimes realistically, sometimes in the most abstract of forms with mere indications of the time and place and nature of the play. If the stage designer is working with a ramp or an arena instead, the problems and their solutions can be varied, for each member of the audience will see the stage from another three-dimensional vantage point. A black cyclorama with some floating shapes might be what the stage designer decides to use, either for esthetic considerations or for

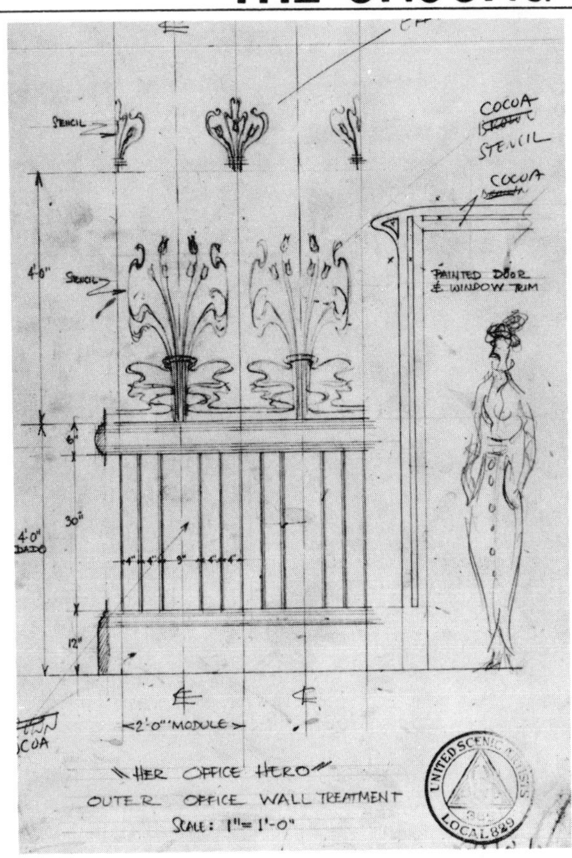

First sketches for set and costume design by Lester Polakov for Her Office Hero.

the mundane reasons of just not enough money. As a result, budding stage designers all over the world are cutting their creative teeth on productions that lend themselves to flexibility, starkness, abstraction—and sometimes realism.

Every once in a while, the film medium allows this flexibility. In the early years of motion pictures, *The Cabinet of Dr. Caligari* was, perhaps, the best example of an attempt at something different; painted stage flats were used in bold designs. Musical comedies have also used abstract backgrounds, and *Anchors Aweigh* (1945) mixed live action with animated drawings. In the field of the business film and the television commercial, scenic designers have also had more freedom of concept, for many of these films are concerned only with the communication of an *idea*, and the design might be based upon a bare white cyclorama or abstract shapes similar to some theatrical concepts.

The sets in the photographs on page 84 are good examples. The sets were designed by Lester Polakov for an orientation film for the Greater New York Fund. Bound by a severely limited budget, he created an art nouveau feeling by using stencils to paint wall designs, placing potted palms at strategic points, renting a few oversized props, and cutting out shapes to represent machines. In a sense, it was still partly "realistic," but it was also an ingenious abstraction of an era and worked well for the film.

For the most part, though, film is very realistic in design and decoration. Whether the designer is working with a period piece like *Barry Lyndon* or *Chinatown*, or with a contemporary story of any genre, he brings to the production a blend of originality tempered with authenticity. As with all the other film crafts, the element of cost control must, of course, also be considered, even in high-budget motion pictures.

All of this is true not only for feature productions, but also in the realm of television film and, generally, commercials. The smallest details are important in the countless living-

room sets, kitchens, and offices used in situation comedies ("sitcoms"), spots, and TV features. Despite a general need for realism, a budget is nevertheless very important in the world of commercials, because producers usually bid competitively to get their jobs from the advertising agencies and a clever designer can save thousands of dollars in production costs.

As more and more film productions have moved out of the studios and into locations around the world, the need for set design has decreased somewhat. For example, instead of building a plantation on a back lot in Hollywood, location scouting discovered hundreds of authentic antebellum mansions on the lower Mississippi River. Small towns were delighted to serve as "set pieces" for film productions, with a side benefit of work, as "extras," for their citizens. Of course, local conditions frequently are *wrong* for photography—or local political situations warrant shooting elsewhere —and thus the beaches of Hawaii were used for *South Pacific* and a good part of *Ryan's Daughter* was shot in Portugal and never even came close to the Emerald Isle.

Still, there is a need for people who can recreate that which no longer exists, and who can convert entire areas into locations that carry the names of other places and other times. When producers began to make "spaghetti Westerns," it was the scenic designers who created Tombstone, Arizona, within Spain and Italy. How many "jungle" pictures were produced within shouting range of Beverly Hills? For a long time, the series "Kojak"—set in New York—was shot on the West Coast. Indeed, the motion picture *New York, New York* was also shot in Hollywood! The "Louisiana" setting for *A Soldier's Story* was really the state of Arkansas. Given the proper landscape, the scenic designer adds a building, some local color, a few new roadsigns and props—and the deed is done.

Makeup and Creature Design Supervisor Phil Tippett adjusts the two-legged walker on the Go-Motion walker set for Return of the Jedi.

In many of the film professions it is a simple matter to take the breakdowns categorized by the unions, and describe each of them. In the case of scenic design, however, this becomes more complicated—almost impossible. First of all, the Hollywood and New York local unions both have different rules and different categories; but, even more important, there is a perplexing overlap in the functions of the locals. Los Angeles has *nine* locals for art directors alone. In addition, on West Coast features and television films the functions of the art director are strictly controlled; while on the East Coast the art director establishes the concept, is allowed to make the necessary drawings, do the drafting, and then direct the prop man in selecting furniture and other decoration necessary for the setting. Beyond this problem, on both coasts there are separate locals for "plasterers" (the people who do the textural work) and set painters (including paperhangers and sign painters). Moreover, costume designers are also members of the scenic artists union.

If we break down the scenic-design and set-decoration jobs by some of the titles used in the field, perhaps you will have a clearer picture of just where you might fit in eventually. Keep in mind throughout, however, that in different parts of the country the jobs overlap, and that in non-union production generally *one* person does everything.

Art Director (or Production Designer). Designs the concept and the look of the set.

Illustrator (or Matte Artist). The illustrator does the color sketches of the set.

Scenic Designer and Model Maker. This individual works from the drawings of the illustrator, and under the supervision of the art director. These two are the people who do the drafting: the ground plans, elevations, and construction

The early German Expressionist film The Cabinet of Dr. Caligari used boldly painted stage flats for its backdrop. However, most motion picture design is highly realistic.

Final sketch for the set used in the General Foods television spot for French Vanilla.

drawings. Many times, a model is made of the set, particularly where a special effect is to be used.

Set Decorator. The set decorator works closely with the art director to collect and assemble all the outside props needed for the set. Frequently the props are rented from antique shops and other furniture suppliers rather than being purchased, and in the larger cities some enterprising retail merchants do a large business with set decorators, renting for productions that will only use the props for a short time, to be returned to their stock when the job is finished.

Remember that you need not set your sights on only one of the jobs described above. Only in Hollywood is the structure rigid and based upon seniority. In New York, and certainly in the non-union area, the jobs above overlap and frequently you find an art director assigned to one picture while working on a different film under *another* art director as a chargeman (the person who hires the work crew and then supervises the construction of the sets).

The area of scenic design is one field in which the beginner can actually take advantage of other opportunities for experience while trying to break into film. Colleges and universities offer excellent design courses, including the technical areas of drafting. In addition, a few courses are given by private professionals on both coasts. And there is other knowledge that can help: art and art history, for example; studies in stagecraft, film history, and architecture are almost a necessity.

Many designers work in the field of the theater and a few move back and forth to film as the jobs present themselves. For the film student and beginner, scenic design is scenic design, and working in off-off-Broadway productions can be good practice, even though the differences in the two fields are vast. Nevertheless, the frame of the proscenium trains the eye, the ramp and the arena challenge the creative juices. College and community productions are another starting place, where the challenge is, of course, compounded by the almost absolute lack of money with which to bring your ideas to fruition.

In scenic design and set decoration, again, there is a chance to show something concrete. The mere fact that you have studied and practiced scenic design will give you a portfolio of your work: samples and drawings and possibly photographs of the work you've done. If the talent is there, you can show it in all its glorious color (or in black-and-white).

As in any tightly controlled trade, the trick is to apprentice yourself to someone who is already established and who works most of the time. Such people do exist and they, in turn, use beginners and talented professionals in the more menial areas. Whether you paint a flat or help someone find the props for an eighteenth-century drawing room, haul lumber to prop up the back of a Western saloon, or refine the drawings of a much-too-busy scenic illustrator, you will be working in the field. And that's what you started out to do, right?

COSTUME, STYLING, AND WARDROBE

If I go out to dinner and I don't have a shopping bag touching my leg, I panic.
—Jo Ynocencio

You have to love clothes. You have to know how to shop for clothes, understand how to break down a script according to characterization and locale. You have to be able to read the mind of the director in order to be successful. But, above all, you have to *love clothes* and be prepared to spend hours and travel miles on two strong legs as you make your way through the department stores, costume houses, and specialty shops of the larger cities.

For the sake of clarity, we might break down the field into two major groups:

COSTUME DESIGNERS On the West Coast, there are two unions, one for the actual costume designer and one for the costumer, the person who works only on contemporary clothes and who does the actual shopping. On the East Coast, the costume designer does *both* jobs. In the field of TV and commercials, the person is referred to as a "stylist."

WARDROBE ATTENDANTS These are the people who actually handle the clothes after they have been selected by the designer, the costumer, or the stylist.

Of course, in the non-union film world, the job lines cross over as they always do.

As in the whole of the film industry, the director is the boss and probably has the most to do with selecting the designer for the film. The work might begin as much as six or eight

Sketches for costume design in Her Office Hero.

weeks before shooting, though much of the selection is done at the last minute, due to delays, trauma, temperament, differences of opinion, and just plain not enough time. In addition to conferences with the director, the script must be analyzed character by character and scene by scene. Each person must be "broken down" in terms of: What does he or she look like? What is the personality of the character? What unusual traits might reflect themselves in how he or she dresses? What ideas do the makeup and hair-styling people have?

In one particular feature film, the lead actress was cast as a car thief. What does a car thief wear? The director wanted sneakers—an obvious costume accessory, he thought, for anyone in that vocation. Fine. But the actress resisted. Sneakers would make her look short and she didn't want to look short. The costume designer suggested construction boots. But the boots would look too heavy. Six weeks went by—the fittings were completed in Los Angeles and the crew moved to the location in Seattle—without any decision made. Finally, on the morning of the shooting, everyone agreed with the designer that Frye Boots would be all right: the actress would be taller and the audience would accept the fact that the car thief would actually look authentic.

The story is a good example of the incredible attention to detail that we find in so many of the crafts in the film industry. Even if the director were to shoot the entire picture in close-up so that no one would even notice the shoes, the important thing was that the designer *knew* that the costuming was right for the role.

At times, actors and actresses can use their own clothes, so the designer must go through their wardrobes to see if that solution is a possibility. More often, however, the personal clothes of the actor cannot be used for the part—and then the designer or costumer or stylist begins the long shopping tour.

Most costume people prefer the West Coast for costume rental—for films where period dress is required and the budget will not allow for the design and manufacture of costumes for an entire cast. Where contemporary clothes are called for in the script, the East Coast (and particularly New York) is preferred because of the vast selection available in department stores, thrift shops, boutiques, and specialty shops. Shopping bags are filled, store by store, as the clothes begin to pile up: a dress for the lead actress, three shirts for the male star, shoes, hats, gloves . . . "The Shopping Bag Brigade" is what they call themselves—and how many have been stopped by store detectives who were convinced that anyone carrying so much merchandise must, indeed, be a shoplifter! Of course, these shoppers are all under the strict confines of a budget. Money is not limitless and it sometimes takes a great amount of ingenuity to dress the cast properly within the budget. A good designer or stylist soon gets to know where the best bargains in town can be had.

Once the clothes are assembled, they are either handled by the non-union stylist all the way through to completion of photography or, in the case of the film unions, they are turned over to the wardrobe attendants. Many attendants work both in film and on the stage, and the job is essentially the same in both areas.

The wardrobe attendant takes care of all the clothing used by the cast, and the more ingenuity one can apply to the job, the more in demand one will be, for the film business is in the constant labor pains of emergency. Ideally, the wardrobe attendant will need these qualifications:

- A feeling for organization, with everything in its place and a place for everything
- How to sew
- How to do quick alterations
- How to maintain clothes—spot cleaning, dyeing, pressing
- How to improvise accessories
- How to "size" people for clothing, gloves, shoes, hosiery
- How to take accurate measurements
- A knowledge of period costuming
- How to improvise when proper equipment is lacking

If the ironing board is missing or has just not been provided for, must be found a better way

Wardrobe people have one of the closest relationships with cast and crew. Many of them work very closely with the stars of a production, under tremendous pressures and frequently under trying conditions. The more levelheaded you are, the more successful you will probably be. Most wardrobe attendants describe their jobs as just having no time to allow themselves their own temper tantrums.

If you eventually join the union, it might help to know just what the job breakdown is for wardrobe attendants:

Dresser. This is the entry-job stage and the dresser generally works directly with the star. Sometimes a beginner is recommended by a member of the union for proven capabilities such as experience in college or summer theater, or a special skill in sewing, for example. In most cases, the star chooses a personal favorite as a dresser.

Supervisor. This is the second stage upward in the union—hired by the First Person, to assist.

First Person. Supervises all costumes on the production, coordinates between the costume designer and the dresser, and must know how to make out payroll sheets, be familiar with hours, benefits, overtime rules, and how to organize the production so that costumes are ready when needed.

Where do you begin?

Colleges definitely offer an excellent opportunity for practice. Courses are available in costume design, and the training will help you in your future research work in the field, for period costuming is a large part of the knowledge you will need.

The stage, especially for the job of wardrobe attendant, probably offers even more opportunity than does film, so many people work wherever the opening presents itself. As a result, school work or community involvement in stagecraft can also be a way of entry into the field.

Some stylists have begun their careers in the field of still photography, for many of the same prerequisites are needed for fashion and magazines: a love of clothes and knowing how to get them and take care of them—and, how to improvise.

If the stylist begins to work in the field of television commercials, the costumed actor may have to fly through the air wearing a dress shirt that must continue to look exquisite as he soars above the cameras. In one such case it was the stylist who designed a harness, used equal parts of tissue paper and plastic under the shirt, and accomplished the feat without a single wrinkle showing in the finished film.

The beginning stylist—much like the gopher—will probably find that the first job includes a great many things that were never taught in school. On your first morning at work, in the midst of making coffee in a small, hot studio, for the models and actors and crew and hangers-on, then being sent out in an emergency to buy some more clothespins with which to tighten a dress, then washing out the dirty coffee cups after work, and learning—always learning—about color and style and dressing, about Scotchgarding the clothes, and how to read people's minds, you will no doubt have a sense of exhilaration at the same time that you wonder what it is you're doing there and why you wanted to get into the film business in the first place. As you drag the heavy shopping bags through the miles of aisles in the department stores, you will come to realize that in this particular craft it helps to be a Jack- or Jacqueline-of-all-trades. It comes in handy!

Stylist Jackie Hickey choosing accessories for a film about dressing for business. Since the production was in black and white, both pattern and tone had to be considered.

THE SCRIPT SUPERVISOR

Sidney Skolsky used to write a daily syndicated column and I remember reading it avidly in the New York *Post*. One of my favorite delights was a section called "Movie Boners"; it was filled with the mistakes of Hollywood, exposed in gorgeous black-and-white for all the world to see. "In the movie 'The Lady and the Woodpeddler,' Gloria Gorgeous comes into the Prince's room wearing a long evening gown and a moment later is seen in a short dress." Certainly an exaggeration, but you get the idea. You've probably seen them yourself: the cigarette in a shot at one angle, empty-handed in another; diamond bracelet one moment, empty wrist the next. Every once in a while they slip through. And somewhere out there the script supervisor winces.

Motion pictures are generally not shot in sequence. In the documentary and in the commercial, this is not too much of a problem, but in the feature film it can be a monumental hurdle just keeping track of everything that goes on from day to day, scene to scene, minute to minute. What is the heroine wearing (down to the last detail)? And what script pages were covered in the last few takes? Which ones were the selected ones—and how will they intercut with whatever else is being shot that day, and possibly seven or ten days later? When they all get into the editing room, they have to mesh. It is too late then to discover that a particular piece of dialogue is missing or that a "movie boner" has inadvertently been made.

So the script supervisor is generally the overworked person who keeps track of everything. And that means everything! The dialogue, silent inserts (MOS), the costume details, movement and placement of the actors and the extras, changes in script made right on stage, the selected sound and camera takes (already double-checked and also written by the sound and camera assistants), director's notes that will later be recalled in the editing room, prop placement for retakes or scenes shot at a later time . . . The script supervisor's notes become pages on the script, lines to indicate the scenes covered and the dialogue spoken, questions asked of the director and crew . . . Writing, always writing.

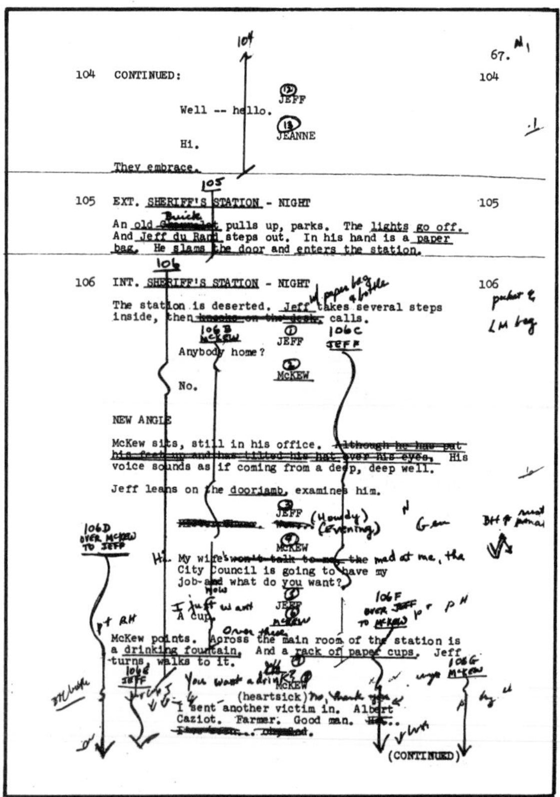

67.

104 CONTINUED: 104

JEFF

Well -- hello.

JEANNE

Hi.

They embrace.

105 EXT. SHERIFF'S STATION - NIGHT 105

An old ~~Chevrolet~~ Buick pulls up, parks. The lights go off. And Jeff du Rand steps out. In his hand is a paper bag. He slams the door and enters the station.

106 INT. SHERIFF'S STATION - NIGHT 106

The station is deserted. Jeff takes several steps inside, then calls.

JEFF

Anybody home?

McKEW

No.

NEW ANGLE

McKew sits, still in his office. ~~Although he has put his feet up and has tilted his hat over his eyes,~~ His voice sounds as if coming from a deep, deep well.

Jeff leans on the doorjamb, examines him.

JEFF

(Howdy)
(Evening)

McKEW

My wife's mad at me, the City Council is going to have my job-- what do you want?

JEFF

A cup.

McKEW

McKew points. Across the main room of the station is a drinking fountain. And a rack of paper cups. Jeff turns, walks to it.

McKEW

(heartsick)

I sent another victim in. Albert Caziot. Farmer. Good man. . .

(CONTINUED)

The same script section as shown on page 30, with the script supervisor's notes. Note the change from Chevrolet to Buick.

In one of those remarkable ballets of the film industry, the script supervisor moves to "where the action is," questions, watches the director, sometimes answers a question as to which scene was covered in just which way, sometimes wearing headsets along with the sound person when the dialogue cannot be heard for some reason (as when the actors are in a closed car and the scene is played while moving), etc.

Although technically a part of the production crew, script supervisors have their own union, and basically all of them have come to their jobs while working in the production area as anything from assistants to gophers. One thing is certain: a script supervisor, like many of the technicians in the field, *must* know just what is going on in all the areas—technical as well as creative—in order to accomplish the job. The slightest nuance must be recorded, the slightest change noted and mentally filed away for the future. Eagle eyes, an alert mind, a well-organized method of working, an ability to see things done in bits and pieces and to put them all together in some kind of form so that they are available to the director and to the editor. A tough job.

An old friend of mine is a former script supervisor and she claims that going to the movies as a spectator has been ruined for her forever. She sits down as everyone else does, ready to enjoy the show . . . the lights dim . . . and automatically she goes to work. She wonders about which scenes were shot on which days, sees the slightest error in movement, costume, or dialogue, mentally breaks down the script, and covers the camera angles in her head. She was, she is, she will ever be a script supervisor—and it was good training, for she is now an associate producer. But it surely makes for bad entertainment when you go to the movies.

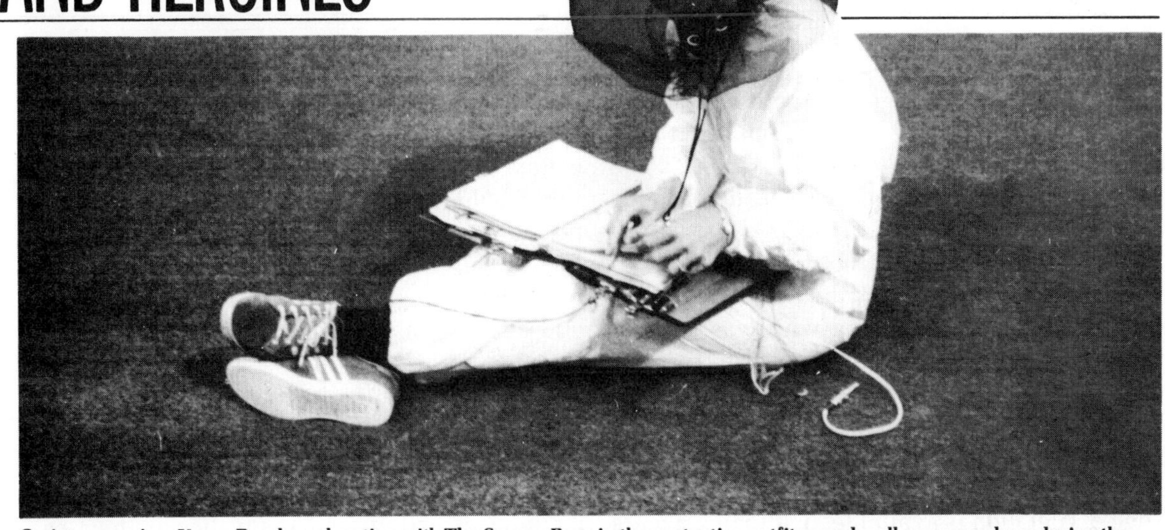

Script supervisor Karen Rasch, on location with The Savage Bees in the protective outfit worn by all crew members during the filming.

CASTING DIRECTORS

The final judge of casting is, of course, the director or the producer of the film. And he seldom gives credit to the person who frequently does the groundwork and, in many cases, the actual casting for a film or a commercial. All *we* see, as an audience, is the final product: the actress who is "perfect" for the role of the vampire, the actor who could have been born into the shoes of the cop, the child who is so cute that every mother in the audience wants the same fame and riches for *her* angel-lamb. But, it takes a lot of people and it's a long, hard process to achieve that perfection. And much of the time it is the casting director who has done the dirty work while the director gets to see only the final applicants.

Certainly, there are good reasons for all of this. Casting takes time. We have already agreed that thousands of actors are competing for the same jobs, and hundreds of agents are involved, all of whom have actors they want to send to the audition, more thousands of unknowns and hopefuls who might one day end up in a film and never be seen again! (Whatever happened to Rose Stradner?)

Of course, the director may be quite instrumental in casting the leads for the film. He has someone in mind for the star of *Saint Joan* and he goes into the project convinced that he will get that person. The contracts and negotiations and commitments are made on a fairly high level—generally the producer and director in contact with high-powered agents. Figures are tossed around in hundreds of thousands and in "points" (percentages) in the film. But we are now speaking of Hoffman or Redford or Streisand.

The casting director, rather, becomes involved when the film has fifty or sixty or one hundred people who must appear. Certainly, no director has the time to look at the thousands who may be considered. The casting director becomes the genius in residence—and here is a classic case where compatibility (even mental telepathy) with the director is important. First of all, the casting director already has a rapport with the director. Then the next step is to break down the script: the number of actors, roles they play, their characteristics, ages. Then the long grind begins. It takes time, and a casting director must get an immediate feeling about an actor who walks into the room. Has he a charisma that can captivate an audience? Out of the hundreds, the casting director chooses a few, the lucky ones who will be presented to the director for final choices.

Some specialize in casting only "principals," the actors who speak lines, and some cast only extras. Film audiences would be surprised to learn that a great amount of time goes into the selection of the people who walk dogs in the background of city scenes, the crowd at a "Six-Day Bicycle Race," the taxi driver, the customers in a department store, the anonymous man who strolls across the street at just the right moment.

Other casting people work on television commercials, with advertising agencies, and

their casting calls are generally right on the agency premises. On a visit to almost any agency waiting room, a casual visitor can see the women and the men and the children who are waiting for those few minutes behind the closed doors so that they can read for fame and fortune. Almost all of these calls are arranged by the casting directors—and most of them use the agents for their first contacts. Remember my agent friend who was looking for a chicken? The call had just come from the casting director of an advertising agency.

Nevertheless, in either case—whether for feature films or television commercials—the casting director must have a working knowledge of just who is available, just which agents are the most reliable, and the "pool" of talent to be called upon for a particular job. As a result, his or her day seldom ends when the office workers and the executives are on their way home (and have you heard this before about the film business?). Many casting directors (and agents) spend their evenings at "showcase" performances, places where actors work for small audiences so that they can be seen. Many of these productions are so far off Broadway that the "bright lights" are not even a glow on the horizon; but many casting directors would rather find new, fresh, talented people for their directors than to use the same faces over and over again. On the other hand, to be fair, many do use the same faces again and again—and some fresh talent withers on the vine in the boondocks.

There are casting directors with offices, and there are casting directors who free-lance and who use any space available for their work. The obvious entry into the field is through the medium of acting, and many began their careers in just that way. Some are ex-agents who know just what actors are around and who can size up a potential talent as soon as he or she enters the room. Most important of all, perhaps, is that I have found most casting directors are very much on the side of the actor—possibly because so many began their own careers on the stage or in film as actors—and their rapport and empathy has helped many a would-be star to win an audition in spite of the newcomer's cold hands and rapidly beating heart.

One of the functions of the "grip" is to move the camera dolly from one location to another.

There was a time that casting directors complained bitterly that they just didn't get enough credit for the job they do. Though they still remain anonymous in areas such as the television commercial, it is not at all uncommon these days to see the names of the casting directors right up there in large, bold type with all the other production credits in feature films. It has taken a long time to receive the recognition, and the casting directors well deserve it.

THE STUDIO TECHNICIANS

The title is a misnomer. They work everywhere: in the studio, on location, in the cold and the heat, under the lights, always on call during the shooting, with names like gaffer and prop and grip. Some are carpenters. And, in the half-darkened theater, as most of the audience are leaving and some are waiting to see the credits, a stage whisper can be heard from time to time, "What the devil is a 'best boy'?" (The first assistant gaffer, or electrician. Now you know.)

On the non-union crew, the title is unimportant—sometimes you'll hear the word "electrician" as a description, but a moment later he's pulling a dolly with a cameraman and an assistant astride the seat, then running to change a light that is glaring, sawing a board to make the dolly run more smoothly, and climbing a ladder to adjust a "barn door" (the small black door on a light that keeps the beam from spreading too far outward).

If he is an electrician who is worth his day's pay, he comes to the location able to figure how the cables are to run, voltage drops, power requirements, how to "tie-in" to the main electrical box. He knows the difference between the lights that illuminate the motion picture industry: midget, dinky, inky, single and double broads, 750 soft light, 750 cones, juniors, babies, 2K and 5K soft lights and cones, 10K pans, titans, brutes, arcs, 170s and B-90s. He is aware that there are also variables in terms of color temperatures and diffusion—and he knows a great deal more. If he were to pick up the *Hollywood Working Manual for Studio Electrical Technicians,* he would really (truly) understand all of the following equipment—and know what to do with it:

Buss lug, spider buss, splicing block, cable, three-wire extension, 6-hole box, 4-hole box, four/ought (4/0), Lundy-lug 2-hole, lamp feeder, tail, head extension, one-hole, one-hole plug, pin connector, T-bone, butterfly, wall plate, wall bracket, pedestal extension, Junior arm, sled, wall-hanger, Trapeze hanger, clamp-on arm, Squatty, sawed-off, turtle, crow-foot, Molevator, hydraulics, air stands, desert dollies, sand carts, Klickety-klacks, trombone, parallel, up and downer, barn doors, blinders, snoots, funnels.

On the structured union crews, the jobs break down (as always) into fairly neat categories. The chief gaffer (electrician) will generally have several assistants under his wing, and the property man will be concerned only with the acquisition and the movement of props on the set or location. We have already mentioned the fact that Hollywood also has the category of outside property man. (Although we have already discussed the prop man in the section on scenic design and set decoration in Chapter 12, his union affiliation falls within this chapter. Another of filmdom's typical overlaps.)

A grip will have a knowledge of carpentry and will be the one who handles the dollies during photography and the movement of equipment from one place to another. In all of "unsung hero" crafts there is a need for physical strength. After a long day of moving equipment, lighting the set, changing locations, the crew consists of a fairly tired bunch of people.

More and more films are using small crews; more and more people are being asked to double up on jobs and, thus, it becomes essential that you become familiar with the functions and responsibilities of several allied departments. Most of the people in the area of studio technician began their careers by just "helping out" on sets: doing anything that needed physical doing, moving things and carrying things and asking questions. Many of them spent Saturdays at film-equipment and rental houses, learning the nomenclature of the technical part of this industry. (Try the *Manual* list again. How many can you really identify?)

The unions occasionally run an apprenticeship program for technicians, but, realistically, it has been practically non-existent in these past years of high unemployment. When jobs do open up, they are naturally in the lower categories and any young person expecting to make a career in this part of the industry must

A "gaffer" changes the setting of a light during the filming of a feature production. Documentary units generally use much smaller lighting setups.

be prepared to have an awful lot of aching muscles after the workday.

A short time ago, we were given the assignment of doing a film on the subject of Western coal and its relation to the energy problem. One of the locations was inside a coal-fired power plant in Arizona, about 160 miles from Phoenix. The shot to be done was the length of a football field and there was no existing light inside the huge ten-story-high room. It has always been a truism that there is no power inside a power plant—they manufacture 500 megawatts for the public, but if you plug into any one of the outlets with a large motion picture light, you'll probably blow the circuit breakers throughout the building. So, the lights and a generator were hauled in from Phoenix—over the mountains—in a truck that could only go about 20 miles an hour with its load. The entire next day, four men worked ten hours to haul the largest of lights, run cable wire to the welding circuits where the power could handle the load, adjust the beams—and finally allow the cameraman to take his shot. The entire sequence lasts twenty seconds in the finished film. We have not yet counted the costs, but we did give the crew extra beer and steak that night. And, as I recall, everyone was fast asleep by 8 P.M.

In addition to electrical knowledge, most people in this field recommend that beginners also study some other important subjects, since the field is changing. Tape is becoming a strong factor in production — and jobs are opening up, however slowly. Sam Robert, of Local 52 (IATSE) in New York, suggests that a study of electronics and electrical engineering might also help in the pursuit of a studio technician's career. The idea is good. Everything helps in this field.

For once my grandmother was wrong. She used to say, "A little knowledge is a dangerous thing." Not if it helps you get a job in film, it isn't.

SPECIAL EFFECTS

The virgin snow lies windswept under the bending trees and the music reaches an ominous crescendo. Down the hill the footsteps walk, each one making its mark in the drifts – just footsteps, not a person to be seen above them! Slowly, slowly coming toward the camera the frightened audience. The Invisible Man. It is movie magic.

Or, the Space Ships from the planet Blotto come roaring through an endless, star-filled universe or we are on a trip to Jupiter, hurled at the speed of light through the colors and the prisms of infinity. Or, tall office buildings catch fire, earthquakes shake the foundation of movie theaters across the country (all in Dolby sound), exorcism and witchcraft float their cosmic tricks before us, mechanical sharks roam the oceans searching for unsuspecting swimmers, visitors from another planet find their way to Panavision screens.

Meanwhile, on the television screen, the craft is alive and well, on a smaller scale, as victims die every few seconds, penetrated by everything from blank bullets to pointed flying salamis. Arrows plunge into the torsos of battling cowboys, and automobiles disintegrate before our jaded eyes. A special-effects technician is at work somewhere, and the craft has changed the look of the industry.

It certainly is not a new craft, though the eighties have opened up new vistas for the art. Back in 1933, *King Kong* was the most popular of special-effects films (along with my favorite, *The Invisible Man* starring Claude Rains). Under the supervision of Chief Technician Willis O'Brien, a group of talented people constructed six different models of the ape, each one a different size. Depending upon the sequence, the angle of the camera and the perspective, a different ape model was used to move the action. Today's special-effects artist still uses models, but the flexibility and the potential of the computer has added new dimensions to the craft.

If ever there was an era of special effects, though, it is the eighties. *Star Wars, E.T., Return of the Jedi,* and the entire range of Indiana Jones adventures are just a few examples, while every "ordinary" cops-and-robbers or sex exploitation films use their own craftspeople to keep the action going and the visual impact strong.

If we had to describe the job of the special-effects technician, we might begin with the word "magician," for they are ingenious, these mad specialists of a make-believe world. Part mechanic, part plumber, part electrician, part carpenter, part model builder, part artist, part electronics and computer expert, their prerequisites also include a fertile and imaginative mind, patience that would try my impatient soul, and an innate sense of timing. Their job is that of deceiving the senses of the audience – and if you look at the box office figures of the top sci-fi films, you know that the audiences love it.

Many special-effects technicians began as stage technicians, some were in the scenic design field, some were model makers with architectural backgrounds, but all of them are aware of one thing: Special effects cannot be found on the

Special effects people had a field day with Indiana Jones and the Temple of Doom with live action, puppets, stop motion and miniatures. (Left) Harrison Ford (Indiana Jones) makes a desperate attempt to stop the mine car, while (right) Stop Motion Animator Tom St. Amand changes puppet positions during the miniature shooting for the same sequence.

shelf. Each job has different specifications. It is the special-effects expert who makes fog over water, rain or snow for a sequence where waiting for the right weather might cost thousands of dollars. It is the special effects experts who, working closely with the cinematographers, discovered that scale models looked real only when shot in slow motion, be it a car going over a cliff or a train wreck on a mountain trestle. How many Hollywood battles and shipwrecks and space epics and catastrophes have been done in exactly that way? They are masters of the "movie magic" that makes hurricanes, they are the armaments experts, the designers of miniature cities, the experts on explosives, for the recreation of war and violence demands that the people who work with them are safe and secure.

Special-effects people are always on the lookout for new ideas: at museums, fairgrounds, expositions, looking for new computer tricks, new mirrors for optical illusions. For the beginner, an occasional apprentice program is available at the networks or with a film unit. But, it is a field of very few experts, though it has grown somewhat in the eighties, and new talent has been a good reason for the growth of science fiction films.

If the craft interests you, try a few tests yourself. How did they get that man to fly? The handcuffs to open without a key? The toast to pop up on cue? And as a test, try making the Red Sea part on your computer terminal!

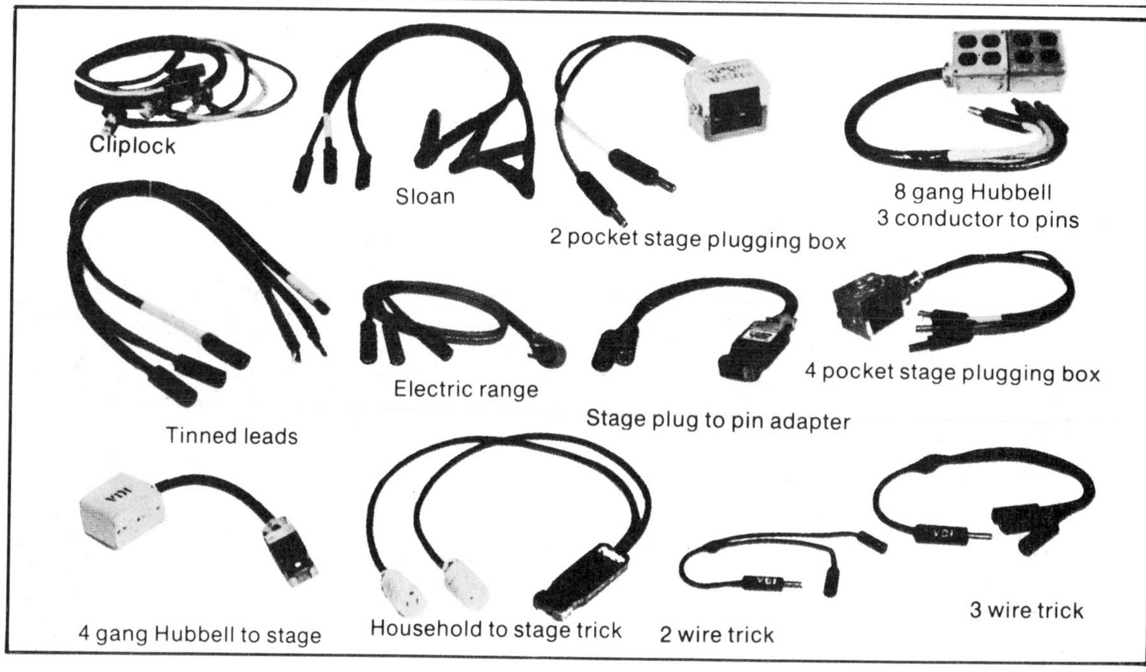

EQUIPMENT TECHNICIANS

For a film crew on location, the *minor* breakdown problems are usually handled by those people who work directly with the equipment. Therefore, the lubrication, cleaning, simple repairs, dismantling, and reassembly of any of the standard cameras is a job undertaken by the assistant late at night in his lonely motel room. (After dinner at The Fox and the Hounds.) The repair of a tape recorder may also be minor, or it may take the ingenuity of the crew who fixed it by telephone—or it may need a major overhaul, just as the family car or any piece of machinery or electronic equipment.

Those of us who work in the industry are completely dependent upon the technicians who overhaul our equipment regularly and who work out all the "bugs" that seem to haunt us from time to time. As examples, cases are dropped by baggage handlers at airports, and the normal wear and tear on a camera or tape recorder will sometimes make itself known by way of a breakdown at a critical time. We always carry backup cameras, but there are limits to the duplication we can provide in planning for a job. In many parts of the world, additional equipment can be gotten to us rather quickly. Unfortunately, standardization has not become totally universal, and some technical material is just *not* around when you need it—a lost case of 35mm Eastman negative film cannot be replaced in Quito, Ecuador, and an Arriflex can be repaired in Munich but not in Bora Bora.

THE UNSUNG HEROES AND HEROINES

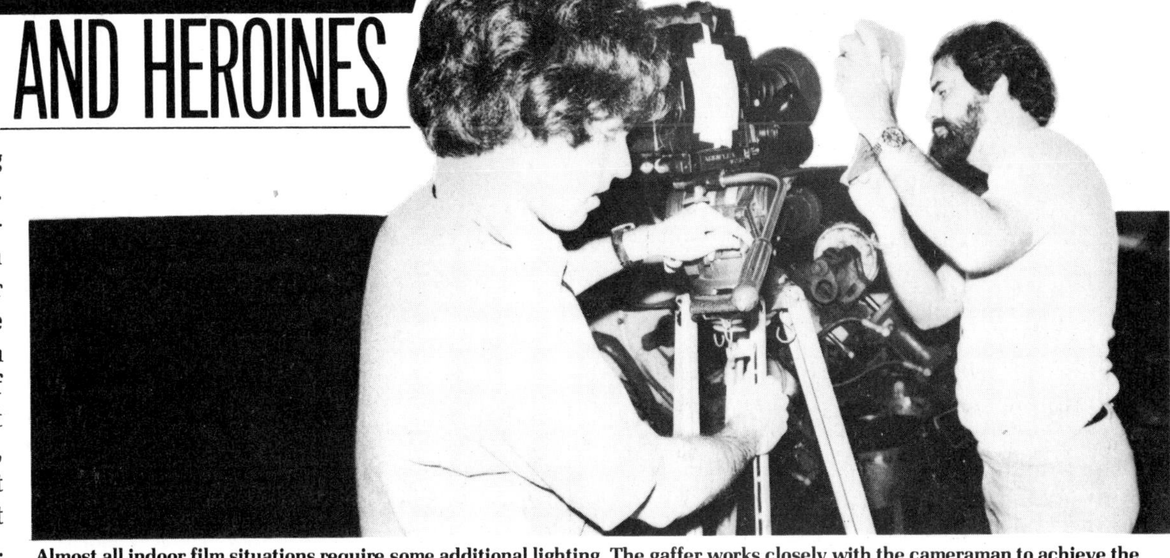

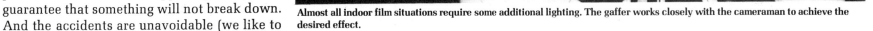

Almost all indoor film situations require some additional lighting. The gaffer works closely with the cameraman to achieve the desired effect.

Some of our technical work is done long before equipment has a chance to break down. Overall, we have found that preventive maintenance helps our equipment hold up well on location trips. Some trips are, of course, better than others, though there are times when the production manager is sent to the airport in the middle of the night to get a broken piece of equipment back to New York on the midnight cargo jet. We happen to own our own cameras, sound, and lighting equipment, but this doesn't prevent accidents from happening, nor does it guarantee that something will not break down. And the accidents are unavoidable (we like to think). And all accidents are not disasters. We were filming in Bangkok some years ago on a short subject for Paramount—and Thailand is a place where you bring *everything* with you. The Customs formalities were completed in a short few hours, the temperature was about 110 degrees (have you noticed how the temperature is always 110 degrees?), and the porters were loading our cases atop one another in a circus array of towers as they hauled all twenty-seven cases away on dollies. Too late we saw the camera case put on top of seven others. The porter headed off at a trot—and the case fell eight feet, right onto the concrete airport floor! The cameraman and I dashed over, holding our breath, looking with anguish at the shattered case lying in front of us. We picked up the camera and plugged in the battery and it worked. It actually worked! The case was shattered, true, but it didn't seem to matter. This was one time we didn't need the repair service back in New York. We aren't always so lucky.

So we have a great admiration for the technicians who work on our equipment—and some people have broken into technician jobs in film by starting their careers in a camera-rental or -repair house. Many of our cameramen have begun their careers by spending weekends in shops and repair rooms—and luckily, for one of the criteria upon which a prospective union member is judged is the ability to break down and reassemble a range of cameras, both 35mm and 16mm. So, the repair technicians become potential production people if that is their goal in the field—and, in turn, production people already at work are far more valuable to a producer if they know something about how the equipment operates and how minor repairs can be made on location.

Most equipment-rental and repair companies require that their employees apprentice for some years on the workbench before being allowed to do a complete overhaul. And, in addition to camera repair work, the experience also includes repair of editing equipment, sound equipment, and even hydraulic equipment. We know of one company (Camera Mart in New York) that hired an automobile mechanic because he had previous experience with hydraulic brakes, and there are occasions when dollies need complete overhaul.

Basically, the qualifications for equipment technician might break down into four:

- It would be helpful if you have a background in electronics.
- It is important that you have mechanical aptitude.
- You should have basic machine-shop experience, and preferably in the detail of small-caliber work.
- It would be helpful to have some knowledge of photography—even as an amateur—since much of the work deals with lenses and their capabilities.

This last point, above, is another way in and is not thought of too often. In the past few years we have heard a great hue and cry about the dearth of good film technicians.

SALES AND SYNDICATION

Everything has to be sold. Whether you are selling yourself as an actor or a free-lance director or selling a two-hundred-thousand-dollar film project to a corporation, you are still selling. Some people are better at it than others, and frequently the superb salesman can win a job against competitors who may be just as good filmmakers, but who cannot inspire confidence and trust in the person who is buying.

There was a time when the salesperson, per se, was much more important to the business and commercial film fields than he or she is today. The salesperson made the contact with the agency or client, screened the sample films, hopefully "closed" the deal, and then turned it all over to the producer and staff. Even then, there were some great ones and some terrible ones, and some wonderful characters. One of the people who worked for me a long time ago was among the best salesmen in the business—up to a point. He just never knew when the sale was made, and I watched in horror as he got the client to the moment of signing the contract and then said, "Wait, before you sign, there's another film I'd like to show you." The client, naturally, hated the film and the salesman would have to resell right up to the contract again.

Everything changes, of course. The supersalesman has been replaced, for the most part, by "the producer who also sells." Film has become more personal—the names of the companies are frequently the same as the man or woman who runs them. As a result, clients and agencies would rather meet the principal of the company that is going to make the film or, at the very least, the producer who will control the project from beginning to end. So, many filmmakers have had to add still another talent to their list and become sales people, too.

My own company is a good example. I make all my own contacts with clients, my own presentations, and then produce the films. I sell—from beginning to end. In competing for films, I often meet the principals of other film companies, also making their own presentations.

Of course, there are production companies that still hire a sales staff—sometimes one or two people to make the rounds of the agencies or to find out which corporations are making films. So it *is* a way into the business, if you like to sell. In the field of the television film many people are in the selling area, mainly in syndication.

My old friend, Wynn Nathan, of RKO Pictures, likes to begin his description of syndication as something it is *not*. "It is *not*," he says, "the Mafia. Everyone thinks you're in the Syndicate..."

To understand syndication, you must first be familiar with how the networks operate in the United States. Under the law, a network can own and operate (called "O&O") as many as twelve television stations, provided that these stations do not collectively reach more than 25 per cent of the nation's viewing audience. They are allowed any number of privately-owned affiliates, with a percentage of their programming done locally and the other shows provided by the network.

Essentially, the networks do not produce the entertainment shows they transmit. In the areas of news and documentaries, where they *do* produce their own programs, it is well-nigh impossible to crack the armor. They just will not let the independents into their domain. Even the public-television (Public Broadcasting System) networks have also withdrawn much of the support they once gave to the outside filmmaker; the remaining opportunities at PBS allow very small budgets. It would seem, then, that the TV entertainment area would be open, even if news and documentaries are jealously guarded domains. Not so. Indeed, not so.

First of all, only so much time is available on the networks. The competition is tremendous because the rewards are of jackpot proportions. In addition to all of that, a screening committee of decision-makers controls the programming and my impression of that group has always been that they are a totally interchangeable committee of gray-black eminences.

A few years ago, we screened a TV Special for ABC before a group of six men dressed in dark suits—all of them without faces. Following the screening, we went to NBC and then to CBS, and in each case we were convinced that it was the same six men who were judging the film. Different networks, same set of characters. The client eventually ended up acquiring time on a series of independent stations in various cities. In that way, the show was shown on 160 stations, with time on each one purchased separately in order to make up the new "network." Of course, the program was shown at different times in different places—sometimes as much as a week or two apart. But what difference does it make if, to the audience, all programming is essentially "local" and no one really cares that Des Moines saw the show three days before Dallas.

This, then, is the method used by syndicators for shows that are not telecast coast-to-coast by one of the networks. Essentially, it is the individual contract with a single local station that puts the program on the air. Sometimes it is the sponsor who buys time, and sometimes it is an agency. Frequently, the show is produced by the syndication company itself, and then sold by the sales people all across the country. "Monty Python," for example, was syndicated by Time-Life Films and sold to PBS. Other programs are illustrated by the publicity material on this page, each of them offered to stations on a syndicated basis.

It takes a large sales staff to sell the programs. Most syndication companies have people in all the major cities in America, though the headquarter offices are generally in New York, with about 20 percent in Los Angeles. There are many companies in the business, with the major studios as the top syndicators: Fox, Paramount, Columbia, and RKO. Others are King World, World Vision, and Don Taffner.

Most syndication executives will strongly suggest that a newcomer in the business can learn it quite easily—that a "salesperson is a salesperson." If you have the personality that loves to sell, then you might make your way into the business through one of the branch offices of a large syndication company. As with any kind of sales, of course, personal

21 new first-run half-hours in color, completed in 1984—and still in production—for a total of 221 programs!
ON-CAMERA HOST: JOHN FORSYTHE
Host/Narrator, John Forsythe adds further distinction to the series. Beyond his current popularity as Blake Carrington in ABC-TV's top-rated series, "Dynasty," Mr. Forsythe is also well known to TV viewers as the 'voice' in "Charlie's Angels."
Spectacular on-location color photography—filmed by 16 camera teams working to capture for television the endless story of wildlife's struggle for survival.
Natural habitats—from the depths of the ocean floor and the African bush—to the American Southwest and the top of Mt. Everest.
Produced by Survival Anglia Ltd.—winners of 46 major television prizes including 2 Emmys and a Peabody Award.
Acclaimed by critics and viewers as the best, most exciting nature program on television:
"Always fascinating—a First Class wildlife series."
—Evening Telegraph
"Hard work, some danger and the patience demanded to wait three days for three seconds of film."
—Daily Mail
"Superb photography."
—Variety
NOTE: Since these programs are primarily designed to further understanding of the natural sciences, they are properly identifiable as "instructional" for FCC logging purposes.
TV SERIES
221 AWARD WINNING COLOR HALF-HOURS
JOHN FORSYTHE'S WORLD OF SURVIVAL
The world's most popular and most successful wildlife adventure TV series!
A SURVIVAL ANGLIA PRODUCTION
RKO PICTURES
1440 Broadway · New York, N.Y. 10018 · (212) 764-6600 · Telex: 881130 RKO PIC UD

An example of a syndicated film show, "World of Survival" is distributed to stations across the country by RKO Pictures.

contacts are important: other sales people are knocking on the doors of the same companies and stations and advertising agencies and clients. You'll have to do your homework, but you need no background in production in order to do a good job. Some people have broken into the field by starting with television stations in a sales capacity.

If you like sales, try for syndication.

BUSINESS MANAGEMENT

For two long years I was the New York executive for a company based in Hollywood, and in addition to the blue-silk-walled office with the chaise longue, I also had a brown telephone (next to the black telephone). It was directly connected with the West Coast—no need to call the operator, no need to trouble anyone with all the mundane things that make life more complicated for the ordinary mortal. We had a direct tie with Babylon. It did not go through my secretary. It went from *Him* to *Me*. And the conversation was always the same:

The brown phone rings. It has its own distinctive, destructive ring.

"Yeah?" There is no need to identify myself. No one else would pick it up.

The voice on the other end: "Hear you sold a film."

"Yeah."

"What's the bottom line?"

Just one single point of interest: "What's the bottom line?" No questions about what kind of film it was—whether it was something that might be important to humanity, a fund-raising film perhaps, a film about the food problem in hungry countries. Nope. "What's the bottom line?" In plain, unadulterated English: "How much profit?"

Perhaps it all sounds crass and commercial, and possibly I would have had my ego stroked if he'd only asked a bit more about the project, but essentially he was doing his job as I felt I was doing mine. Now, as a partner in a thriving and active film company, with a payroll each week that would stagger the Jolly Green Giant, I am just as concerned about the bottom line as my friend on the West Coast. For the bottom line is essential to survival. It is the business part of the business. It is the dollars-and-cents profit, the domain of the accountant, the realm of the comptroller; but it is also the responsibility of the producer, the independent, the staff of the organization. It is everyone's concern, for though it seems wonderful to think of film being made in a comfortable ivory tower, safe from the real world while we think through our problems, the reality is, simply, that we cannot survive without meeting our financial obligations.

There are people in the field who are specifically charged with the business management of their companies. Their day-to-day work is taken up with budgets, cost control, cash flow, profit and loss. But don't be frightened away. It is another way to get into this business and, as I shall strongly insist later on, *everyone* in the film field should know about the business of doing business. If your background is in the financial area, if you have a talent with figures, if accounting was your minor or major subject in school, this might well be the way in. The gentleman who once called me on the brown telephone is now co-producer of one of the highest-grossing feature films produced in the past ten years. He must have been doing something right!

The smaller film companies, however—the people in business film, the small commercial producers (as opposed to producers of films for entertainment), the one-, two-, and three-person production companies—certainly cannot afford to have one executive who handles only the financial burden. That, in itself, would be uneconomical; so that the dollars-and-cents part of each project, and of the company itself, is handled by the individual producer. If you are going to work anywhere in this business, you—yes, even you—will somehow be involved in business management. You should know what goes into budgeting a film and you should know how to budget accurately. Every film project has someone asking, "How much will it cost?" You, too, should be able to answer the question.

We've talked about "the bottom line" (and hopefully you will never forget the term). There are hundreds of items that can affect that figure, and some of them will probably pop into your head even if you're guessing. To simplify matters, the industry has come up with standard items, and the budget has been divided into two parts: "above the line" and (naturally) "below the line."

"ABOVE THE LINE" These are budget costs that are concerned with the creative end of the film. Interestingly enough, if you look at the items carried in this part of the budget, you can readily see why it is generally the highest portion of the total cost of a feature film—particularly if the stars are paid astronomical sums.

THE UNSUNG HEROES AND HEROINES

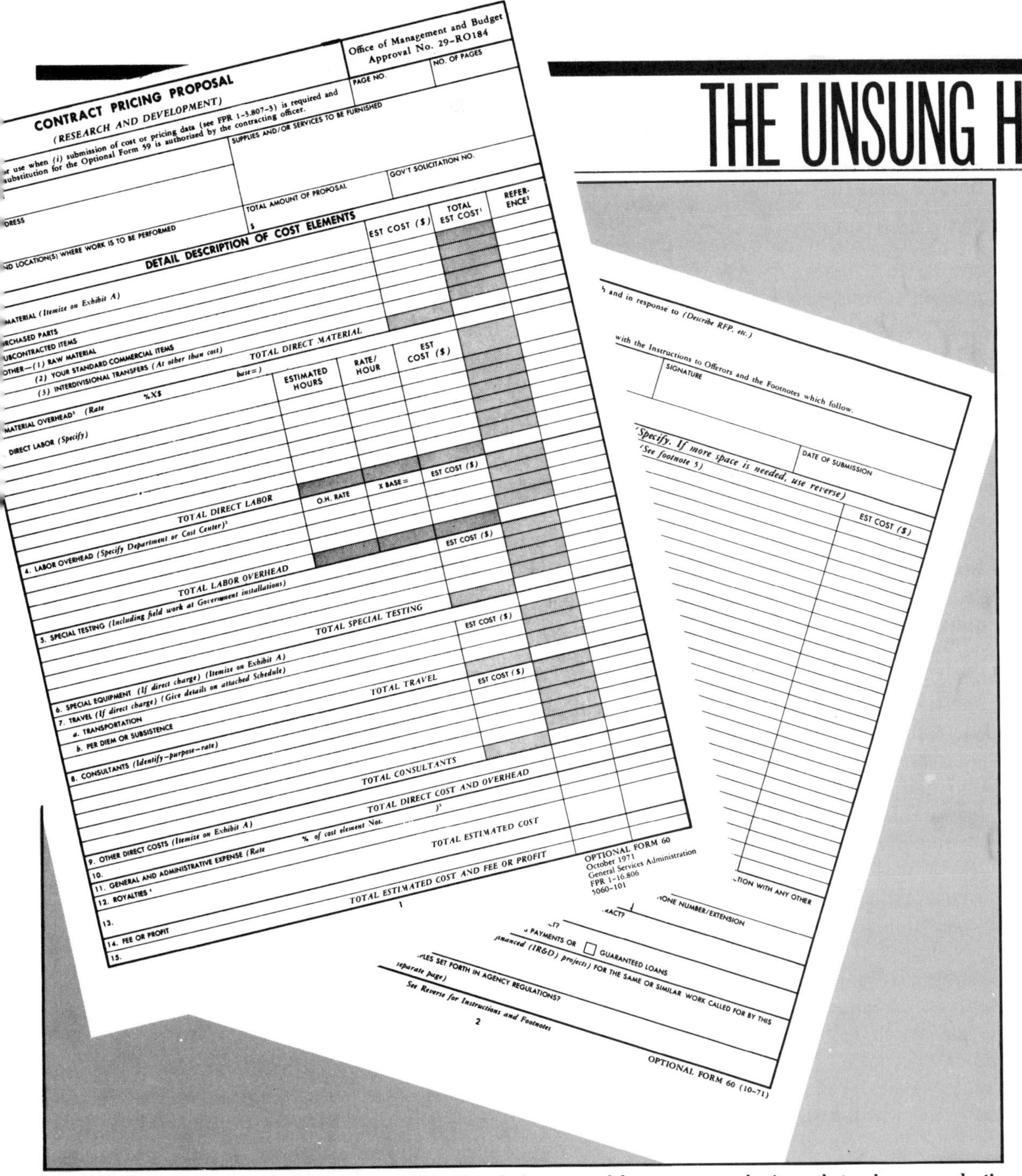
CONTRACT PRICING PROPOSAL
(RESEARCH AND DEVELOPMENT)

Office of Management and Budget Approval No. 29-RO184

PAGE NO. | NO. OF PAGES

...r use when (i) submission of cost or pricing data (see FPR 1-3.807-3) is required and ...ubstitution for the Optional Form 59 is authorized by the contracting officer.

SUPPLIES AND/OR SERVICES TO BE FURNISHED

GOV'T SOLICITATION NO.

...DRESS

TOTAL AMOUNT OF PROPOSAL
$

...ND LOCATION(S) WHERE WORK IS TO BE PERFORMED

DETAIL DESCRIPTION OF COST ELEMENTS

EST COST ($) | TOTAL EST COST[1] | REFERENCE[2]

...MATERIAL (Itemize on Exhibit A)
...RCHASED PARTS
...UBCONTRACTED ITEMS
...OTHER—(1) RAW MATERIAL
(2) YOUR STANDARD COMMERCIAL ITEMS
(3) INTERDIVISIONAL TRANSFERS (At other than cost)
TOTAL DIRECT MATERIAL

...MATERIAL OVERHEAD[3] (Rate %X$ base=)

ESTIMATED HOURS | RATE/HOUR | EST COST ($)

DIRECT LABOR (Specify)

TOTAL DIRECT LABOR

O.H. RATE | X BASE = | EST COST ($)

4. LABOR OVERHEAD (Specify Department or Cost Center)[3]

TOTAL LABOR OVERHEAD

EST COST ($)

5. SPECIAL TESTING (Including field work at Government installations)

TOTAL SPECIAL TESTING

EST COST ($)

6. SPECIAL EQUIPMENT (If direct charge) (Itemize on Exhibit A)
7. TRAVEL (If direct charge) (Give details on attached Schedule)
a. TRANSPORTATION
b. PER DIEM OR SUBSISTENCE

EST COST ($)

TOTAL TRAVEL

8. CONSULTANTS (Identify—purpose—rate)

TOTAL CONSULTANTS

TOTAL DIRECT COST AND OVERHEAD

9. OTHER DIRECT COSTS (Itemize on Exhibit A)
10.
11. GENERAL AND ADMINISTRATIVE EXPENSE (Rate % of cost element Nos.)[3]

TOTAL ESTIMATED COST

12. ROYALTIES[4]
13.
14. FEE OR PROFIT
15.

TOTAL ESTIMATED COST AND FEE OR PROFIT

1

OPTIONAL FORM 60
October 1971
General Services Administration
FPR 1-16.806
5060-101

...and in response to (Describe RFP, etc.)

...with the Instructions to Offerors and the Footnotes which follow.

SIGNATURE

DATE OF SUBMISSION

...Specify. If more space is needed, use reverse)
(See footnote 5)

EST COST ($)

...TION WITH ANY OTHER

...ONE NUMBER/EXTENSION

...ACT?

...PAYMENTS OR ☐ GUARANTEED LOANS

...nanced (IR&D) projects) FOR THE SAME OR SIMILAR WORK CALLED FOR BY THIS

...PLES SET FORTH IN AGENCY REGULATIONS?

...separate page)

See Reverse for Instructions and Footnotes

2

OPTIONAL FORM 60 (10-71)

A budget form used by some government agencies. Though the proposal form may vary, the items that make up a production budget are fairly standard throughout the industry.

Story. This includes story purchase, writers, and all research.

Producer. This category also includes the assistant producer and secretaries.

Director. This item doesn't include assistant directors.

Cast. This includes stars, feature players, extras, stunt people, plus all pension and welfare costs.

Casting Director. This category fluctuates. Occasionally it can be found "below the line."

"BELOW THE LINE" The costs concerned with production, technical areas of the project, and the staff that may be needed to complete the film are "below the line."

Production Staff. The production manager, unit manager, assistant directors, dialogue and script supervisors, and dance director are in this category.

Production Operating Staff. This takes in all of the camera crew, including assistants. It also includes the sound crew, wardrobe department, makeup and hair styling, set dressing, grips, property people, electrical department, special effects, carpenters, and painters.

Set Design and Construction. This includes art directors, draftsmen, and materials and supplies.

Set-Operation Expenses. All the purchase and rental of equipment for all departments are included here.

Editing. This item includes editors, assistants, sound and music cutters, and a negative cutter; also cutting-room rentals.

Laboratories. This includes all developing, the printing of both picture and sound, the titles, fades, dissolves, opticals, and stock shots.

Music. One of the strange things about this category is that it includes the composer, who

might well be considered an "above-the-line" cost, along with the writer and director. This item also includes conductor, musicians, singers, copyist, arrangers, royalties, and instrument rental and cartage.

Sound. This is not to be confused with the sound department in production. It includes all dubbing and mixing, as well as any studio sound needed for narration or recording music.

Transportation (Studio). These are car, truck, and bus rentals, plus gas and oil and drivers.

Location Expenses. These include travel costs, hotels, meals, car, bus, and truck rentals, scouting and pre-production, gratuities, permit costs, night watchmen, and location-site rentals.

To all of this, the "below-the-line" items of studio rental (if necessary), insurance, taxes, licenses, and even details such as coffee for the crew and cast are also included. And, finally, the "little" item of *overhead* must be added: office expense, secretaries, entertainment of clients, legal fees for the corporation, public relations, and any other cost that cannot be attributed directly to the production of the film.

We add the "above-the-line" costs to the "below-the-line" costs, deduct from the amount of money we are receiving for the project—and we are, hopefully, left with a bottom line that shows a profit, however small.

We realize that your first, perhaps experimental films may not have as complicated a structure; but knowing all the pitfalls can alert you to budget properly. Most filmmakers—and this includes a great many professionals—do not budget realistically. There is a tendency to "hope" that rain will not fall on a day scheduled for sunny exteriors. The amount of film stock to be exposed is generally underestimated and therefore laboratory costs for developing and printing rise accordingly.

The worst area of budget failure is generally found with corporate or "in-house" films. Time and again we have found executives who tell us that they don't use professional film companies because the last film they made cost only $15,000, while every bid they got from the outside was twice or three times that amount. When you look closely at the $15,000 you begin to see why they can make it for that figure (or think they can). The answer is that they conveniently eliminate a great many of the costs that should honestly be added to the budget. "I work here anyway," the vice-president says, "so I don't charge my time to the project." They find that travel expenses, secretarial costs, typing, production time of executives, are somehow conveniently lost in the shuffle. Properly budgeted, their film, however, generally comes out closer to the outside bid than the corporation would like to think.

On the other hand, some corporations can keep an entire staff at work in an audiovisual department because the sheer amount of film work utilizes such staff members throughout the year. But even then, the overhead of such an operation is quite high.

All of us in the business—whether commercial filmmakers, business filmmakers, or documentary filmmakers—generally work out a budget based upon the specifications listed above. Of course, these are much simpler for smaller crews, and when there are no actors and little travel, but film stock exposed is still film stock, no matter who is shooting it. We have learned how to budget because it is our method of survival. Government films are bid in the same way, and all proposals must contain a complete budget, broken down item by item. (See the illustration on p. 103.)

Whether you are making your first film as an independent or working for a small company, you are in constant competition with other filmmakers for the available business. The answer to "What is it going to cost?" may well determine whether or not you get the job. If you have bid incorrectly, you might well have the job, but how are you going to make up the loss because you unrealistically figured the shooting days, the crew costs, or the film to be exposed? Those who work in this business *must* know how to break down story boards in order to figure shooting days, cast costs, special-effects charges, etc. Even documentary treatments must be broken apart in order to figure how many travel days there will be in specific locations, how many shooting days in each, the hotel and meal costs, and all the other budget problems that arise when you begin to analyze how your film is going to get done. In the business film, budget is always a factor, and accurate "educated guesses" sometimes win the job over the competition.

One of our favorite clients came to us this year and asked us to present a budget for a film that would take *five years* to complete. All that he could provide was a list of approximate locations and potential shooting days through the five-year period. We knew nothing else about the project, yet we had to figure on educated estimates as to costs—including constantly rising air fares, crew salaries, and the normal inflation that has driven our budgets ever upward. And, with all of that, we were competing against two other companies. Well, the budget was done—partly through experience, partly through finger-crossed guessing, partly through hard information. We got the job. And in five years we'll tell you just what the bottom line is.

Through the months of doing research for this book, I spoke to friends of mine who work in the various crafts, and I spoke to strangers who were willing to help. All of them felt that potential film people *should* know what the field is really like. All of them were asked to dig deep down and describe their jobs. All of them told us that they work hard, and all of them told us that it is important to get along with people. But the most obvious thing that *all* of them had was an innate pride in their jobs and in the roles they play in the film industry. All of them felt there was something special about what they did. And, they *are* special, for we could not exist without them.

Some years back, we had a job in Italy: a film about food and wine. Of course, it was a glorious job, for we photographed the food of the country and then we ate what we had photographed! Naturally, the crew gained ten pounds per person, but we would do it again in a minute.

One of our crew members was an Italian gaffer named Marino, who had just come off the huge feature production *Cleopatra*. But, rather than feeling that our small documentary crew was beneath his dignity, he reacted in quite the opposite way. Marino became the resident expert in everything, moving from place to place to help, driving cars, setting the electrical equipment and lights . . . When we were filming in a small trattoria, trying to redress it to look like a turn-of-the-century restaurant, Marino helped build an open fire over which to cook the pasta, and as we were about to shoot, one day, he stopped us with a wave of his hand. Quickly, he moved across the room and covered an open fuse box with a string of garlic, explaining that they didn't have electricity in such a place in 1900. About the second day of shooting, during a lunch break, Marino came over to me and asked me for a script. Curious, I told him that I had an extra one, but wanted to know why he was asking for it.

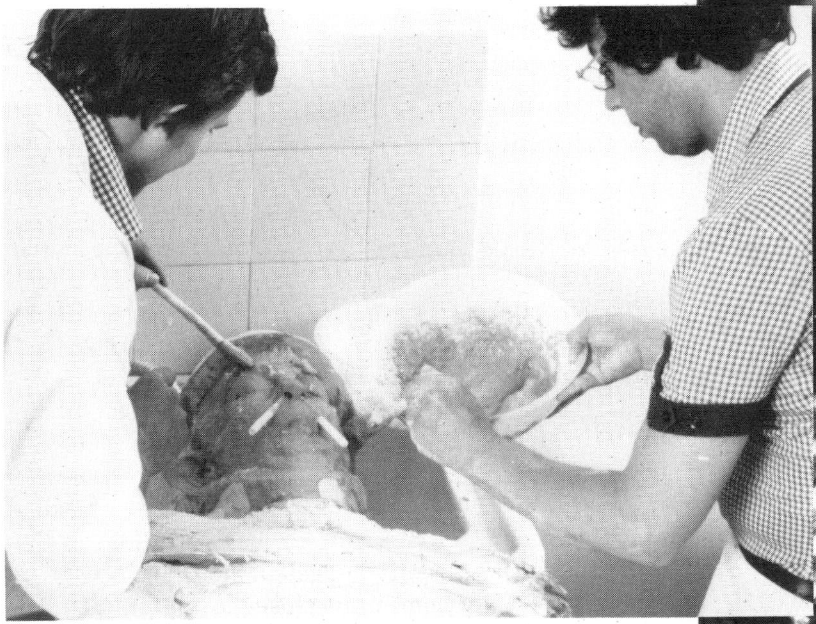

Makeup artistry and special effects played a critical role in Raiders of the Lost Ark. (Left) Tom Smith, working with Christopher Walas and pyrotechnician Thaine Morris, developed a life mask that would explode when actor Paul Freeman (Belloq) unleashed the monstrous power of the sacred Ark of the Covenant. (Right) Belloq screams in horror before his head "expodes" on cue.

"You see," he explained, "if you tell me to move a table, I will move it. If I know *why* I am moving it, I can do it better."

Marino was a man with pride in his work.

Robert Flaherty on location for Louisiana Story. The film, produced and directed by Flaherty, was one of the first successful business films to use the documentary form. The sponsor was Standard Oil and the film set the pattern for many subsequent productions for large corporations.

CHAPTER 13

THE DIRECTOR AND THE HYPHENATED FILMMAKER

Where It All Comes Together

If you've just picked up this book and you have turned immediately to this chapter (because everyone wants to be a director), it might be wise to close the book again and go right back to Chapter 1. Then, working your way slowly to this page, you will finally be rewarded, and right before your very eyes you will find all the rules that tell you how to become a director with your name spelled out on the back of a chair.

Except that there *are* no rules. (Not even "You take two eggs . . .") And, in twenty-five years as a director, I have yet to sit down long enough to warrant having my name on a chair.

It has been said, however (and truthfully), that film is a director's medium. If one job in the industry brings it all together, it is this strange, complex, and rewarding craft.

For the beginner, it would be enlightening if any one of us could post a set of rules that lead to becoming a director. It would be wonderful to be able to say that the first step is to learn to read, so that you might understand a script, followed by the sound of your voice calling, "Action!"

We are not certain, however, that some directors can read, and in the documentary, if it's a non-actor film, even the word "Action" is seldom heard. We find, when we film in areas where the general public is allowed to observe, that most people expect film crews to use the clap-stick slate while someone yells, "Quiet on the set!" and the director calls,

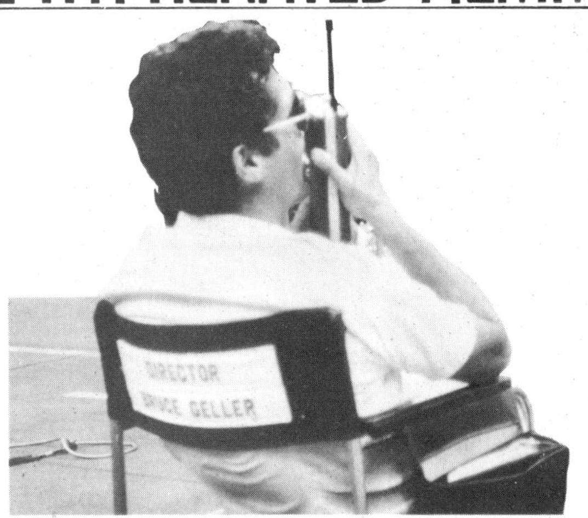

"Lights, camera, action." Well, the old slate has, for the most part, been replaced by electronic slating, and many documentary crews indicate their scene numbers on anything from index cards to small plastic slates hanging around the neck of the assistant cameraman. The director, in turn, may operate so unobtrusively that the watching public may not even recognize that the person with a bleeding ulcer is in charge of the whole operation.

There are, of course, directors who yell and scream. There are directors who are talented, quietly efficient, and in absolute control. There are directors who are instinctively cost-conscious, bringing in the most complicated productions on time and on budget. There are others who couldn't care less about the dollar (or lira or franc). In one company, we had a West Coast director who complained bitterly to his East Coast production manager when a cameraman was hired at ten dollars over scale. The director then flew in to New York, First Class, was met by a limousine at Kennedy International Airport, supervised one hour of shooting, stayed in a suite at the Plaza, and then returned to California the next day! There are directors who are former stunt people, directors who first worked as production assistants for other directors, directors who learned film as camera people, directors who began as gophers, others who came right out of school with a sample film and then started their careers as feature directors. And there are directors who are starving—just like so many actors, free-lance writers, and Edsel car salesmen.

The one common denominator, however, is the fact that the director is the person in charge, the one who should understand *all* of the crafts well enough to put them together in a structured working unit. Of course, it is not necessary for the director to know how to *operate* the camera, nor must the director be familiar with all the technical aspects of all the crafts that have preceded this chapter. But the director—the successful director—is either a genius at hiring the right people to do those jobs, or is familiar enough with the film jobs to demand and get the optimum performance required in order to put the film together. The director need not make the film splices in the editing room to know the difference between an effective cut and an editorial mess. Most of all, the good director probably has to know more about handling people and getting them to work as a unit than almost any other person on the crew; everyone has his own way. And if we considered a hundred directors, each would approach the film subjectively, each getting the result according to personality, talent, and individual neurosis.

In an interview with Jeanne Moreau, who

was directing her first film (*La Lumière*) at the time, a newspaper quoted her as follows: "With me what was unexpected was the exhilaration when I got on the set. It's like being in battle. You have all the actors and crew waiting for you. You feel alone and selfish; you don't care about anyone's problems, you only care about your film." Of course, most of us would not describe directing as a "battle," but this was her personal view. She went on to describe how Joseph Losey always developed an allergy before shooting and couldn't breathe, how Truffaut walked up and down in his room all night, and how Buñuel would touch each object on the set just to reassure himself.

Whatever the director's personality on the set, whatever the personal inner conflicts or unique way of working, you will find that all good directors are an awesome combination of psychiatrist, salesperson, traffic cop, jigsaw-puzzle enthusiast, persuader, administrator, diplomat, and artist. The days are spent in listening, absorbing, straining ideas, accepting, rejecting, thinking, planning—and, above all, deciding. Someone must be in charge of the collaboration that brings success or failure. The director is that person.

In the field of television commercials, Lenny Hirschfield (right) has successfully combined the jobs of director and cameraman in producing his films.

Though any director who works in film must be (should be) well grounded in the crafts and professions that make up the industry, personality plays an important role in determining which sector of the film medium best suits a particular individual. There are successful directors of feature films who would make inefficient and ineffectual documentarians, and the directors of commercials must have very special talents.

THE DIRECTOR OF THE FEATURE FILM

If any part of the film business could be compared to working with an army, the feature film would be the prime candidate. The very complexity of the feature requires an approach and a mental attitude quite apart from any other film form. The logistics are staggering, and since the majority of films have moved from the studio out to locations, the problem of moving people and equipment, while still maintaining some sort of schedule, has grown to astronomical proportions. Budgets, of course, are much larger than for any other type of production and money can be eaten up in huge gulps. As a result, the staff complement for a feature becomes the army of which we spoke. The production manager, if the job is done properly, could easily earn four stars in an infantry division. But it is the director who through efficiency eventually moves the production, or stalls it with indecision, who sparks the crew into vitality, or creates underlying dissatisfaction and inefficiency.

Added to all of this, the feature director generally does not get to shoot a script in sequence. Therefore, for the director, as well as for the actors, there is the constant need to mentally hold on to some sort of continuity. On the stage, the action naturally flows from the opening curtain; through Acts I, II, and III, on to the closing curtain, the play has been performed with a specific and unchanging continuity. In the feature film, this is just not possible. Frequently, the end sequences are filmed first, and more often than not Scenes 17, 165, 304, and 345 are all done on the same day merely because they take place *at the same location.* The crew is there, the actors are on call, and the director must do his work so well that the audience will never be able to tell that the complete ninety-minute film was not shot in a long, continuous schedule beginning with Scene 1.

Some time ago we filmed a documentary about an NBC feature film, *The Savage Bees,* directed by Bruce Geller. It was a classic case of shooting out-of-sequence, the ending of the film photographed on the first days of the schedule, with the rest of the film to follow. Since the Superdome in New Orleans was only available to the crew on two specific days, the last scenes of the picture were shot first. The heroine was trapped in a tiny Volkswagen, millions of vicious African bees swarming around the car, the level of performance at near-hysteria—would she be saved in time? (Of course, she was!)

It is the director's function to make decisions as to whether or not the performance will fit with scenes that are not even completed at that point. The "working up" to the climax, as in a stage play, simply cannot be there. And yet when it gets to the editing room, it all has to fit together. Generally it does.

It is the director, then, who makes the major decisions as the production progresses. Not only does the role include a close relationship with the cast, script clerk, and production personnel, but communication with the director of photography and camera crew is also of prime importance. The director, the director of photography, and the camera crew decide upon the final angles and the framing of the shot and whether or not the scene is a "take" and is to be printed by the laboratory. Certainly the "army" is essential. The many people who eventually touch that production are as important, each and every one of them, as any other person on the crew or in the pre- and

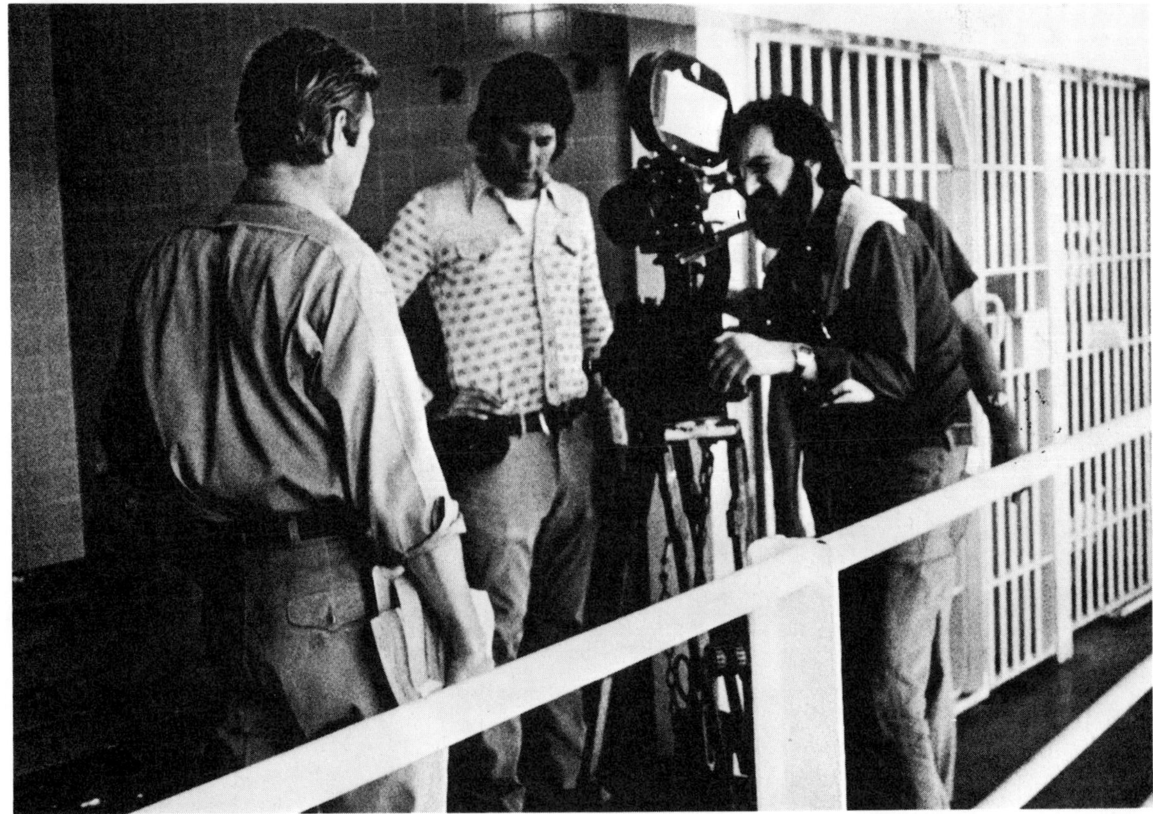

Another filmmaker who acts as both director and cameraman is Chuck Braverman. Here, he lines up a dolly shot with actor James Franciscus for the title sequence of a pilot film, Hunter.

post-production phases. But there can only be one person in charge.

Once more, personality is an important attribute. It is fascinating to watch directors at work. When you begin to know what the ideal director should know and do, you can begin to see why one crew works well under one person, gives loyalty and sweat and uncomplaining hours, while another crew seems to slow down as the day progresses and indecision seems to be the prime element of the production. Many comments have been made in the field about people such as Robert Altman, who work closely with cast and crew to achieve the end result. Other directors come across as tyrants, but still achieve a work of perfection.

On the set or on location, the director is the "traffic cop" who controls the efficiency as well as the creative aspects of the film production.

THE DIRECTOR OF THE COMMERCIAL

Really only one star is on stage at the filming of a commercial: the product. Even if the spot is designed for "soft sell," it is nevertheless structured to sell *something*. One of our favorite clients has a painting in his office (which he did himself) showing a sound stage filled with people shooting a commercial spot. Account executives, lighting technicians, script supervisor with stopwatch, camera crew, sound crew, director, art directors—twenty or twenty-five people in all. And there, in all its glory, brilliantly lit on a small cyclorama, is a small can of "the product." To the director of the commercial this emphasis on the product is not so farfetched, for many people have made their reputations as being the best "beer director" or the best "car director" in the business. As a result, careers rise and fall with amazing speed and the "fair-haired" people in the industry appear as meteors in the agency sky, only to burn out quickly as someone new replaces them.

The commercial field is volatile, and yet it is challenging in that the very same qualifications and functions necessary for feature production must be scaled down to the rigid demands of time. The commercial is produced for sixty seconds or thirty seconds or ten seconds, and (with rare exceptions) no other time frames exist.

There are many similarities, nevertheless, in the jobs of commercial director and director of features. Both work with actors, both must know the techniques of production, the function of camera crews, sound and lighting people, special effects, editing, animation, laboratories. But there is one prime difference in the jobs: the director of commercials works quite closely with the advertising agency and the finished spot is as much a function of the agency as it is of the production company—sometimes more so. Chapter 14, on advertising agencies, goes into more detail about their function in the field. Briefly, however, the director is seldom the final arbiter on the design, filming, or finishing of the spot. With the art director, copy chief, account executive, and client all involved to one degree or another, the director may also have to be a diplomat in addition to all the other functions necessary for his creative survival. Many of the film techniques now accepted as standard have either been developed *through* the television commercial or have been adapted from other film forms and then given to the public *via* television. But always keep in mind, if this is to be your field of work, the product is king, queen, and crown princess.

Back in the early sixties, I was asked to do a commercial for one of the larger agencies, the product being a well-known toothpaste. The production would have done justice to a feature film: two-story set, cast of ten including a charmingly spoiled seven-year-old whose mother kept telling me that they treated her better on the "Horn and Hardart Children's Hour" (which none of you remember), a full camera and sound and stage crew, and eleven people from the advertising agency.

The day went beautifully. By three in the afternoon we were actually finished, except for one shot. In that final close-up, we were to film the toothpaste being squeezed onto a brush. Extreme close-up. No problem at all. We did the shot in two minutes. All set to wrap up the day, not bad at all. One could even get to like toothpaste. But wait!

The account supervisor walked over and told us that the toothpaste had been squeezed all right, but that when the tube was pulled away a little tiny tip was left at the end of the tube. Couldn't we manage to *cut it off sharply*? I tried to think back to my sleepy morning brushing. Did the toothpaste cut off sharply when I took it away from the brush? I just couldn't remember, and I doubted it, but times like this are not for logic. We tried again. A little tip. Again. And again a little tip.

At *11:30 that night,* a prop man invented a tube which cut off the toothpaste without leaving a little tip at the end. Eureka! We were saved. The day ended with thousands of dollars in overtime and an exhausted crew glad to be in the film business for the "glamour" and "excitement." The end of the story is even more fascinating.

The spot was edited and because of the limitation of the sixty seconds, we had no time to let the toothpaste squeeze out to the neat, sharply cut-off end. We dissolved out of the shot in the middle and showed the name of the product. Our lovely eight-hour production of a glob of toothpaste squeezed without a tip *was never even seen!*

THE DIRECTOR OF THE DOCUMENTARY

The director in this film form is quite different from his brothers and sisters who do features and commercials. The field is less structured, the major difference being, of course, that the documentary director deals with "real people" rather than with actors. The situations are real and the problem is to achieve the naturalness that communicates the emotion of the moment and at the same time almost belies the presence of camera and crew. This is most difficult to accomplish and much of the criticism of the documentary has come in the area of just this problem: How can anyone ignore the fact that there is, in reality, a camera present? Well, some are just better than others. Frederick Wiseman, Francis Thompson, Pamela Yates, Marcel Ophuls, and Bill Jersey sometimes succeed where others fail. Imagine the tension, the feeling of walking on a tightrope that Barbet Schroeder must have had in producing *Idi Amin Dada,* in working with a man who had been known to imprison or execute people on a whim.

Documentary directors must learn to take advantage of events as they happen and, as a result, probably find themselves in more awkward situations than they care to, only topped, perhaps, by newsreel camera crews. We were filming in a slum in Ecuador when a local citizen came up to us and put his gun to the head

of our cameraman and told us to get out. At times like this, you have no room for argument. Certainly, the documentary director lives a calm and peaceful existence on most of his films. He experiences very little danger for the most part—I have only been arrested three times in my career, and have once been chased out of an area by a rock-throwing mob. But all of us are aware of a prime factor in our daily work: we are always working with "real people," and their approval or disapproval can determine whether or not we get the sequence for which we traveled eight thousand miles.

Documentarians travel more than any other film people—whether to make travel films, business films, or the feature documentary. The hours are long; the need to "think on your feet" is paramount. Generally, there is no structured script—the crew is provided with merely a treatment or an outline from which to shoot. The reason is simple: no one really knows what "real people" will say once the cameras are rolling. Some of the most forward and aggressive people "clam up" when the camera is there and some of the quietest become complete hams. The documentary director takes advantage of every situation, changing concept if necessary, to fit the flexibility of the moment. If you were on a travel-film location and you happened to stumble on a rain dance given by Amazon Indians, would you not shoot it because it was not in the treatment? (Of course, if the Indians turned out to be hostile, you might very well *not* shoot it.)

One major difference stands out in the life of the documentary director when he is compared to the directors of other film forms. His crews are generally a lot smaller, sometimes as few as two or three people doubling in their jobs. Each person on the crew therefore ends up with more responsibility for the efficiency of the project. The fewer people traveling to a distant location, the fewer logistics problems. It is far easier to move a station wagon and a sedan from one place to another than it is to move a convoy of trucks, vans, people, and equipment. For the director this creates an additional closeness with the crew as well as an ability to cover more sequences in a shooting day.

THE "HYPHENATED FILMMAKER"

The film field was more tightly structured twenty or thirty years ago than it is today. Categories were fairly well defined and seldom did anyone cross over. The writer gave the script to the director, who chose a cameraman and then turned over the footage to the editor. In today's film world, however, we often find that the best-known people are the "hyphenated filmmakers": director-camera-person or writer-producer-director or just "filmmaker." The supervisory control of the finished product then becomes the responsibility of one person. And, more often than not, the hyphenated filmmaker includes the function of the director. Claude Lelouch, for example, directs and is his own director of photography and camera operator. Haskel Wexler also handles much of the hand-held photography in his films. In the documentary, filmmakers such as Francis Thompson, Joan Kuehl, Frederick Wiseman, and even this author all perform more than one role and thus the films are more total reflections of their individual personalities. The perceptive viewer can almost sense a "signature" in their work. Even in the commercial field, the director-cameraperson has become important—Len Hirschfield, Steve Horn, and Bill Fertik, for example.

For the beginning filmmaker, this change in the structure of the directorial field presents another opportunity for entry—for the acceptance of the hyphenated filmmaker allows samples to be made by only *one* person and many film students are producing, directing, editing, and writing their own productions—which leads, naturally, to the very important subject of how in heaven's name you become a director.

I had no intention of being facetious, earlier, with a description of how some directors get their jobs. Generally, the director "eases" into the job through one or more circumstances, some of them quirks of fate, others a determined effort to achieve the role. There is no one way. Some young people I know are starting their own film companies right from scratch—in spite of all the competition from producers with much more experience in the field. Some will fail to get clients to support them, others will be as successful as one lawyer-turned-filmmaker who took a job away from us though he had never made a film before. In general, the role of director is not an entry job in the film world; you will usually have to begin in some other category and then take advantage of opportunities as they present themselves. Of course, the roadblocks put in the way of beginners have not stopped some people from merely putting the entire "package" together—raising the money from friends and investors, producing, directing, and then finding distribution for their films. The film industry has not been noticeably kind to minorities, nor has it encouraged the development of women as filmmakers. Nonetheless, the field has been cracked by people who just went out and found a way.

It is not easy, but there are shining examples of the battles against the Hollywood and New York establishments. Melvin van Peebles produced his *Story of a Three-Day Pass* in Paris, and found distribution in the United States. Joan Miklin Silver's *Hester Street*, Sylvester Stallone's *Rocky*, John Sayles' entire output of features, Edward James Olmos' *The Ballard of Gregorio Cortez* are but a few more glowing victories. The establishment gives way slowly and reluctantly, and the success stories are rare. But it can be done, and there are ways. You may observe a director from the vantage point of a gopher or as an assistant director, and you will comment that you definitely could do it much better. But there may come a time when you will find yourself directing and you will be hard put to describe just how you got there. As a young writer–assistant-director (hyphenated) in television, I introduced the director to his future wife. When they got married and took a two-week honeymoon, I directed the show in his absence. I was a director!

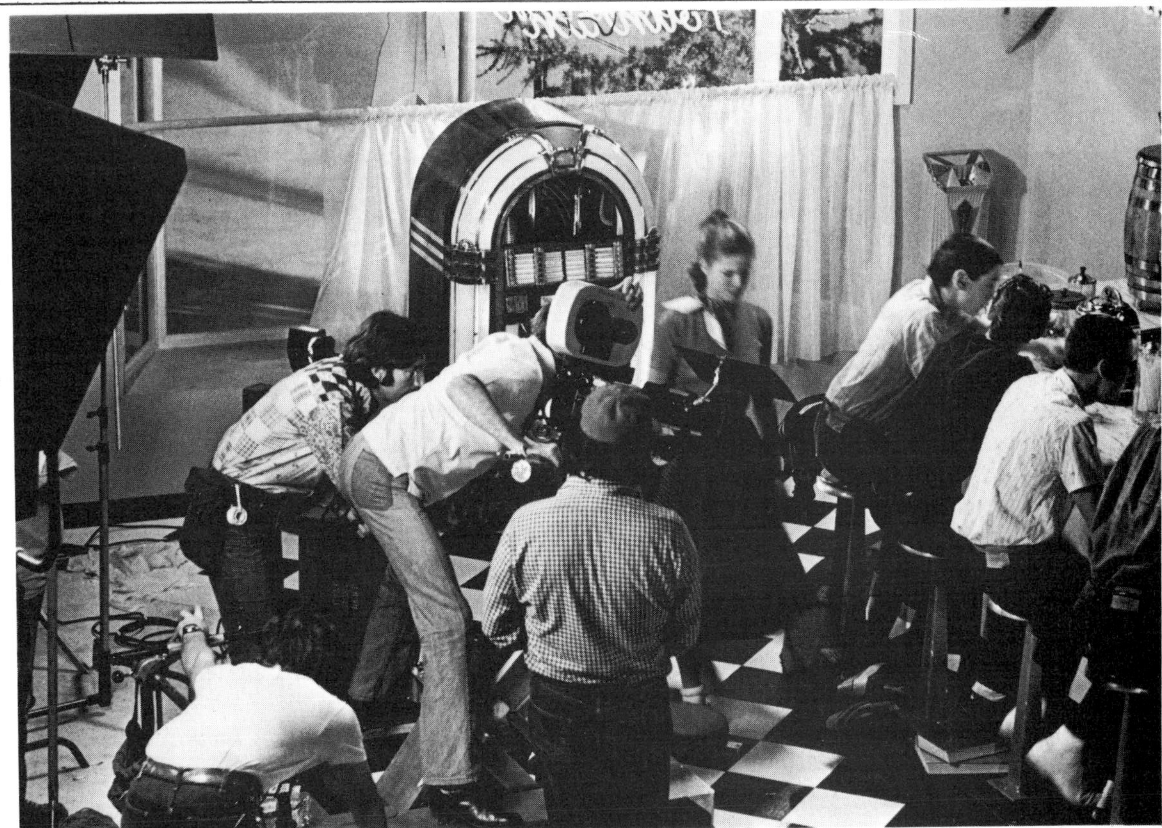

Filming a commercial for Levi Strauss in San Francisco. There are some training programs which enable young filmmakers to observe productions such as these right on set with the crew.

In the chapters dealing with schools and grants, you will find some information about an internship training program run by the American Film Institute and funded by the Academy of Motion Picture Arts and Sciences. The people chosen to participate are given an opportunity to learn the art of directing by observing established directors at work during the making of a film. But the entries are severely limited, though the talented few have a superb opportunity to learn from the masters of the field. I have watched their progress with interest. Some years back, a young filmmaker named Martha Coolidge moved from documentary films (*Not a Pretty Picture*) through the program and into features with Robert Wise's *Audrey Rose*, followed by the film *Valley Girls*.

Perhaps one of the most important programs to be designed for those interested in the production end of film has been the one instituted by the Directors Guild of America in conjunction with the producers in the industry. Started in 1969, it is still going strong, though only a few people are accepted from the thousands of applicants who apply for the New York and Los Angeles programs. (It is not available in Miami or Chicago.) Here is a brief summary:

The program is designed to emphasize the administrative and managerial functions characteristic of Assistant Directors and to familiarize the trainees with the paperwork and proper maintenance of records, including the preparation of call sheets, production reports and requisitions; to acquaint them with the working conditions of the collective bargaining agreements of industry guilds and unions; and to give them a basic knowledge of the administrative procedures in motion picture production, including production and some post-production operations.

During their training, trainees will have the opportunity to improve their skills in the handling of the people, learn how to call actors, extras and other personnel, how to assist in the staging of background action and the giving of cues to actors, how to determine compensation adjustments for extras and stunts, how to make arrangements for facilities and rental equipment, how to break down scripts, and how to schedule and budget pictures. They will be able to acquire some knowledge of looping, recording wild lines, characteristics of camera lenses and matching of angles for editing.

The program will include both on-the-job and off-the-job training. On-the-job training encompasses up to 400 work days during a two year program. Employment will be subject to all applicable collective bargaining agreements and studio or producer rules and regulations. Consistent with the collective bargaining agreement referred to above and the Trust Indenture under which this program operates, trainees are employed and paid by signatory producers. Upon satisfactory completion of the program, the trainee will be accepted into the Directors Guild of America as a Second Assistant Director.

To be eligible, an applicant must meet all of the requirements outlined by the guild, available through an information sheet mailed on request. For example:

• Experience in the motion picture industry or the suitable equivalent in accredited technical training schools or graduation from a four-year college or university. Evidence must be clearly documented.

•At least two letters of reference from motion picture or related industry employers or from an educational institution

The letters should include comments on such qualities as:

(a) excellence of performance
(b) organizational experiences and ability
(c) capacity to give orders and also accept and execute orders
(d) administrative ability (planning, scheduling)
(e) skills in dealing with people
(f) consistency of behavior
(g) versatility
(h) ability to work effectively under pressure.

•United States citizenship or permanent residence status

•Good health and character

There are, of course, other prerequisites and you can write directy to DGA (East) at 110 West 57th Street, New York, N.Y. 10019 or DGA (West) Training Program at 14144 Ventura Blvd., Sherman Oaks, CA 91423 if you'd like to apply.

The interesting thing about all the requirements is that they succinctly outline *all* the attributes necessary to be a good production person and—eventually—a good director. The description of the program outlines almost every area of film craftsmanship: acting, directing, budgets, equipment, camera. Most of all, note the phrase, "trainees will have the opportunity to improve their skills in *the handling of the people*" (Italics mine). This is the prime attribute of a good director.

Let me close with a story about being a director. I wrote at the beginning of this chapter that I had never had a director's chair. Actually, I did have one. It was placed in a prop truck prior to leaving on an eight-week location trip to Pittsburgh . . .

When I work, I pace a lot. I walk three feet off the ground during production and normally never have time to sit. And so, for all of the eight weeks the chair lay securely wrapped in the back of that truck. Until the last day.

The weeks had taken their toll on the crew and on me. I was tired, glad that the job would soon be over. Eight weeks in a hotel had worn me down. That very last day, working in the toughest neighborhood in Pittsburgh, protected by at least eight policemen, I turned to my production manager and said, "Bring out my director's chair." Then I turned back to finish a sequence.

When I turned again and walked over to sit down, the toughest-looking teenager was sitting in *my* chair and just daring me to ask him to get up. I turned again and decided not to press the issue.

So, I *have* had a director's chair. I just never sat in it.

CHAPTER 14

THE ADVERTISING AGENCY

"Some of My Best Friends..."

In many respects, the advertising agency is not really a part of the film-production industry; the people who work there do not fit into any of the categories described in the previous pages. Much of their work is involved with print advertising in newspapers and magazines, and on billboards, statistical research in the marketplace, the purchase of TV air time and newspaper space, and, in many instances, includes public relations for their corporate clients.

In many respects, nevertheless, the advertising agency *is* very much a part of the film industry. The entire field of television commercials would have to find a different structure if it were not for the role played by the agencies—and, more important, the job market for the beginner is vast and many directors of commercials began their careers in the TV production departments of the ad agencies.

The field is much maligned, sometimes with good cause, but often because it is not understood. The role of anyone in the middle is generally a difficult one—and that is exactly where agency people stand. On the one side is the client, possibly an executive or a committee of executives in an industrial organization. On the other side are the suppliers who work with the agency in film, art, graphics, and space and time sales. In the middle is the advertising agency: controllers of the product image, creative psychologists—and sometimes very neurotic from always being in the middle.

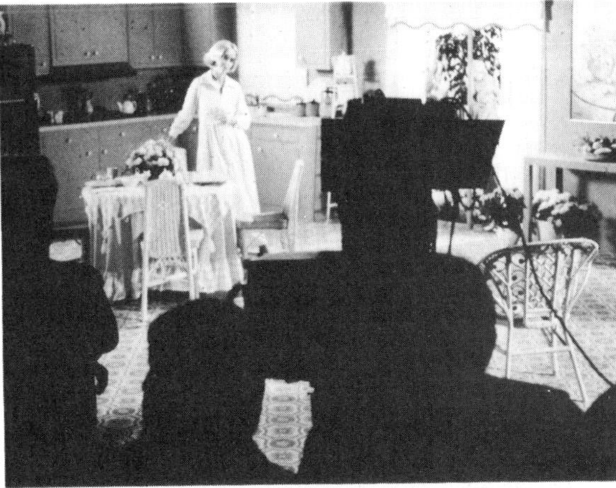

Shooting a Solarian floor-covering commercial for Armstrong World Industries.

We will try to stick to the role of the agency in television commercials, and even then we must take a middle course, for all agencies operate differently. In the smaller and medium-sized companies, one person may double or triple in jobs; that is very much the structure of any small corporation. In the larger agencies, however, the job functions are more severely divided, though the titles may be vague and overlapping.

The marvelous thing about the agency business is that, as in the business film field, you are exposed to the potential of hundreds of industries; and if you are working on an account, you have an obligation to learn about that industry or product before you can even begin to consider advertising their products or services. The agency staff, then, must research the product, check the important consumer points, and then find a vehicle with which to advertise that product. If we consider that the average TV viewer sees between ten and fifteen thousand television commercials a year, we can begin to understand why the TV departments of the advertising agencies have grown so big, and why the job market has increased over the last twenty years.

SPOT PRODUCTION The job of the agency in spot production can be broken down into three areas:

- Creation of a campaign or the direction a spot will take
- Developing the campaign or the spot to a final "story board"
- Contracting the production of the spot to an outside film or tape company

Certainly, the agency will eventually also buy the time on the stations or the networks and certainly agency research has gone into all of this, but remember that we have narrowed the job to the film end of the business. The balance could take another book.

The production of a spot by an agency involves the following people:

The Client. The first stage in the development of the spot generally involves a client decision on some level of his company, possibly by the vice-president in charge of advertising. A new product or an idea must be communicated. The next step is to contact the advertising agency.

The Account Executive. This function is generally performed by the agency's "in-house psychiatrist"— the account executive, who is the liaison between the client and the agency's creative staff. Account execs are familiar with marketing, research, the product, the client corporation, and they tread a thin line in keeping everybody satisfied. Some large agencies

have executives for each individual product.

The Copywriter. After several meetings to discuss strategy, the agency's copywriter will develop a script that outlines the form the commercial will take. Sometimes this job is done *after* the next one on our list, for the art director (see below) occasionally designs the style of the commercial before the copy is even written.

The Art Director. This is a role that has increased in importance over the years and many art directors are also the agency producers on the spots they create. Essentially, the art director develops the visual concept of the spots, and in time a story board will evolve, giving the entire message in picture and word form.

The Producer. This person generally gets to know the most about the film and tape industry, for the agency producer is responsible for the entire production, casting, timetable, budget, and the legality of the commercial.

The Assistant Producer. This is, once again, a job category that is hard to define. All assistants do whatever jobs are assigned to them; and all assistants are overworked and underpaid, even assistants who don't even work in the film field. But what a place to learn! And it's a good entry-job area for the beginner.

In addition, the agency generally has its own casting director and many auditions are put directly onto videotape so that the client may be shown the selection at a later date. Many times the final casting session is held in conjunction with the director from the film production company and the agency producer.

There are, of course, departments to handle the agency's business affairs—paperwork, budgeting, invoicing, contracts, and financial analysis—and departments whose only job is to keep track of the residual payments due the actors and then send out the checks on time.

I've mentioned that the film and tape jobs are contracted out to production companies—and generally this is the job of the agency producer. The bidders are chosen for various reasons: their previous experience with the agency, a good reputation, or a "hot" director whom everyone must get. Some production companies are adept at doing certain types of commercials (such as hidden camera work); others are superb with product; some do animation and nothing else. The agency producer must know enough about the budget process to be able to tell if their bid is correct.

The agency generally gives the story board to several producers. The number can vary from two to twenty-two. Generally, three or four bid on the board. An agency friend of mine tells the story of giving out three boards for bids. One of the producers came in with a

Designer's drawing for the setting of the Armstrong World Industries commercial. The agency was BBD&O.

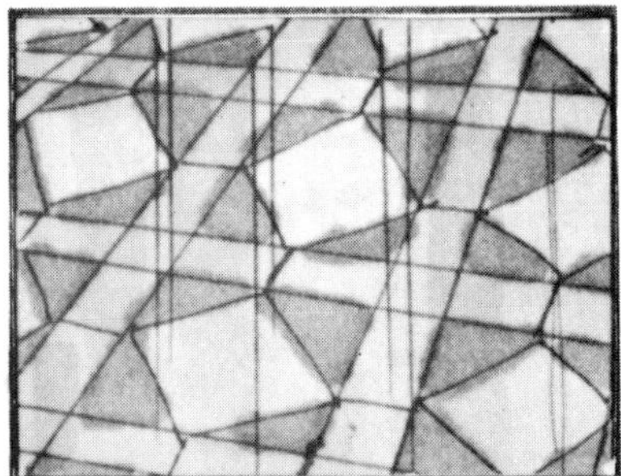

The rough story board for the Solarian commercial, prepared by the advertising agency's art director and copywriter. Scenes from the completed commercial as they appeared on television with narrative from the script can be seen on page 118.

budget many thousands of dollars below the other two. Since the production company was well known to the agency, they were questioned rather firmly and they stuck to their figure. When the job was awarded to them, the agency discovered that one entire page was missing from the story board and that that was the reason why the producer had come in with a low bid; he had only seen two thirds of the commercial! From that time on, the agency has insisted that each story board have numbered pages and that the total be put right on the first page, where it can be clearly seen.

What eventually goes out over the air is a spot that begins with the client and the agency and wends its way through production to the TV sets of the nation. But in between, a lot happens before we hear the dulcet tones of the announcer saying, "We now interrupt this commercial for another commercial . . ."

You can't say just anything in television advertising, and a broad range of organizations control any spot between its inception and air date. If any of these "powers that be" feel that the audience will infer something stronger than the claim you are actually trying to make, the agency may be asked to change the wording of the commercial. On the federal level alone, the content of TV commercial advertising is controlled and regulated by the Federal Trade Commission, the Food and Drug Administration, the Federal Communications Commission, and the Treasury Department (Bureau of Alcohol, Tobacco and Firearms). And, if that's not quite enough, the networks themselves have their own self-regulating group, the National Association of Broadcasters.

The rules of these agencies are rigid, the structures outlined in no uncertain terms. You cannot use the word "free" in a commercial unless you are actually giving away something without any purchase whatsoever. Superlatives cannot be used: you may not say, "the *best* coffee . . ."; but you can claim, "a better coffee . . ." We used to ask, painfully, "Better than what?"

Finally, eighteen other organizations hover in the background, each concerned with its own particular industry and just what is to be shown and said about its products. The beer industry, for example, has its own governing body, which has dictated that no person may be shown actually drinking beer in a commercial. It is not illegal; it's just an industry dictate. In a recent case, the ban against showing models wearing bras was again renewed, in spite of the fact that we claim we are living in a more enlightened era. Despite all of these confining measures, nevertheless, the television commercial has managed to break free in many areas of film creativity—and the annual awards festivals are a joy to behold.

Of course there are times when the advertising agency's being in the middle creates tension and insecurity, for the responsibility of the agency to its client is a large one and sometimes millions of dollars in billings can depend on one campaign. Corporations are notorious for changing agencies after twenty years of loyalty and, naturally, the loss of an account can also mean the loss of jobs. So, insecurity is a natural adjunct of the field. The stories abound.

One of my acquaintances was in charge of the music session for an airline commercial. The control room was filled with about fifteen people, all surrounding one of the vice-presidents of the agency. This was his "baby" and

LADY: An Armstrong Solarian floor is like letting the sunshine in.

Because Solarian is the sunny floor that shines without waxing.

Look how it shines. It's easier to care for than any floor Armstrong has ever made.

And it shines far longer than an ordinary vinyl floor.

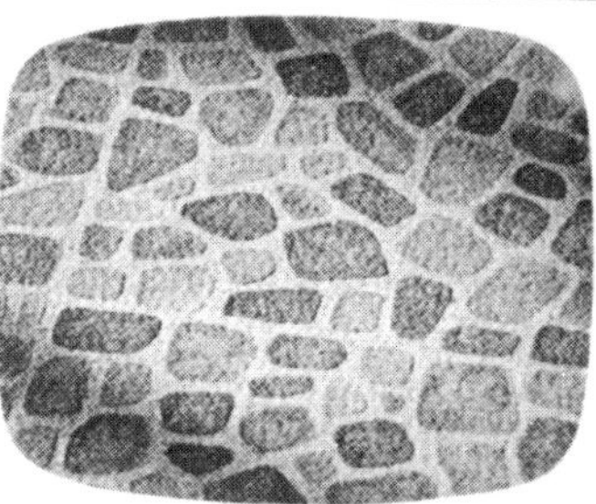

get Armstrong Solarian.

The completed Solarian commercial.

the thirty-second spot had to be right. Through two hours of a grueling session with a large (and expensive) orchestra, everyone kept looking to the top executive for approbation. He never smiled. The session went on. Finally, after two more hours, a grin lit up his face and he said, "That was good," and everybody collapsed.

A short time before, someone had ordered coffee and sandwiches for the musicians and the agency people, and at just that moment the deliveryman walked into the control room, put down the carton, and waited to get paid. The loudspeaker played back the selected take, the deliveryman took his money and went to the door. As he opened it, he turned and muttered quite audibly, "Ecchh, that stinks!" and then slammed the door. The executive was stunned at what he had heard. This was, after all, the reaction of the common man—the very man they were trying to reach with the commercial. He shrieked, "Go find that guy!" and two people ran out into the hall after him. He was gone—down the elevator—and lost somewhere on Broadway. For two more hours, the arguments went on, and the spot was played bit by little bit trying to analyze just what it was that the deliveryman didn't like. We still don't know.

For the professionals in the advertising business, its film aspects provide an unlimited opportunity to be the Renaissance people of the twentieth century: they must know about film production, theater, music, finances, travel, art and graphics, and a hundred other subjects. This suggests that, in order to break into the field, you must have a rich background and interest in the areas of film, or art, or graphics—*and* a vital interest in the field of advertising. Portfolios, film samples, and anything you might have to show are important "door openers." And from that open door in advertising, many have gone out into the film field per se with production companies—as directors, producers, writers . . .

Under normal circumstances, this short chapter might end here. It is another lead, another way you might break into the film business. Another open door. But I hear, in response, the plaintive wail of dissatisfaction about advertising. In a recent Gallup poll, the survey took into account the public's feelings about honesty and ethical standards of the various professions. At the top of the list were doctors, engineers, college teachers, and journalists. At the bottom were advertising executives—below labor-union leaders, congressmen, senators, and business executives.

The question has been raised time and again about the companies who make the commercials for the products manufactured by America's corporations. Does the film company *always* agree with the philosophy of a client when it is selling his product? Certainly, no film field is perfect, and perhaps there are some agencies and film-production companies who would advertise anything; but we know of many agencies that will withdraw from a client or an account if they have reservations or serious questions about the morality of advertising a particular product. Many of my agency friends in hiring positions claim that some young people come in for interviews with the question: "What is the morality of what you do?" A classic answer was given by a man in one of the larger advertising agencies: "Tell me, have you thought of joining the clergy?"

CHAPTER 15

THE FILM UNIONS

"Don't Eat the Label"

Like all young children brought up in the Bronx, my introduction to the unions came at an early age, probably four or five. Bread baking still took place "while you sleep" and the packaged, tasteless, plastic, thin-sliced white commercial loaves had not yet come to fill the shelves of the local grocer. My mother bought her bread in a bakery and each golden-brown rye loaf carried a union label, a small white sticker affixed firmly to the pointed end of the bread. Since, like all children, I wanted the end (a strange need, which still remains with me today), it was torn off—label and all—and I can still hear my mother's strident warning: "Don't eat the union label!" Today, as an amateur bread baker, I keep wondering whether it might not be a stroke of whimsy to put my own union label on the results of my Sunday labors—except that my union is the Directors Guild of America, and I wonder how that would look on a loaf of rye bread.

The unions are a fact of film life, and throughout the book I have spoken of the various unions and guilds that are very much involved with the industry. This has also been an excellent way to explain how the jobs and categories are broken down. In this short chapter about the film unions, I would like to give some further information, as well as some possible help about your eventual role with these organizations.

We might as well begin by saying that you do *not* have to belong to a union in order to work in the film industry. Across the country there are independents, small production companies, educational film producers, corporate audiovisual units, and commercial producers who do not have union affiliation, never will have it, and will probably go on throughout their entire careers without filling out an employment form such as we have shown on page 76.

If you plan, however, to go on to the larger production companies, or if you decide that television or tape or features or big-city commercials (Hollywood, New York, Chicago) are the stars in your future, then the unions become important and, at some time, you will have to become a member of a local in either the International Alliance of Theatrical Stage Employees (IATSE), the National Association of Broadcast Employees and Technicians (NABET), or, perhaps, the International Brotherhood of Electrical Workers (IBEW).

For the most part, film unions are under the jurisdiction of IATSE, while television is the domain of NABET. The various *locals* refer to the film crafts controlled by a particular group in a particular area. For example, Local 798 refers to the makeup and hairstyling artists who work out of New York, whereas Local 706 is a member of the same union for the same people in Hollywood. In New York, the cameraman's local is 644; in Hollywood it is 659. And though each is a member of IATSE, the rules and regulations, initiation fees, dues, and residency requirements are different on both coasts. You will find this to be true throughout the guilds and unions in the industry. The best way to find out just what they require is to write the local of your choice and ask for information. Dues and regulations also change from year to year, so a long listing of specifications here would be out-of-date within the next few months. However, what I have tried to do at the end of the chapter is give you the names and addresses of the film unions as they appear at the time of this printing. A letter to a specific one will certainly bring a response.

For too many years the unions were rigid and unbending in their demands of the film producers, though this was not all as bad as it sounds, for the union structure has provided job benefits that would have been almost impossible to achieve without them. Wages are excellent and pension and welfare plans are strong throughout most of the film trades. Working conditions, craft guidelines, and effective bargaining procedures have also been brought into the industry. But there have also been ripples that were not quite as beneficial. Primarily, it has become more and more difficult for the beginner to crack the union barrier. The people in any organization have a tendency to protect themselves; therefore, so often we hear the complaint, "I can't get into the union."

The rules are stringent, and in many cases quite unbending. This does put up a wall for many young people, though in spite of it, many do get in and move through the categories to the top-paying jobs. The trick is to begin early, and know what's ahead of you before the union problem even comes up. The longer you work in the field, the more friends you will make, the more information you'll get, the more valuable *you* will become to the potential union or guild. Time and time again there have been people—stage technicians, cinematographers, designers, etc.—who can provide a special talent, or who have a particular skill that cannot be equaled by anyone else; they have continued to work in the industry until offered their memberships in the respective

locals. You will not begin your career as a union member, but you will probably have to face the situation at some later date.

Qualifications differ. Some unions give a written exam and require some background in the craft, either in school productions or in stage work or in non-union work in the same field. In all of them some type of executive-board approval is needed for new members, followed by a vote by the general membership. (One good sign recently has been the trend toward younger people running the executive boards.) Some unions will take you on immediately if you can get a job in the field (notably, the locals involved with television, in NABET). In other cases, being hired by a signatory of a union contract—such as the Writers Guild—automatically makes you a member after thirty days. Still others have usually tightly closed doors that occasionally open for a small apprenticeship program. Of course, under the Taft-Hartley Law, should you get a job with a union producer, the local must accept you as a member or allow you to work without joining. Under the same law, any union employer can hire you—even if union acceptance has not been given—just so long as you have expressed a willingness to join the particular local that covers the craft, and if the union cannot provide a member who can do the same job and is acceptable to the producer.

From time to time, training programs have opened up in the various craft unions, sometimes in conjunction with major studios or supported entirely by the guilds themselves. However, you must keep in mind that everything depends upon the current economic conditions in the industry, what percentage of union members is currently out of work at any given time, and the amount of help offered by government grants and funding. These past few years have not been good, and much of the grant money has dried up in Washington. Programs begun by groups such as the people at the old Astoria sound stages in New York, have not been able to continue, since much of their support came from HEW and the city universities. Nevertheless, it is a good idea to keep your eyes open by reading the trade papers and magazines, and when such a program does become active, and it meets your own career goals, apply as quickly as you can.

Almost all unions require an initiation fee once you are accepted, and these also vary depending upon conditions. They generally run from about $500 to as much as $3,500; after that, a small percentage of your yearly salary will be paid in dues. Pension and welfare costs are generally provided by the employer each time you work on a production.

Interestingly enough, after all the legitimate complaints from beginners about the tightness of unions and the difficulty of making that first break, I was fully prepared to meet some union resistance to the writing of this book, even though I am a member of a guild. To the contrary, I found the unions' business agents open, receptive, available, and, above all, sympathetic to the plight of the young filmmakers who will eventually fill out their applications. Each union representative was aware of just how difficult it is to break in and each, in turn, was a staunch supporter of any apprentice program that might be developed in the future. But if all of us have to face reality, so do the executives who run the labor unions in the film industry—there are just so many jobs to go around and just so many openings that occur each year.

The best advice, then, is to work in the field any way you can possibly get into it—union or non-union. Your experience will eventually bring you face to face with the decision about either joining or being rejected, and you can fight the fight at that time. Meanwhile, it would pay you to learn about the qualifications for the local that covers your eventual craft category. Write to the local. Learn about its rules and apprenticeship programs. And every time you meet union cameramen or scenic designers or directors, ask them questions. Pick their brains. Every bit of information you can get will eventually help you.

Here are the names, addresses, and telephone numbers of the unions and guilds in Hollywood, New York, and Chicago:

HOLLYWOOD

(Area Codes 213 and 818)

American Federation of Musicians 213-462-2161
817 Vine Street Los Angeles 90038

Directors Guild of America 213-656-1220
7950 Sunset Blvd. 90046

Film Technicians (Laboratories) 213-935-1123
6721 Melrose 90038

I.A.T.S.E. 213-876-2010
7715 Sunset Blvd. 90046

I.B.E.W. 213-877-1170
5643 Vinland Ave. N. Hwd. 91601

THE FILM UNIONS

International Sound Technicians 818-985-9204
11331 Ventura Blvd. Suite 201
Studio City 91604

I.P.M.P.I. (Cinematographers) 213-876-0160
7715 Sunset Blvd. 90046

Make-up Artists and Hair Stylists 213-877-2776
11519 Chandler Blvd. N. Hwd. 91601

Motion Picture Costumers 213-851-0220
1427 N. La Brea Blvd. 90028

Motion Picture & Video Tape Editors 213-876-4770
7715 Sunset Blvd. 90046

Motion Picture Illustrators 213-876-2010
7715 Sunset Blvd. 90046

Motion Picture Electricians 213-466-4209
3400 Barham LA 90068

Motion Picture Studio Grips 213-931-1419
6926 Melrose 90038

N.A.B.E.T. 213-462-7484
1800 N. Argyle 90028

Publicists Guild 213-851-1600
1427 N. La Brea Blvd. 90028

Screen Actors Guild 213-876-3030
7750 Sunset Blvd. 90046

Screen Extras Guild 213-851-4301
3629 Cahuenga Blvd. West LA 90068

Script Supervisors 818-784-6885
14724 Ventura, Sherman Oaks 91403

Set Designers and Model Makers 818-784-6555
14724 Ventura, Sherman Oaks 91403

Society of Motion Picture Art Directors 818-905-0599
14724 Ventura, Sherman Oaks 91403

Sound & Cine Technicians 818-985-9204
11331 Ventura Blvd. Studio City 91604

Studio Lighting Technicians 818-891-0728
14629 Nordhoff, Panorama City 91402

Writers Guild (West) 213-550-1000
8955 Beverly 90048

NEW YORK CITY

(Area Codes 212 & 718)

American Federation of Musicians 212-869-1330
1500 Broadway 10036

Directors Guild of America 212-581-0370
110 West 57th St. 10019

I.A.T.S.E. 212-730-1770
1515 Broadway 10036

I.P.M.P.I. (Cinematographers) 212-247-3860
250 West 57th St. 10019

Make-up Artists & Hair Stylists 212-757-9120
1790 Broadway 10019

Motion Picture & Video Tape Editors 212-581-0771
630 Ninth Avenue 10036

Motion Picture Lab Technicians 212-757-5540
165 West 46th St. 10036

Motion Picture Studio Mechanics 212-399-0980
326 West 48th St. 10036

N.A.B.E.T. 212-265-3500
1776 Broadway 10019

Screen Actors (Screen Extras) Guild 212-957-5370
1700 Broadway 10019

Screen Cartoonists 212-354-6410
25 West 43rd St. 10036

Screen Publicists Guild 212-673-5120
13 Astor Place 10003

Script Supervisors, Production Office Coordinators 718-706-0204
Kaufman Studios
34-31 35th St. Astoria, NY 11106

Theatrical Wardrobe Attendants 212-221-1717
1501 Broadway 10036

United Scenic Artists 212-736-4498
575 8th Avenue 10018

Writers Guild (East) 212-245-6180
555 West 57th St. 10019

CHICAGO

(Area Code 312)

Directors Guild of America 644-5050
520 N. Michigan 60611

I.P.M.P.I. (Cinematographers) 341-0966
327 S. LaSalle St. 60604

Motion Picture Lab Technicians 922-7105
327 S. LaSalle St. 60604

Motion Picture Studio Mechanics 922-5215
327 S. LaSalle St. 60604

Moving Picture Machine Operators 787-0220
875 N. Michigan 60611

Screen Actors Guild 372-8081
307 N. Michigan 60601

Theatrical Wardrobe Attendants 477-4952
3500 N. Lake Shore Drive 60657

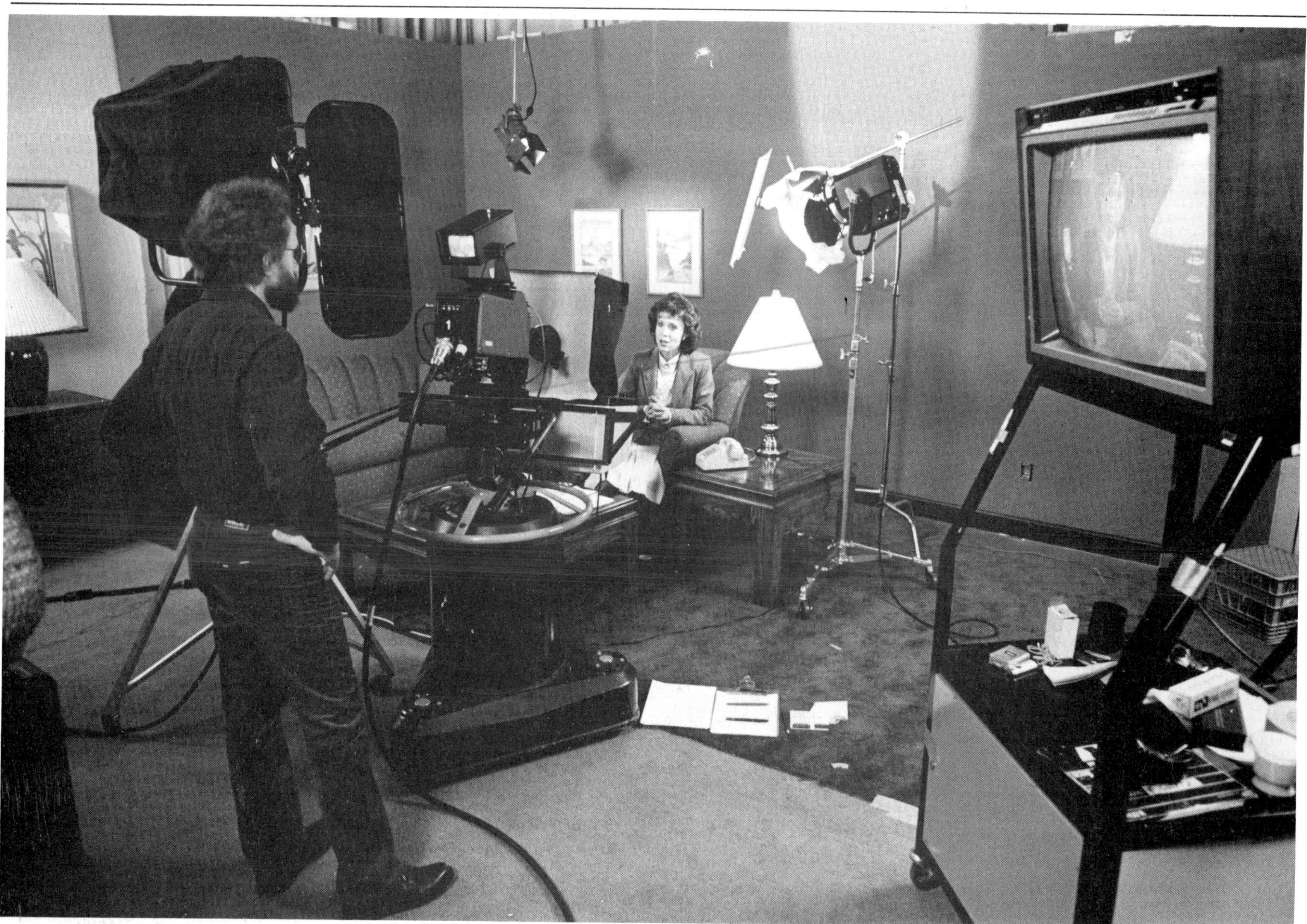

A sequence being shot at Ohio Bell's television studio. Video tape has become an important communications tool for industry and vies with film in use and popularity.

CHAPTER 16

FILMS VERSUS TAPE

"It's Time for a Truce"

Tape has been called the "engineer's medium"—and at one time it deserved the title. Some think it still merits the name. Others violently disagree—and the more sophisticated tape has become, the more it has warranted a closer look. No one will ever solve the argument as to which medium is more effective or more practical. Film people will be forever bound to Celluloid and tape people will swear that they are just as "creative." Column after column in trade newspapers and magazines such as *Millimeter* and *Backstage* are devoted to the discussion of tape versus film. Cheaper? Faster? Better? Worse? It doesn't really matter, for all that should concern us here is that tape has opened up another job market in the industry and is worth a good, close look.

Back in 1956, most television programs were produced live, and some of us still remember with fondness and trembling the trauma of putting on a coast-to-coast show, knowing that the mistakes as well as the genius could well go out over the air. How many stagehands walked in front of the cameras while the actors were still emoting? And one of the classic stories still talked about is the "corpse" who got up and walked off the set before the scene was over.

I can laugh now at one of my own live shows, when we used dry ice in hot water to make smoke for a lovely cello solo, envisioning wispy clouds filling the screen as the cellist played *The Swan*. Unfortunately, before our horrified eyes, the water froze. From New York to Los Angeles, the viewers were treated to a beautiful shot of dry ice in freezing water in a galvanized metal pail!

But the networks had a more severe problem with live TV than just a few funny "goofs." If a show was produced in New York at 9 P.M. and it was to be shown in Los Angeles, the network had several choices, and none of them was really the best answer to the problem. The program could go out live to the West Coast, simultaneously—in which case the audience there would be viewing the show at 6 P.M., not a very good prime-time hour. Or, they could rebroadcast the program live at midnight, in which case the three-hour time lapse would bring the show to the West Coast at the "same" time that it had been seen in New York. Or, the third possibility was to kinescope the show and rerun it at the proper time. Kinescopes were nothing more than a

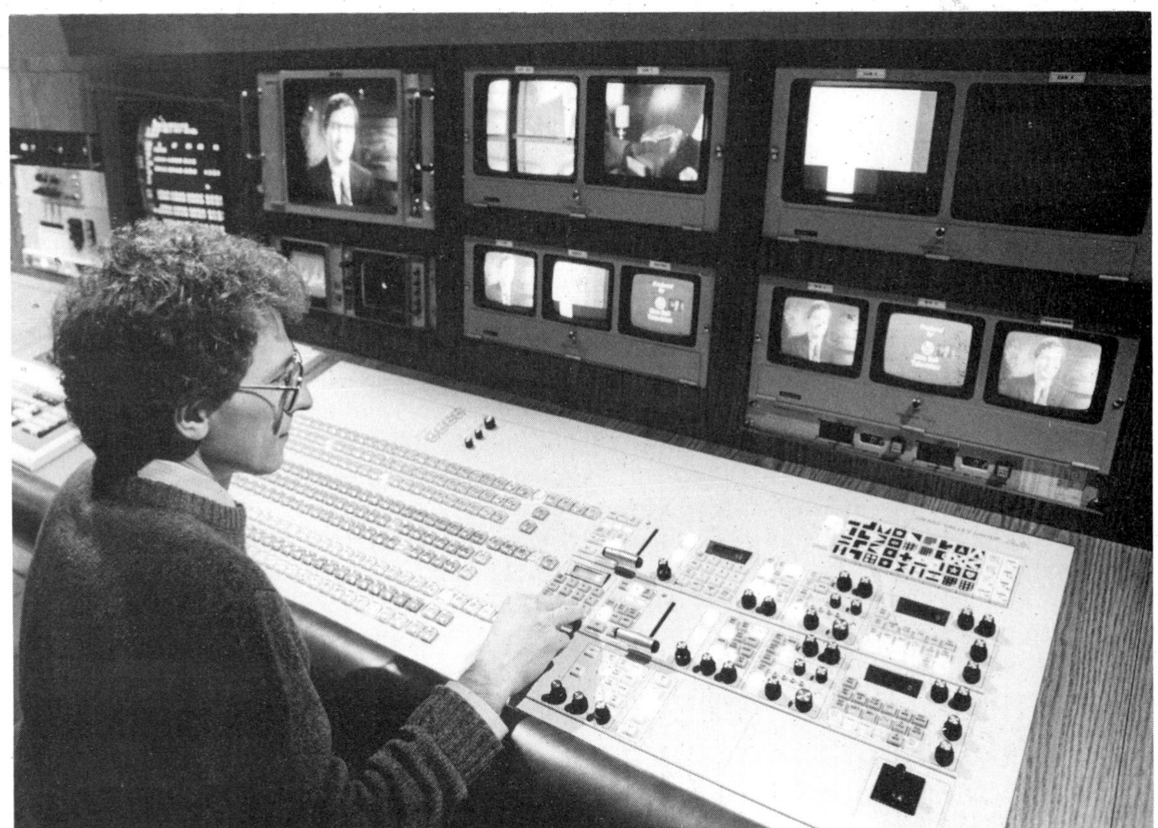

A state-of-the-art switching system at the Ohio Bell Visual Communications Center control room in Cleveland.

film taken from the TV screen and the grainy black-and-white was immediately recognizable for what it was: a very poor film. Tape solved the problem of America's time zones.

If tape were used just to reproduce a program, from beginning to end, it was great. The quality, even then, was far superior to the kinescope and it was reproduceable into many copies, if the need arose. Nevertheless, editing it was a tedious, time-consuming, almost impossible task. Since the networks now had the chance to remove the mistakes, the tape could be edited, and the show rebroadcast after the polishing job. Each cut, however, took anywhere from ten minutes to half an hour; the tape had to be started many sequences before the edit spot, then stopped accurately, and the cut made with a razor blade; next, a piece of metallic tape was pulled over the wound and the tape was run on a monitor—if the splice had been made incorrectly, if the razor blade had not been sharp enough, the monitor showed jagged electronic lines and the whole thing had to be done over again! I remember doing my first dramatic shows on tape and we spent all night trying to make editorial changes that would take a few minutes today. Some editors were just better with the razor blades than others.

But the editing of tape had begun, and it was started by engineers: the people who designed the systems, the television hotshots who understood the technical language and who worked in control rooms and with complicated switching systems and inadequate lighting systems. Videotape was quick but it was cumbersome—and it soon developed the reputation of being singularly non-creative. The argument resumed: Film was the answer to anything that had production value. Film was creative. And everyone forgot that film, too, once had hand-cranked cameras and slow film stock, and lights that were too large for one person to handle comfortably.

The technology of tape has improved. Film people are beginning to use the medium—and more tape people are experimenting with film. The editing has become electronic and totally flexible. Color and contrast are sophisticated, more attention is being paid to the lighting of the set or the location. The equipment is still designed by engineers—but the *thinking* about tape is changing. Moreover, along with these improvements, the two main factors that first made tape so valuable are still with us: speed and immediate playback.

Each year, almost twenty thousand commercials are produced in the United States alone, about 25 percent put on tape for national distribution. The regional figures are even more impressive, with about one third of all spots produced in the medium. And this does not include other uses of tape: for television shows, industrial and corporate use, and in education, for example.

For the commercial field, tape has been a great boon. There are times, in shooting a commercial film, when the director is quite certain the last take is all right, the cameraman agrees, and the agency producer is not quite sure. Since the aim is to please the client—and the film will not be developed for a day or so, too late to come back and shoot it again—the tendency is always to "do a take for protection." Twenty-seven takes later, they finally get the shot to everyone's satisfaction (or else they're all too tired to care), and the crew prepares for the next scene. The next day, screening the rushes, everyone sees that Take Number One was really the best one, after all. Of course, it seems like a waste to introduce a whole new technology just so that the client can see the playback immediately and thus save the rest of the time spent in "protection," but it *is* an advantage.

Tape can now be transferred to film and this is being done quite successfully. It can go the other way too: film to tape. Feature films are also using tape sequences for special effects. A Universal remake of *The Invisible Man* used tape for certain sequences while shooting film for the balance of the picture. And Francis Ford Coppola has begun to use entire tape monitoring facilities even though the picture is being shot on film. *Cotton Club* was produced in exactly that way.

The networks are beginning to phase out film in their news departments. With the invention of the Minicam, an eleven-pound portable TV tape camera, news crews find that their coverage of live events has improved because of the weight and the flexibility that comes from a more compact unit. The crew consists of two people attached by a ten-foot cable—the cameraman carrying the camera and a backpack with power supply, the second person hauling the videotape cassette.

Certainly, then, there are places where tape should be used in place of film, and other places where film is the obvious choice. In terms of speed, live coverage, and the ability to play back at once, tape far surpasses film. In other areas, however, tape becomes cumbersome, expensive, a bad choice under the best of conditions. You would not, for example, try to take a tape unit through Asia to do a travel documentary (though some have tried it). Some years ago, I produced a fashion show for NBC in Rome (another one of those "glamorous" locations again!) and the only solution for the job was tape, since the show was to be shot over a weekend and was to be on the air the very next night. We edited through Sunday night, made the morning plane to New York, and had it on NBC prime time Monday evening. But I would not normally want to take a tape unit around the world to do a fashion show. In fact, I would normally prefer the quality and response of film in photographing any kind of clothing on location. I try to choose the medium that best suits the job.

One of the most effective and superb uses of tape production was in the documentary *The Police Tapes,* produced by Alan and Susan Raymond and presented over the Public Broadcasting System. It was a classic case of the proper use of the tape medium, for film could not have performed in the same way. Living with the police of a busy, hectic, crime-ridden New York precinct, the producers needed a medium that would be unobtrusive and still allow them to record incidents at night under low light level and in very tense situations. The feeling of "presence" and the fact that the cameras were ignored for the most part by the participants were tributes to the choice of tape.

Is tape cheaper? No. And—yes. It depends again upon your specifications and your needs. You can use tape to get your materials in one day—and everyone can look at it and go away happy. But then you begin to edit. I've men-

Corporations have begun to use both live and tape teleconferencing as a means of communicating with large groups of employees. Here, Playback Associates producer Denny Crimmins directs three senior corporate managers in a videotaped discussion.

tioned that editing today is not what it used to be. Razor blades are used only for shaving. All editing is now done electronically on sophisticated machines. By the touch of a wand, the edit is made. But editing is expensive, terribly expensive. You have saved all that money by shooting in one day—and you can easily spend as much as $15,000 to edit the spot! This has been done, and even that figure is conservative. Some agency producers have gone running back to film after just such experiences.

Cheaper? Not if you haul a fifteen-person crew to Kenya and Greece, as a recent network producer did. (Though in all fairness, part of his crew costs could be attributed to a decision to take drivers, interpreters, and spouses as well as the tape technicians.) The same job could have been done by a three-person documentary film crew at much less cost. In addition, the original investment for a tape operation can run from ten to one hundred times the cost of basic film equipment, though this is generally brushed aside by the tape industry by explaining that you can use the tape stock over and over again. But the cost of the tape *stock* is an infinitesimal part of the investment. Tape got its reputation as a more economical medium during the days when the lights were turned on, never adjusted, and the narrator or host was put in front of a gray cyclorama and told to speak. You could shoot twenty commercials in one day—and, of course, they were budgeted at very low costs. But, if you bring in people who care, if you use a director who demands quality, a lighting person who takes time, a crew that wants each shot to be perfect, then the costs mount and tape today may not be the more economical medium. Again, you have to make the right choice.

It all boils down to two major problems: The *thinking* in each medium is different and the "hardware" in tape keeps changing so that many of the systems are not compatible with other systems. Even in home video, VHS cannot be used with BETA, and Kodak cannot be used with either one. In addition, film producers find difficulty in making production and editing decisions all in the same day. There is an initial discomfort with the ambience, with the complex editing systems, with the computerized commands and thinking. At the beginning, a whole new world has to be learned. But, as I look at the growth of video tape, I find that most of my film friends are working successfully in *both*.

In professional video tape, masters are generally made with one inch tape stock to assure top quality.

One of our favorite film people was asked to work as a video cameraman on a production out in California. The director had seen his film work and was duly impressed with his ability to pick out shots, to find unusual angles and good coverage at an event. The cameraman felt flattered—it was his breakthrough in the videotape field. He states:

Well, we started and I was camera number one and they had a two and a three. A technician came out and began balancing the camera with the color charts and we started. I immediately began to do what I do when I'm shooting film—looking around for what might make a good close-up or an interesting shot—and suddenly over the headsets I hear this voice out of nowhere yelling at me, "Camera number one, get a medium of the nurse." Here I was, trying to help out and this disembodied voice, a comparative stranger, is in a truck yelling at me—"zoom in, zoom out, pan up, number three get a two shot, tighter, looser, pan down." Well, when it was all over after three days of this, I went up to the director and said, "Thanks, I appreciate your introduction into the videotape field, but I think I'm over-qualified."

If anyone is thinking about getting into videotape after doing film work, he's going to have to expect this, because that's what it's all about. Videotape is becoming a very mechanical process and I look for the time that they won't even need cameramen out there on the floor. They'll use robot cameras and they'll do everything from the booth! !

The fields just grew differently, and when you work in videotape after many years in film, the differences are magnified. My own background was in live television, then film. But I know what our cameraman meant. After five years in film production, and the redevelopment of my pacing in producing a show—from the tension and quick decisions of the control room to the more deliberate movement of taking a film from beginning to end—I was asked to direct several dramatic shows on videotape for PBS. The experience drove me back to the film business again.

It was the difference in *thinking* that counted. The television mind versus the film mind; the need to produce and get on to the next job versus the feeling that something could be thought through and worked on. My five years in film created the problem of my wanting to do an entire act over again because I thought I could do it better the next time, while the TV producer kept insisting, "You've got it. Go on to Act Two." I was never very happy with the results, but this too might be different today. I just don't know. My orientation is film and it will probably stay that way.

But the tape field is going to grow in spite of me and in spite of my cameraman friend. It is growing, and not just in the realm of the commercial and the television show. It is a remarkable tool for training, and educational groups and corporations have begun to use it as a part of their programs.

Out in the world—the one that is not concerned with "show business"—tape has been used along with film for sales training, technical training, customer education, and for teleconferencing. Companies have found that the latter use of live television combined with tape has grown *not* because it especially saves travel time to a conference point, but because they can now include *more* people in their seminars and meetings, all of them in different cities across the country. Once participants become comfortable with the studio setup, usually with well-hidden cameras, the meetings flow easily and effectively. The Atlantic Richfield Company, for example, has a large and sophisticated internal network. Equitable Life Assurance Company, Sears Roebuck, Datsun, and Xerox are other companies with networks of their own. Certainly, these are expensive to set up and to operate, but over the years they pay for themselves in allowing distant communications with the entire organization. Some of them produce their own sales-training vehicles, some have regular executive conferences both live and on tape, some produce their own customer-information cassettes for distribution to dealerships. It's an effective way to sell and it works in getting product information to the consumer.

Producer Web Golinkin (right) and director Don Goodwin (center), of Playback Associates, supervise a corporate videotaping session on location.

The job market in tape includes everything that was once confined to the film field: television, independent production companies, and in-house corporate production. The latter often use free-lance writers and designers. And, as more and more commercial spots are made on tape, the job opportunities will open in that area, too.

Entry categories in tape are very much the same as in film, with the addition of many more technical jobs. Thus, a background in electronics can help, and training in both television and film production can also be an asset. The production jobs are essentially alike in both crafts and many small companies use the same people for their tape operations and their film production.

Whether I prefer tape or film is not important. What is really happening to the audiovisual field is all that is going to matter to those of you who are thinking of entering the industry. Tape is growing. It is continuing to grow at an incredible rate, so it is not to our advantage to debate the issue of film versus tape. Both have their advantages, both are here and both are going to stay. If you are in the wave of the future, then *you* are going to have to become familiar with the advantages and the disadvantages of both mediums. You will have to be well versed in tape and in film, for they have stopped growing separately and have begun to blend. It is no longer a matter of film *versus* tape. You'll just have to begin thinking of film *and* tape.

(Left) While still a student at the University of Wisconsin, Michael Camerini produced several films about India. (Right) He is now a successful producer/cameraman and president of his own company. He is shown on location in Arkansas with Soundman James MacDonald and a local newspaper reporter, for the film Good Crop, funded by the National Endowment for the Humanities.

CHAPTER 17

SCHOOLS AND TRAINING PROGRAMS

Breaching the Ivory Tower

The marvelous thing about absolutes is that there aren't any. For years I had been saying that if I had a choice, I would rather hire someone with one year of industry experience than a graduate of film school with a degree in communications. This was an absolute. I had no doubt in my mind that I was right—and just like never ending a film with a sunset or an American flag, I broke the absolute into a thousand shattered fragments of good intent. One of the most talented people with whom I have ever worked is Jon Fauer and he came to our company right out of school—Dartmouth, to be exact. Now, Dartmouth was not a school known for its film courses and I had no job opening at the time.*

It occurred to me, however, that we were in desperate need of some research. At the time, we were competing against six companies for a large-budget television special and I thought that a college-trained researcher would know just where to go to find the information we needed in order to complete the treatment proposal. He went to work—at a minimal fee—and in a few days came up with some of the most original ideas I had seen. The treatment was written, based totally upon his research, and we won the job, eventually entitled *Celebration* and starring Lorne Greene.

Once he had proven to us that he could be valuable, Jon was gently eased into production, finally put on staff, and in six years he went all the way through production management to assistant cameraman to full cameraman (with a union card, no less). His current role is that of cameraman on a range of film projects including features, documentaries and commercials. And all of it began with just a few days research. So much for my theory about not hiring people directly from film schools!

It is important to understand, however, that a graduate of a school, holding a degree in communications, is not necessarily equipped or ready for a career in film. Much is dependent upon just what the school emphasizes in its curriculum, how much practical work is involved in the four years, and the caliber of instruction. Thus, it is no accident, I feel, that the new generation of filmmakers who have come out of film school to careers in the feature field, have generally been trained at the best of the "working" film schools such as USC and NYU.

And with the emergence of that group has come a change in the attitude toward film school grads. At first it was the Californians—Coppola, Spielberg, Lucas, along with Martin Scorcese from New York. But suddenly, in the eighties, the East Coast made itself felt, with a young and talented group who had all graduated from New York University at some point in their careers: Joel Coen (*Blood Simple*), Susan Seidelman (*Smithereens* and *Desperately Seeking Susan*), Amy Heckerling (also from AFI with *Fast Times at Ridgemont High* and *Johnny Dangerously*), and Jim Jarmusch (*Stranger Than Paradise*).

And it has happened not only in the field of feature films. Students to whom I lectured in graduate and continuing education courses, have also begun to surface as real-honest-to-goodness professional filmmakers. While writing this chapter, in fact, I received a call from a man I'd met while speaking to a Directing class at NYU. He was the oldest in the class by far, in his mid-thirties at the time. In a few short years, he has organized and established his own very successful commercials production company in New York, Parineu Productions, and Michael Zellen is now a professional filmmaker, and a good one at that.

The greatest problem, however, is that too many film schools are graduating people who are not prepared for the world of the professional, for the job hunt, and for the day to day problems of making films and *making a living* at the craft. There are far too many philosophy and history of film courses and not enough of the pragmatics of production. To some extent, the problem is being mitigated by an effort in some schools to strengthen the faculty with active filmmakers: producers, directors, writers, and production people who can bring to their courses a practical viewpoint of the industry. Another development has been the return to the campuses of filmmakers and experienced film teachers, some of whom are working on advanced degrees and others who simply want to catch up in a field that is constantly changing and growing.

As always, even though it is sometimes not too evident, the people in the industry itself are trying to work with the universities. Through programs supported by American Film Institute, professionals in the field have given seminars around the country on the subjects of writing, production, acting, television, cable, and advertising. In addition, working filmmakers have always conducted workshops and seminars as well as offering their services as guest lecturers

*Though a list of Dartmouth film alumni would make any school proud: Budd Schulberg, Joseph Losey, Bob Rafelson, Buck Henry, Walter Bernstein. Merely proving again the last sentence in this chapter.

in communications schools. All of this helps, of course, in bringing a touch of reality to the isolation of "book learning."

But let's speak now about how good the schools are and what you can get out of them. I address myself to you as two basic groups: (1) those who are already enrolled in a school, and (2) those who have not yet chosen a school. The first group of you is the easiest to advise, for you are already there. Your school's curriculum was known to you, to a great extent, when you made your choice. Even if you are already on your way to a degree in filmmaking, though, there are some other things you might want to consider.

The best thing you can do, now that you are enrolled in communications or film techniques or film production or video tape production is to make a good film or tape sample—a really good one that can be shown when you get out. If you can make the entire film yourself, so much the better. It's obvious that working only as a production assistant on a film sample is a difficult way to show just what it is you'd like to do—or can do. If, on the other hand, you can produce a complete film or tape project—work on it and make it yours—you'll be that much further ahead when you call later for an appointment.

Several years back, when the first edition of this book was in the final rewrite stages, I was visited by a young filmmaker by the name of Michael Camerini. He showed me one of his sample films, produced while he was in college. It was superb, but furthermore, the subject was awe inspiring. He had actually gone to India for his film project and the resultant sample was one of the best I'd seen in some years. The college had a "Junior Year Abroad Program" so Michael borrowed a Bell & Howell, found five thousand feet of black and white negative, borrowed $3,000, and made a first film: an impressionistic study of a city, entitled *Benares*.

After the project was completed, he wrote and printed a flyer about the film, sending it to every college and university that had a department of religion, anthropology, or Indian Studies. Eventually, the film was shown in over two hundred colleges and universities, some of them renting a print from Camerini each and every semester. It didn't make him rich, but it paid his back debts and gave him enough of a sample to get the funding for another series of films in India. But it was also a start for his eventual career, for he is now an established producer as well as a director/cameraman with his own company (World View Films). He is also active in the fields of the documentary and the business film, and is currently working on his first independent feature.

More recently, while lecturing at a tape seminar at The Global Village in New York, the very same thing happened. A young woman named Sally Simmons showed me her sample tape, a documentary about a shadowy New York character who spent his nights painting black figures on empty walls, leaving them for the morning crowds to wonder who was doing it and why. She and her crew found him, though no one in the city had been able to uncover his identity before, and they got him to agree to being taped. I was so impressed that a few weeks later I hired Sally to work for me on a new tape project that we were beginning for one of our large clients.

From the story that began the chapter right to this point, I suppose I am saying as often as I can that the real world is not interested in seminars in film history or film as art. You are much better off spending four years in school working on a good sample. If you graduate with honors but come out telling me that you "didn't have time" to make one during those years, is it any wonder that for so many years I felt that I would rather hire someone with one year as a gopher than any film student just out of college—especially someone without a sample. Jon Fauer, Michael Camerini, Sally Simmons, all of whom were hired by me at some point early in their careers, all had superb samples of their work. They could have made them in Boy Scout or Girl Scout Camp for all I cared. They were beautiful and effective and very professional.

Certainly, *in their place*, college courses like those I've mentioned are valuable, exciting, provocative, informative—and really quite necessary if you want a well-rounded film education. I am only saying that we eventually come back to the student. What are *you* willing to do to show that education worked for you, when you go out to get a job?

And so, my lecture completed, you will begin to work on that film sample that we will screen together when you come up to see me one blustery winter's day; it will be a pleasure to sit in the warm, dark screening room anticipating that a genius will be there beside me, reflecting an as yet undiscovered talent up there on the screen. And sometimes this happens! The cold of the winter manages to disappear for the rest of the day.

Now, what about that second group of you, who are just starting out. What school do you choose?

There are almost a thousand schools teaching film and TV (with only about one quarter of them offering film-related degrees, however). Currently there are almost fifty thousand students pursuing those degrees with more than twice that number enrolled in various other communications curricula such as Continuing Education and technical courses, all with an eye toward an eventual job in the field.

The best book for learning about such schools is *American Film Institute Guide to College Courses in Film and Television*, (7th Edition, 1980. Peterson's Guides, P.O. Box 2123, Princeton, N.J. 08540). The price is now about $11 plus postage, but it's a worthwhile investment if you're looking for a school. About eight hundred schools are listed in the book, each one with an outline of the courses, the thrust of the curriculum, and the faculty. (See a sample of the listings on pp. 134-36.)

What school should you be looking for? After all, out of eight hundred entries, even if you eliminate the smaller schools and film cooperatives, the choice is difficult. Although many factors may affect your choice (not the least of them personal ones such as tuition costs, geography, travel home during vacations, or having an old chum or lover who is now attending a college in Lower Seepage nearby), you will have to consider at least three important areas:

THE SCHOOL'S COMMITMENT TO FILM OR TAPE. The attitude of the school is of primary importance. If the feeling is that film is just another course they have to offer (like driver education), then it may not be the place for you. Some schools are committed to the *philosophy* of film rather than to the practical *application of techniques* or *production*. Some of the most valuable pieces of information given in the guide I've suggested are the "Area Ranking in Films" and "Emphasis on Filmmaking" data. Where film production or film history is first in emphasis, you might well investigate the school more thoroughly, if film production is your eventual goal. On the other hand, if film history and criticism are listed *without* film production, read the balance of the curriculum more carefully. Of course, film history may well be your major interest, but it might not help you get a job in the industry if it stands alone without the support of courses in practical filmmaking.

THE SCHOOL'S EQUIPMENT. You can't compete in the film or tape field if your experience has consisted solely of making films with a Cine-Special or an 8mm Canon Scoopic, or if your tape experience is limited to a home-video VHS or Beta setup. The real world uses Arriflexes and Mitchells and Panavision and Eclairs and Ikegamis and sophisticated tape decks and editing equipment. Our sound equipment is not the Sony recorder you use at home—you'll have to know about the Nagra and the microphones that go with it. Some schools list fairly impressive production courses, but the equipment lists contain only 8mm cameras or—even worse—no equipment at all.

If the commitment is there and the attitude seems to be one that insists film will be taught properly, then the school *must* also commit itself to the purchase of equipment to do the job properly! The best of universities and colleges have a full complement of the latest cameras, sound equipment, editing equipment (including the most modern flatbed models), projectors, lighting equipment, and even some studio space. Of course, this takes money, but if they can equip the football team, they can provide the tools for their film students.

THE FACULTY. It is not necessarily true that only working film people can teach well. Some superb craftspeople are inarticulate when it comes to communicating ideas (look at some directors!); others can work well with their hands (such as editors) in a darkened, lonely room and yet be unable to tell anyone what it is they're doing. On the other hand, the schools that can command the services of active filmmakers will generally provide a more realistic view of the industry.

The universities that are in the most important film areas, geographically, can draw easily upon experienced film talent for their faculties. It is no accident that the University of Southern California and New York University can draw upon a faculty that includes some of the most important names in film and television, or that even in a course such as Richard Brown's *Filmmakers on Filmmaking* at New York's New School, such names as Richard Attenborough, Dustin Hoffman, Robert Duvall, Warren Beatty, and Ellen Burstyn appear with regularity. Of course, USC and NYU have evolved the best reputations among the film schools, for many of their students have gone on to greener pastures. But remember too, that enrollment in film schools is so large that many graduates have also disappeared from view and have never been heard from again! Again, don't be swayed by Hollywood and New York. There are other places where people go to school, where they work and where they thrive in the film business.

The University of Pennsylvania and Temple University have developed fine film programs, as have the University of Michigan, Syracuse University, and Ohio State. You will also find film schools overseas, some of them equal to or surpassing the instruction given here at our own universities. Some years ago, we worked with the London School of Film Technique and I remember going to Shelton Street the very first time. British taxi drivers fortunately know their way around London, and we soon drew up in front of the seediest little building in the tiniest

alley in the city. I climbed four flights of rickety stairs and came upon a gold mine of talented young people, all of whom were in love with film. One of the most marvelous afternoons I've ever spent was in their creaky screening room, sitting on a hard-backed chair for three hours and watching student work. The physical "campus" doesn't really matter much, after all.

But film does not exist in a vacuum. It lives in a real world filled with other, completely different skills and crafts. The good filmmaker is a vital part of that world, as the world itself is reflected in his or her visual statements. The school you choose must offer more than film production or the history of cinema. It is up to you to take advantage of more of the school's facilities than merely the twenty-seven Arriflex cameras in the supply room. In giving advice to would-be directors, Elia Kazan suggested that they become knowledgeable in theater, opera, music, sculpture, the history of art, costuming, lighting, color, and camera, as well as literature, aesthetics, philosophy, psychology, economics, sociology, and audience research.

Professor Robert Wagner of Ohio State goes even further in stating, "More will be required of the film student in the future. If experienced teachers and some expert filmmakers are to be believed, students of cinema will have to be superstars." So, on the one hand, film students today are becoming specialists in fields other than the profession of the cinema. And, on the other hand, those students who major in non-film fields as diverse as sociology, agriculture, law, and nursing are also studying visual communications for eventual use in their careers.

I have mentioned before that, from time to time, programs of study other than those in schools and

School provides an opportunity for the film student to produce, direct, or edit a personal film sample. Later on, after graduation, that sample can mean an open door to the job interview.

colleges open up in the field, sometimes supported by unions such as Directors Guild of America, and sometimes sponsored by foundations or organizations dedicated to film as art and a career. For many graduates, these programs are a way to encounter the practical aspects of filmmaking under the guidance of working professionals. For example, the American Film Institute offers several programs at their marvelous campus on the West Coast. Though the competition is keen (and where is it not?) and there is certainly no guarantee that you will end up with a mansion in Beverly Hills after graduation as a top-flight director, you might still want to write for information to: American Film Institute, 2021 North Western Avenue, Los Angeles, CA 90027. Tel: 213-856-7600. Here is just a brief outline of their programs:

- Center for Advanced Film Studies. A one year Curriculum Program in the art of filmmaking. This is open to filmmakers who have already attained some degree of proficiency in the craft. However, applicants in related fields such as theater, literature, music and photography, as well as the fine arts, will also be considered. The program covers screenwriting, directing, cinematography, production, and production design.
- A Conservatory Program. A second year of training, open only to those who have completed the Curriculum Program.
- Directing Workshop for Women. Open only to professional women who are experienced in some facet of filmmaking. The thrust of the course is basically to open opportunities to women in the field of the feature and television.
- Seminars and Workshops. These are held in many cities across the country, and though the program has been severely cut back in recent years because of the drying up of funding, you can keep up with the schedule in AFI's magazine, *American Film*.

You might also make note that the American Film Institute, just like the rest of us out there in that other world, will require some example of your work: film, tape, script—whatever best shows your talent in the field. Incidentally, another program that I've also mentioned in the chapter on directing, the AFI Academy Internship Program—supported by the Academy of Motion Picture Arts & Sciences—also requires an example of your work. It provides an opportunity for a limited number of promising new filmmakers to learn by observing established directors at work during the production of a film. In addition to *two* film samples, the most provocative question on the application is: "Note six directors you would like to intern with and your reasons for choosing each."

Of course, the one question uppermost in your mind after all of this is: "Will it help me find a job?" Begging the question just for a moment, let me quote from an introduction to an early edition of AFI's *Guide to College Courses in Film and Television*. It was written by professor George Stoney of New York University and, at least, it approaches the problem honestly and directly:

"While a surprising number of film school graduates find work in some branches of the industry, only a handful have hit the big time either in theatrical films or TV. Most work in some phase of non-theatrical production...or around a local TV station. Overall, their pay is not good, compared with the income received by their classmates who went into business administration or computer science. In general, their job security is non-existent. Worst of all, they are not doing what they had their hearts set on when they first decided to major in films."

A young graduate recently wrote me an effective letter; he had a good resume attached, several film samples produced at Ohio State, and an urge to get into the business. It was late, the office empty, I was fairly tired, and I thought it might be nice to telephone him and speak of making an appointment at some future date. I called—and got his mother on the telephone; the young man was not at home. Nevertheless, I passed on my feelings about how talented I thought her son was and, rather than getting a parental glow in return, I found the women quite depressed. Yes, of course, her son was talented—certainly her son spoke glowingly of the excitement of film, the people he'd met, the dynamism of the industry. Then why, I asked, did she seem so depressed? "Well," she answered, "I wanted him to be a doctor!"

For those who want to work in film, the pay will not seem too important at first. And for those who are going to school and reflecting upon the competition of fifty thousand students who will be getting degrees and then go pouring out into the film world in a deluge, there will somehow be a way to do it. The feature field is not the end-all of the business; many of us are working in those "other areas" and getting well paid for it, traveling around the world to any place we want to go, and meeting the most exciting people who live on this volatile planet. School and training are but a first step. And along with all the Latin inscriptions on your university seal, put down the words my grandmother used to say:

"You get out of it what you put into it!"

NEW YORK UNIVERSITY

Graduate Institute of Film-TV, 40 E. Seventh St., New York City, 10003, (212) 598-2416. Contact: Mel Howard, Chairman.

Degree Offered: M.F.A. in Film.

Film Majors: 120 graduates.

Scholarships: Approximately $19,450 per year is distributed in scholarships among nine students plus Martin Luther King grants. Five student assistantships are also available (tuition remission and stipends of $1800 each).

Distinctive Programs: A film major may complete a film project in lieu of a thesis.

Department Chairman: Mel Howard. **Full Time Faculty:** Beda Batka, Eleanor Hamerow, Roberta Hodes, Mel Howard, Ian Maitland. **Part Time Faculty:** Arthur Freed, Milton Moses Ginsberg, George Griffin, Marketa Kimbrell, Saul Levitt, Jim McBride, Lee Minoff, Frank Perry, David Sovel, Andrew Ferguson.

Summary: "The school is production-oriented. Our academic calendar is divided into segments of approximately seven weeks of class study and seven weeks devoted to production. All students are expected to write, direct, produce, and edit 16mm or 35mm films. The major learning experience occurs through production and faculty responses to student films."

Area Ranking in Films: 1-film production. **Emphasis in Filmmaking:** 1-documentary, dramatic fiction; 2-experimental, animation.

Course Titles:

Production Workshop I & II (G)
Beginning Camera (G)
The Movies as Medium I & II (G)
Writing for Visual Medium I & II (G)
Acting for Filmmakers (G)
Directing for Filmmakers (G)
Television Production (G)
Beginners Still Photography Workshop (G)
Advanced Still Photography Workshop (G)
Color Camera I & II (G)
Motion Picture Camera Technology I & II (G)
Film Editing I & II (G)

Course Titles:

Film Editing III & IV (G)
Motion Picture Production Techniques, Methods, and Organization I & II (G)
Motion Picture Production Techniques, Methods, and Organization III & IV (G)
Directors Seminar (G)
Production Crews I & II (G)
Production Crews III & IV (G)
Writing for Film I & II (G)
Script Analysis Seminar I & II (G)
Practicum in Film Directing (G)
Film Production Seminar I & II (G)

Film Equipment: (9) 16mm cameras; (4) 35mm cameras; Super-8 camera; 35mm still camera; (3) still cameras with a variety of lenses; wide range of lenses; (5) slide projectors; wide range of meters; tripods; (8) portable recorders; large number of microphones; wide variety of lights; (6) 16mm projectors; Super-8 projector; (2) 35mm projectors; etc. **Facilities:** sound studio; mixing room; editing rooms; photography laboratory; sound transfer facilities; TV studio; 35mm screening theater seats 80.

NEW YORK UNIVERSITY

School of Continuing Education, Division of Liberal Studies, Room 21, 2 University Place, New York City, 10003.
Contact: Raymond P. Zelazny, Director.

Summary: "We offer students a thorough foundation in basic and current techniques and practices of film production. The student is given the opportunity to demonstrate progress through varied independent and group productions. Production emphasis is complemented by lecture-discussion courses which students may elect to further develop deeper appreciation and awareness of the historical, aesthetic, and experimental aspects of film. Students study for non-credit or certificates in the Division of Liberal Studies. These non-credit courses are offered part-time in the evening and full-time in the summer. Admission into the program is at various levels, depending upon the student's previous training in film." **Course Titles:** Introduction to Film Production, Film Production I & II, Film Editing, Sound for Film, Animation, Writing for Film & TV, Advanced Writing for Film & TV, Radio & TV News Writing, Writing Commercials for Radio/TV, The Musical Film, Video Tape Workshops: Basic & Studio, The Filmmakers, The Documentary Film. Two full time Film Production Workshops are offered. Each provides an intensive, comprehensive program which includes over 100 hours of lecture-discussion, plus more than 100 additional hours of independent field and cutting room experiences. For further information, contact Raymond P. Zelanzny, Director.
For further information, contact Raymond P. Zelazny, Director.

NEW YORK UNIVERSITY

Undergraduate Institute of Film & Television, 51 West 4th St., New York City, 10003, (212) 598-3703.
Contact: Haig P. Manoogian (film), Irving Falk (TV).

Degrees Offered: B.F.A. in Film; B.F.A. in Television.

Film Majors: 350 undergraduates. **TV Majors:** 200 undergraduates.

Distinctive Programs: We offer a comprehensive film and television production program. Students have the opportunity to intern in media positions at New York television and radio stations.

Department Chairman: Haig P. Manoogian. **Full Time Faculty:** Haig Manoogian, George Stoney, Irving Falk, Richard J. Goggin, Peter Glushanok, Jaqueline Park, Mark Chernichaw, Charles Milne, Thomas Drysdale, Barry Sherman, Nicholas Tanis. **Part Time Faculty:** Raymond Broussard, Ms. Red Burns, Patricia Cooper, William Etra, Kenneth Fishman, Andrew Ferguson, William Godsey, Murray Gross, Venable Herndon, Chester Higgins, Jr., Marketta Kimbrell, Daniel Kleinman, James Lardner, James Manilla, Andrew Mann, Phillip Messina, Tad Mosel, Vincent Novak, Eli Noyes, Lee Osborne, Robert Pinto, Irving Oshman, Paul Owen, Bruce Rasmussen, Marcia Resnick, Flora Roberts, Charlie Russell, Lawrence Silk, Dadiv Sobel, Thomas Zafian.

Summary: "The film and television curriculum is structured, and the courses are designed to provide the student with a variety of creative experiences in both the conceptual and production phases and with the technical skills for bringing these concepts to the audience. An extensive critical and historical frame of reference, an understanding of the relationship between society and the visual and sound media, and a personal philosophy that embraces

Excerpt from the American Film Institute's Guide to College Courses in Film and Television. The guide is now published by Peterson's Guides (7th Edition, 1980. P.O. Box 2123, Princeton, NJ 08540). There are nearly a thousand schools now teaching film or tape as part of their curriculum.

the potential of these media as a means of expressing and communicating a wide range of human experiences are considered important aspects of this program."

Area Ranking In Film: 1-film production; 2-writing; 3-film history/criticism. **Emphasis In Filmmaking:** 1-documentary, dramatic fiction, experimental; 2-animation. **Area Ranking In TV:** 1-television production; 2-broadcast history; 3-writing. **Emphasis In TV Production:** 1-studio production; 2-exterior production, experimental.

Course Titles:

History of Broadcasting I & II (U)
Film History (U)
Broadcasting, CATV & New Technology (U)
Programs & Program Building (U)
Mass Media & Contemporary Civilization (U)
Community Information Systems (U)
Aesthetics of the Film (U)
Contemporary Cinema (U)
Advertising, Audiences, Marketing (U)
Broadcast & CATV Programming (U)
Aesthetics Principles & Problems in Broadcasting (U)
Station Management (U)
Film Industry: Changing Picture (U)
Introduction to Half-Inch Video (U)
Production Techniques to Half-Inch Video (U)
Nonverbal Communication (U)
Motion, Matter, & Meaning (U)
Language of Sight & Sound (U)
Beginning TV: Production-Direction (U)
Cable TV & the Community (U)
The Actor's Craft (U)
Camera Technology (U)
Editing Technology (U)
Electronics Technology (U)
Portable Half-Inch Video Workshop (U)
Media Internship (U)
Intermediate Still Photography (U)
Advanced Still Photography (U)

Course Titles:

Documentary Workshop (U)
Animation Workshop (U)
Narrative Workshop (U)
Experimental Workshop (U)
Senior Production Workshop & Seminar (U)
Sound: Recording Methods & Techniques (U)
Music for Film & TV (U)
Motion Picture Editing (U)
Cinematography (U)
Lighting: Motion Pictures & TV (U)
Creative Sound Workshop (U)
Directorial Problems (U)
Experimental Video Workshop (U)
Television Producing & Directing Workshop (U)
University Broadcast Lab (U)
Producing for Film (U)
Producing for Broadcasting, CATV, & Cassettes (U)
Introduction to Dramatic & Visual Writing (U)
Screenplay Structure (U)
Script Clinic (U)
Seminar in Writing Problems (U)
Advanced Writing Seminar (U)
Independent Study (U)

Film Equipment: (32) 16mm cameras; (7) synchronous recorders; wide assortment of mikes & accessories; completely equipped experimental sound laboratory; lighting equipment; (12) Moviolas, etc. **TV equipment:** (2) completely equipped TV studios. **Facilities:** (22) complete editing stations; (2) screen rooms; sound transfer facility; recording studio; (2) TV control rooms; sound laboratory; animation studio; sound shooting stage; 16mm film library.

UNIVERSITY OF SOUTHERN CALIFORNIA

Division of Cinema (film), School of Journalism (TV), University Park, 90007, (213) 746-2235 (Cinema), 746-2166 (Journalism).
Contact: Bernard R. Kantor, Chairman, Division of Cinema; Joe Saltzman, Head of Telecommunications Sequence, School of Journalism.

Degrees Offered: B.A., M.A., M.F.A., Ph.D. in Film; M.S. in Film Education; B.A., M.A. in Journalism with an emphasis in radio-television.

Film Majors: 200 undergraduates, 250 graduates. **Journalism Majors:** 200 undergraduates emphasizing television.

Scholarships and/or Assistantships: 14 assistantships available to cinema majors who have been at USC one full semester (free tuition & $3000); 5 Cinema Circulus Scholarships ($3000 each); George Cukor Scholarship ($2000); William Morris Scholarship ($1000); CBS Foundation Scholarships ($100 awarded by the faculty on the basis of need and talent).

Department Chairmen: Bernard R. Kantor, Cinema; Joe Saltzman, Journalism. **Full Time Faculty:** William H. Allen, Irwin R. Blacker, Joseph Casper, Gene Coe, Herbert E. Farmer, Trevor Greenwood, Richard Harber, David W. Johnson, Bernard Kantor, Edward Kaufman, Robert Kaufman, Arthur Knight, E. Russell McGregor, K. Kenneth Miura, Eugene Petersen, William Sabador, Melvin Sloan, John R. Taylor, Wolfram von Hanwehr, Daniel Wiegand, Frank Withofp, Morton Zarcoff, Joe Saltzman, Don Smith, Edward Borgers, Ernie Kreiling. **Part Time Faculty:** Marty Blake, Charles Bloch, Paul Boris, Robert Churchill, Jarvis Couillard, Lin Dunn, Robert Ebinger, Blake Edwards, Ken Evans, Nuri Ertuck, William Froug, Jack Garfein, Sheridan Gibney, Bernard Gruver, Ross Hunter, Stephen Karpf, Joan Keller, Anne Kramer, Don Kranze, Russ Leadabrand, Sol Lesser, Jerry Lewis, Leonard Lipton, Stephen Longstreet, Jack Mahoney, Michael Ludmer, Jerry McGuire, Marc Mancini, Arthur L. Mayer, Margaret Mehring, Bill Melendez, John Milius, Eric Morris, Edward Mosk, Art Murphy, Lester Movros, Sherwood Omens, Mike Rachmil, Ken Robinson, Leon Roth, John Schultheiss, Richard Smith, Ralph Sogge, Sidney P. Solow, Leonard Spigelgas, Norman Taurog, William Tuttle, King Vidor, Malvin Wald, Bernard Weitzman.

Summary: "We hope to educate the film artist who will fulfill the traditional role of the artist in society, using his art not only to reflect but to improve, for social change. Our approach is professional in the best sense. We equally offer emphasis in history/criticism or production in film. The goals of our options in the telecommunications sequence, broadcast management and broadcast journalism, are to produce a graduate who has the skills necessary to produce and write various kinds of public affairs programs, and who has the appreciation and background in the world of television. We stress creative concepts."

Area Ranking In Film: 1—film history/criticism; 2—film production; 3—electronic. **Emphasis In Filmmaking:** no emphasis. **Area Ranking In TV:** 1—television production, professional skills; 2—broadcast history; 3—educational media. **Emphasis In TV Production:** 1—exterior production, news-documentary; 2—studio production, experimental, educational.

Course Titles:

Freshman Seminar in Film & Writing (U)

Course Titles:

Motion Picture Sound Recording (U)

Introduction to Film (U)
Techniques in Motion Picture Production (U)
Fundamentals of Film (U)
Visual Communication (U)
History of the American Film (U)
Language of Film (U)
Filmwriting (U)
Photographic Communication (U)
Image of the Film (U)
Motion Picture Camera (U)
Motion Picture Editing (U)
Writing the Short Script I (U-G)
Advanced Writing (U-G)
Motion Picture Script Analysis (U-G)
Photojournalism (U-G)
Make-up for Motion Pictures (U-G)
Advanced Photographic Communication (U-G)
Advanced Camera and Lighting (U-G)
Production Planning (U-G)
Photography in Scientific Research (U-G)
Photo Instrumentation Research Problems (U-G)
Motion Picture Processing (U-G)
Animation Camera (U-G)
Introduction to Film Graphics-Animation (U-G)
Advanced Production in Film Graphics (U-G)
Animation Theory and Techniques (U-G)
Art Direction (U-G)
Film Business Procedures and Distribution (U-G)
Film Genres (U-G)
Informational Film Symposium (U-G)
Theatrical Film Symposium (U-G)
The New Filmmakers (U-G)
Film Style Analysis I (U-G)
Directing of Informational Motion Pictures (U-G)
Basic Film Theories (U-G)
Ethnographic Film Production (U-G)
Practicum in Pre-Production I (U-G)
Production Workshop I (U-G)
Cinema Workshop (U-G)
Production Workshop II (U-G)
Special Problems (U-G)
Senior Film Seminar (U-G)
Film Directing (U)
Colloquium: Motion Picture Production Techniques (U)
Art and Industry of the Theatrical Film (U)
Documentary Film (U-G)
Film History and Criticism (U-G)
Literature of the Film (U-G)
Filmic Expression (U-G)
Censorship in Cinema (U-G)
Analysis of Contemporary Cinema (U-G)
Studies in Film (U-G)
Photojournalism (G)
Practicum in Makeup (G)
Seminar in Production Planning (G)
Seminar in Camera (G)
Seminar in the Film (G)
Special Effects in Cinema (G)
Development of Prototype Materials (G)
Seminar in Film Editing (G)
Practicum in Sound (G)
Seminar in Motion Picture Engineering (G)
Animation Camera Workshop (G)
Studies in Film Graphics-Animation (G)
Advanced Studies in Film Graphics (G)
Seminar in Film Graphics (G)
History of Film Graphics (G)
Production Design (G)
Seminar in Motion Picture Distribution, Budgeting and Management (G)
Publicity in the Performing Arts (G)
Seminar in Motion Picture Business (G)
Seminar in Film Genres (G)
Seminar in Film Analysis (G)
Seminar in the Theatrical Film (G)
Film Style Analysis II (G)
Seminar in Film Direction (G)
Practicum in Film Directing (G)
Critical Film Theories (G)
Graduate Production Workshop (G)
Educational Film Workshop (G)
Historiography and Methodology in Film Studies (G)
Graduate Film Seminar (G)
Directed Research (G)
Historical and Critical Research Methods (G)
Seminar in Film Research and Testing (G)
Seminar in Cinema History and Criticism (G)
History of Motion Pictures (G)
History of the Sound Film in America (G)
Seminar in Film Literature (G)
Creative Cinema (G)
Film and the Classroom Teacher (G)
The New Language in Film (G)
Censorship in Cinema (G)
Studies in Film (G)
Seminar in the Documentary Film (G)
Writing the Short Script II (G)
Basic Screen Writing (G)
Practicum in Screenwriting (G)
Advanced Motion Picture Script Analysis (G)
Practicum in Writing the Nonfiction Film (G)
Designing Large Group and Multimedia Presentations (G)
Historical and Critical Research Methods in Communication (G)
Seminar in Instructional Technology (G)
Advanced Programming for Individual Instruction (G)
Basic Principles of Broadcast Production (U-G)
Broadcast Newswriting (U-G)
Broadcast Reporting (U-G)
Principles of Documentary Production (U-G)
Principles of News Special Production (U-G)
Principles of Broadcast News Production (U-G)
Principles of Public Affairs Production (U-G)
Thesis (G)
Special Problems (G)
Introduction to Dramatic Writing (U-G)
Composition for Films and Television (U-G)
Music in Motion Pictures (U-G)
Ethnographic Film Analysis (U-G)
Use of Instructional Media in the Elementary School (U-G)
Process and Theories of Communication (G)
Research and Theory in Instructional Technology (G)
Learning, Perception, and Mass Communication Theory Applied to Mediated Instruction (G)
Direction of Instructional Materials Centers (G)
Evaluation of Instructional Media (G)
Individual Production Study (U-G)
Basic Newswriting/Reporting (U-G)
Basic Copy Editing (U-G)
Telecommunications Regulations (U-G)
Social Responsibility of Broadcasting (U-G)
Reporting Public Affairs (U-G)
Radio-TV Programming (U-G)
Broadcasting & Social Change (U-G)
Public Educational Broadcasting (U-G)
Introduction to Telecommunications (U-G)
Broadcast Censorship/Criticism (U-G)
Radio-TV Advertising (U-G)
Broadcast Management (U-G)
Broadcasting as Art (U-G)
Radio-TV Continuity Writing (U-G)

Film Equipment: very well-equipped for all types of 16mm production, etc. **TV Equipment:** full complement of VTR color cassette equipment; portable units for video tape in the field; fully-equipped TV studio; fully-equipped audio studio; portable studio/van. **Facilities:** editing rooms; mixing rooms; screening rooms; processing lab; TV studio; audio studio; 35mm screening theaters seat: 1700, 350, 150, 90; very large film library comprised of 16mm and 35mm prints.

CHAPTER 18

FILM GRANTS

"Daddy, Can I Have a Hundred Thousand Dollars to Make a Movie?"

Once a young filmmaker called to ask me for an appointment to show me his film. We met early one morning, if I remember correctly, and he showed me his work. It was fair, at best, but it covered the entire country, parts of France, and a bit of Africa. Even the subject escapes me at this late date, but I do remember thinking that it was a lot of film for an independent project and it probably would have cost a client of ours upward of $100,000 if we were even to begin to produce the same film. He left, disappeared into the world outside, and I never saw him again. But a few weeks later I happened to mention the filmmaker to an acquaintance of mine who knew his background, and I finally got the whole story. *His father* had given him the money to make the film. It was a personal grant to his son and was, of course, something that any father would do—if he were a millionaire!

In the world of poor fathers, however, a film grant may be a more reasonable solution, though the problem of getting one can be terribly difficult, especially in these days of government budget-cutting in order to balance an inflated deficit. For the filmmaker who reads that the President wants to slash Federal support in media grants by almost 8 percent, and with those grants ranging in minimal amounts of $500 to $10,000—hardly enough to produce a film—we begin to understand why a great many of us spend *most* of our time just putting enough money together to begin. Some filmmakers, in fact, have spent from three to five years in raising the money, and only one year for total production!

Nevertheless, by learning the world of film grants thoroughly, many filmmakers have learned how to combine grants from government agencies, foundations, corporations, and even from affluent relatives in order to compile a budget that gives them the independence to put their message on film. Certainly, expenses are very much smaller than for professional film companies, and certainly you can produce your film without the costs that professionals face every day: overhead, high wages, expensive hotels, cars, and client entertainment. But, as you go after those first hard-won dollars, remember too that film stock costs you the same as it does us, and even if film equipment can be rented cheaply, laboratory costs are deferred, and you live on the campus common in a sleeping bag—the few thousand will disappear very quickly.

However, the financial grant is an important part of the film business. Some excellent low-budget films have been made on grant monies, with the filmmakers going on to other things as a result of the single sample made with foundation or personal or corporate support (or all of them). If the sample is a good one, it can be a giant step forward.

Two major divisions exist in the field of film grants—and the second one is, unfortunately, seldom thought of:

- Foundations, organizations (including some in the film industry), government—federal, state, and local, private corporations, television stations, festivals, all of whom may offer financing specifically for the production of a film.
- Foundations and organizations who may be involved with a *specific field*, such as archeology, architecture, urban planning, or anthropology, and who might be interested in funding a film on their individual specific subject.

In the first edition of this book, I wrote that financial assistance might also be available from sources other than the normal government and foundation channels, and I suggested that a grant seeker might well look into areas *other* than film by consulting grant programs outside the categories of "motion pictures" or "cinema arts" or "film." Occasionally, in the grant literature and the books on the subject, a film project may be lurking under some other fertile major category: anthropology, education, religion, humanities, special projects, or community arts. In writing of this often ignored potential, I used as an example the fact that an anthropological association might be interested in financing an ethnographic film on the native cultures of Micronesia. Not too long after, I received a letter from a young filmmaker based in Guam, who had taken my example as advice and who searched until he found an expedition on its way to Micronesia that needed a filmmaker to go along—and he got the job!

Under the guidance of Ms. Anne Schlosser, the chief librarian of the American Film Institute, I have looked at a great many of these "hidden" grant potentials. Some time ago, in the National Endowment for the Arts brochure on architecture and the environment, I found just such a case in point. Buried deeply in the specifications, was the little word "film" as a vital part of the grant.

Basically, you have to look and you have to look carefully and deeply into *everything* available on the subject. One of the best overviews on the topic is a section of Leonard Maltin's book, *The*

Whole Film Sourcebook (Universe Books/New American Library, New York, 1983), in which Thomas Zummer outlines the world of film grants. His subjects are fairly complete and they give the new filmmaker a good view of just where the money might be lurking. Thus, his first subject is, rightly, "The Search for Money." The other areas covered well are:

- Government Grants
  Federal Government Programs including the National Endowment for the Humanities, National Endowment for the Arts, The American Film Institute Independent Filmmaker Program (funded by NEA)
- Public Television
- State Arts Agencies
- Regional Arts Agencies
- State Humanities Committees
- Community and Local Sources
- Foundations
- Corporate Grants
- Trade and Service Organizations

In addition, he mentions groups that may give some help in the actual production costs of your film, plus a bibliography of books, catalogues and pamphlets. The book is a good place to begin your search.

Another source of excellent information is the good old public library. Not only can you find the listings for foundations that give grants, but also a great many books on how to write successful foundation proposals and how to fill out their application forms—sometimes no mean feat in itself! In the chapter on the writer in film, I made the point that *all of us*, whether we plan to be the writers of screenplays, or directors or independent filmmakers, *all of us* must practice the craft of writing a proposal or a letter that will convince someone that we are the person for the job or the grant. This is a prime example of just what I'm speaking of. Many times, the cover letter or the explanation of our thinking is more vital to a decision in our favor than the neatest and the best of application forms.

If your public library is fairy large, you might try to locate the catalogues and publications that give grant or foundation information. For example:

- Annual Register of Grant Support
- Foundation News
- Taft Corporation Directory
- Foundation Commentary
- NEA Guide to Programs
- NEH Program Announcement
- NEH Humanities

Ask the librarian for help. In many of them, you'll be able to locate the names of the people to contact, the types of grants offered, the size of those grants, deadlines for entry, and the specifications and prerequisites for applying. In addition, there are some important books in the grants area, many of them available in the research sections of your library:

• *Foundation Grants to Individuals*, 2nd edition, New York, Foundation Center, 1981.

The book covers about 200 foundations, all of whom give grants to individuals. Though grant amounts vary from year to year, the total funding from this group has reached almost $100 million per year.

• *The Foundation Directory*, 8th edition. Published by the Foundation Center, distributed by Columbia University Press, 1981.

This publication will not give much guidance on film grants, per se, but it is quite valuable in the "subject" area and the potential of "hidden" film grants mentioned previously. It contains about 3,000 entries, but does not include government agencies.

• *The Foundation Grants Index*.

Issued annually, it lists over 20,000 actual grants made by foundations in the previous year. By giving the researcher a specific listing of the size of grant, the recipient's name and location, and the grant description, it is an excellent guide to just where the grant money is going.

• *Grants Register*, New York, London: St. James Press.

Also updated every few years, the book includes some 1,300 entries covering organizations in the United States, the United Kingdom, and some developing countries. For the most part, the film grants are not listed separately, though we have been able to find a few scholarships and grants that are supported by large universities. Scan the lists for subject matter rather than outright grants for filmmaking.

There is one more potential goldmine of information in the world of grants: the networking of filmmakers themselves and the attendant publicity that comes with the unveiling of a successful film project. In reading the literature of film, in scanning the reviews of independent film projects that have made it to festival or theatrical release, we constantly find mention of the fact that the filmmaker produced the project with the help of NEH and/or NEA and/or the Jerome Foundation and/or Corporation for Pubic Broadcasting and/or parents, relatives & friends, and/or the local bank or credit card company. Within these stories and from your filmmaker friends who are struggling just the way you are come the tips and the advice that you might well heed in your own quest for funding.

Keep your eyes open. Every once in a while you'll see an item in the local paper or in a flyer for a film festival or in the college periodicals or in trade magazines—and even on the lobby bulletin board of a film school. Send for any and all applications so that you get good practice in filling them out—and be prepared to be quite overwhelmed when they arrive and you have to meet the requirements. You'll have to fill them out with some degree of adroitness and creativity, for others will be competing for the very same scarce dollars.

With some grants, funding will be given only if you can show a guarantee that other sources are available to add to your budget. And, in fact, many filmmakers use the first grant as a psychological wedge with which to get the next grant from another foundation or corporation, or even from their family and friends. However, with other grants, there is a stipulation that you *cannot* receive a grant from two organizations at the same time (AFI and NEA, for example). Some grants are limited to U.S. citizens, others are bound by rules of age and experience, many will accept applications from co-filmmakers, and almost all of them require that you are able to succinctly outline your goals, give a synopsis of your project, and offer some supporting material that shows your capabilities as a filmmaker. A sample of a film or tape may be a must.

On the last subject, I cannot urge you too strongly to make a personal film sample while you are studying the craft of film. During the four years at school—or in the time that you are taking technical training, utilize the facilities and the equipment and the friends in order to make even a short sample of your work, be it in animation, computer graphics, or documentary film. It is a subject, in fact, that you will come across again and I discuss the job hunt later on in this book. It may well be your entry not only into the world of the film grant, but also a key to making your mark in your first job interview.

There is one other area that you will probably have to show some understanding of in applying for film grants: production know-how. You will have to offer a budget, indicate how much you will spend on production, stock, equipment rental, lighting, lab and processing, post-production, rights and releases, and the treacherous area of contingencies.

For those of you who are making your career in the world of video tape, the story is pretty much the same, and there has been a slight increase in the grant potential for this growing area of communications. I note, for example, that the American Film Institute now includes video grants in its Independent Filmmaker Program. Global Village in New York and The Film Fund and others are also encouraging the production, distribution and promotion of video works for dedicated and talented people.

I suppose that the question that keeps coming to mind as you read this, is: Is it at all possible? Have others made it on grants? Have they made their films in independence (more or less) and without spending so much time writing out applications that they have no time to produce their film projects? Well—yes. There are some, and a few have even made a bright reputation while doing it.

Emily Hubley, for example, is a young animator, not yet 30 years old at the time of this writing, and her history of film is based upon the grants method of funding. Her film, *Emergence of Eunice* was made back in 1980 with an AFI grant, followed by *Delivery Man* funded by the Jerome Foundation, and her latest project in 1984, a collaboration with her painter sister, Georgia, on a grant from the NEA for a film called *The Tower.*" And with each film, her reputation grows. Yes, it can be done. It really can.

Even with the tightening of the money-belt in these days of difficulty for the independent filmmaker who works on grant money, and even with the added problem of just plain survival during the years of producing that personal and important film project of yours, the film will probably be made because it *deserves* to be made and don't let anyone deter you from that goal. Someone will eventually listen to you, even if it's not the rich father you never had.

There are people out there pulling for you, though it's sometimes hard to believe. When the Administration tried to cut the humanities budget, Congressman Tom Downey, who chairs the Congressional Arts Caucus, stated in no uncertain terms that, "We should understand that when we starve the endowment budgets, we starve our own soul, and that's a bad and stupid thing to do!"

Amen.

The ABC Entertainment Center, site of the annual Los Angeles International Film Exposition.

CHAPTER 19

FILM FESTIVALS

"Oh, By the Way, You Were Nominated for an Academy Award"

The telephone rang late one night. It was the overseas operator calling from New York and I was soundly sleeping in Caracas (still *another* great location). My assistant got on the telephone and talked for almost a quarter of an hour (at $12 for each three minutes) —and at the end of that time he had merely small-talked. Finally, in tired exasperation, I said, "Gus, what did you call for?" A silence at the other end of the line, and then, finally, "Damned if I can remember. I called you for something, but I just can't think of it now."

We hung up and our crew continued its trip through South America, returning to New York two weeks later. I had forgotten about the telephone call. It was only a dim recollection, the urgency of a desk piled high with "emergencies" now taking priority and the real world crowding in upon me. It must have been a month after that, when my wife turned to me and said, "Oh, by the way, you were nominated for an Academy Award while you were in South America." I looked up, startled. "Didn't Gus call you in Caracas to tell you?" she exclaimed. She seemed surprised. Confronted with this the next morning, Gus threw up his hands and laughed, "I *knew* there was something I wanted to tell you when I telephoned!"

If the filmmaker is interested in collecting experiences, the Academy Award ceremonies in Hollywood might well be included as being among the most unusual. Because of the time differential between both coasts, their televising begins at a time that most West Coast residents would call early evening. The award ceremonies are very specifically played out for the wide-ranging public and the potential box-office bonanza that will result from naming the winners. Even in the field of the documentary, the independent film, and the short subject, the Academy Awards become important for the potential sales effect on new clients and for future grants.

There is no doubt in mind that my own nomination has helped me through the years. Of course my mother only remembers when "Debbie Reynolds said *your* name." (My dear old grandmother was not alive to enjoy it.) I suppose that I most remember the fact that the hotel voluntarily changed my room from a small closet to a golden suite when they found out I had been nominated. I didn't even know enough people, then, in Hollywood to hold a party in that oversized ballroom; it was, naturally, called "the Cinema Suite."

The Academy Awards are, perhaps, the only large festival known to the general public, since the main thrust is toward promoting the feature—eventually with a screaming advertisement headline of "Nominated for Twenty-Seven Academy Awards!!" Whatever its shortcomings—that it is self-serving, that it is incestuous (by only allowing about 3,400 members the right to vote), that it gives awards *this* year for the fact that an aging star was a nice guy *last* year, that it is everything we have come to expect it to be in terms of ballyhoo, slickness, and "show biz"—the Academy Awards are still an important part of the film-festival world, and will probably remain an important part for years to come, if the industry has anything to say about it.

It may come as a great surprise to learn that the Academy has an intense interest in the beginner's world, too. Perhaps more quietly, but just as importantly, the Academy of Motion Picture Arts and Sciences is supporting a program of Student Film Awards (in conjunction with American Telephone and Telegraph Company). There are five areas of competition:

- Dramatic
- Animated
- Documentary
- Special Jury Award (for films that do not fit into any of the above categories)
- Experimental (an optional category for student films that are free-form, non-narrative, and non-explanatory)

The awards for each category give $1,000 to the winner and $250 to each runner-up. In terms of judging, the country is broken down into ten regions and nearly four hundred films are submitted throughout the country each year; about fifty are selected for final competition at the Academy.

This is but the tip of the iceberg for the young filmmaker, for the world of exhibition possibilities and festival recognition is open to everyone who is trying to find some niche in the industry, whether you are involved with commercials, documentaries, television specials, or experimentation with film or tape. In fact, it is this "other" world of the small film festival that is so vast, so impossible to catalog, so difficult to define. They exist almost everywhere, both here and abroad. They are supported by foundations,

universities, the film industry, museums, television stations, independent groups, specialized societies, and cities, states, and countries. They can be found from Avignon to Zagreb.

Though we are familiar with the Oscar, we are certainly less familiar with the Golden Dove, Golden Eagle, Golden Ear, Gold Boomerang, Golden Rocket, and Golden Thistle awards. Not to mention the Hitchcock Cup, Gandhi Awards, Gran Premio Bergamo, Espiga de Oro, the Rajah Soliman Trophy, and the Prix Bell Telephone. Each year, more are added and some disappear. Probably a hundred or more festivals have special categories for the student, for the amateur, and for the independent filmmaker. Some of the festivals are, unfortunately, "rip-offs," pandering to the egos of the filmmaker while collecting huge entry fees for each film submitted to the juries. In this latter category, one festival in New York (and a rather well-known one at that) takes a large fee for submission and then notifies some of the participants that they are now in the "finals"—and that for only *one hundred dollars more* they will be allowed into the judging for prizes. It pays to read the rules carefully before you enter.

However, there is no doubt that the festival world can be of inestimable value to the beginner:

- It is a place to show your films to other professionals in the field, a place at which to meet other filmmakers who are active in the art.
- Ego aside, it is a great way in which to build your credits and your reputation.

Many festivals manage to get some of the best-known filmmakers to appear as judges or as seminar participants.

- Some festivals, especially those catering to the student and the independent filmmaker, award cash prizes or grants that can help considerably in producing that next project.
- At times, an independent film shown at a festival is then selected by a distributor for inclusion in a catalogue.

In the feature field, Jim Jarmusch's *Stranger Than Paradise* first won major prizes at Cannes and Locarno, while *Blood Simple* got rave reviews at the New York and the Toronto Film Festivals before the major studios began to take notice. When Jon Fauer's Dartmouth film, the documentary *White Water* was seen at CINE (Council of International Non-theatrical Events), thirty prints were subsequently purchased for distribution in Afghanistan! Other documentary filmmakers and animators have also found their first recognition at these events, while commercial producers use their festival awards to tempt future agency business.

It would be impossible to list every festival now in existence throughout the world, for the chapter would be out-of-date as soon as these words came off the typewriter. One such attempt was made by Shirley Zwerdling back in 1970, and she laboriously compiled the most complete film festival book of its time, but it was impossible to keep up with all the new Golden Pomegranate awards that constantly cropped up, and the project was eventually abandoned.

The obvious way in which we all keep up-to-date (in addition to the yearly promotional mailings by the well-known festivals) is by reading the trade publications, such as *Backstage, Variety* and *American Film. Film Comment,* published by Lincoln Center, carries new listings of competitions in each issue, as does the magazine *Film News*. And, frequently right within the editorial content itself, you may pick out the name of a festival you've never heard of before: Cartagena Naval Sea Films Week or the Cat Festival in Cambridge, Massachusetts.

Possibly one of the best sources for continuing information about upcoming festivals, dates, prizes, and other specifics about each one is in a monthly bulletin called "The Independent," published by the Association of Independent Video and Filmmakers. In order to receive the bulletin, they ask that you become a member, and fees vary depending upon whether you are a student or professional. You can contact them at 625 Broadway, New York, NY 10012. Telephone: 212-473-3400. In my last discussion with Bob Aaronson, he mentioned that the association was working on an anthology to be published yearly in order to update all the festivals that were current, to give their specifications, and to comment on prizes, dates of entry, and costs. Knowing the difficulties which I've already mentioned, the target date is still vague, but I do wish them luck.

As you progress through the industry, you will become familiar with the standard festival listings. For those of us in the documentary field, and for the commercial filmmakers who are active in television, sports, and business films, the names are well known and the award plaques cover the walls of screening rooms, client offices, and hallways. Of course, it has been suggested that *anyone* can begin a festival—by merely choosing a name and then issuing entry blanks. Someone will always enter. The integrity of certain festivals, however, has assured their success and their longevity: San Francisco, American Film Festival, Columbus, Annecy, and Zagreb (animation) have all been around for years now.

Even the larger festivals have special arrangements for the independents and for the student, with lower entry fees (or no special entry fee at all, in some rare cases) and with special award categories that take into consideration the cost of making films in this inflated marketplace. Thus, the proliferation of 8mm categories and videotape awards, and the awarding of prizes to films that may only run two to three minutes in 16mm. However, keep in mind that each time you enter a competition, you will have to submit a print or a dub and that it may not be returned to you for several weeks—or, in some cases, several months. Sending prints for screening has sometimes been compared with lending your favorite book to a friend and then never getting it back, even though your name was written all over the flyleaf! This may be an important consideration when you decide just which festivals are worth entering, particularly if two or more happen to fall in the same month.

For the independent and the beginner, there are some fascinating opportunities in the festival field, since some of them are closed to professional filmmakers. I remember, some years ago, hearing of the Sinking Creek Film Celebration and thinking that someone had made up the name. Since then, I have become friends with Mary Jane Coleman, who runs the celebration with George Griffin, and it is, indeed, a real and worthwhile place to enter your films.

Each year, the celebration is held on the Vanderbilt University campus in Nashville, Tennessee, supported by the National Endowment for the Arts, the Tennessee Arts Commission, and the university. It's been going on for nearly twenty years now, and it's open to any U.S. student or in-

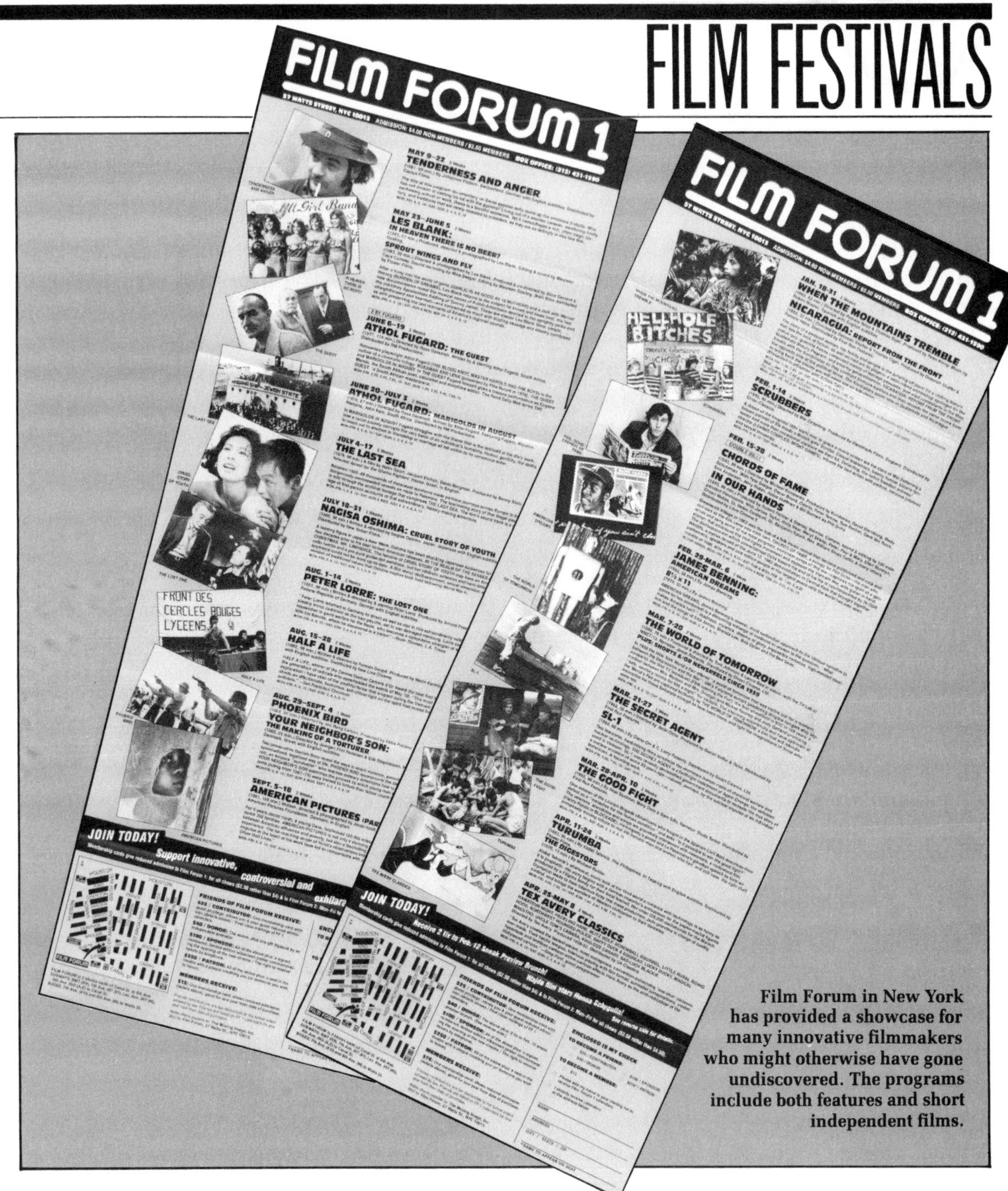

Film Forum in New York has provided a showcase for many innovative filmmakers who might otherwise have gone undiscovered. The programs include both features and short independent films.

dependent filmmaker. There is no entry fee, and the winners are showcased at the festival that follows the competition. Filmmakers such as Les Blank, Carmen D'Avino, and D.A. Pennebacker come down to the celebration to screen their work and to discuss film in general, while others like Karen Cooper of Film Forum, George Stoney, and James Blue have judged the entries. The festival awards prizes totalling $7,000, apportioned among these categories:

- Film by a young filmmaker under the age of eighteen
- Film by the college filmmaker
- Film by the independent filmmaker
- Film with special appeal to children.

In the past few years, Sinking Creek has also included video in its range of competitors. If you'd like further information, write to them: Creekside Farm, Route 8, Greenville, TN 37743, or call Mary Jane Coleman at 615-638-6524.

Possibly the oldest festival of its kind in the United States is the Ann Arbor 8mm Film Festival, open only to nonprofessional filmmakers who shoot in the smaller format. It's perfect for young filmmakers who cannot afford the expense of 16mm film. Write: Ann Arbor 8mm Film Festival, PO Box 7571, Ann Arbor, MI 48107. They will let you know about dates, small entry fee and other rules.

There are many more for the beginner and the nonprofessional, but perhaps it would be worthwhile to mention one last contest open to student films. Each year (for almost ten years now) the FOCUS awards have been given to student films in a range of categories, and with substantial scholarship prizes for the winners. The competition is partially sponsored by the Nissan Motor Corporation, with prizes contributed by such sponsors as Universal Pictures, 20th Century Fox, Eastman Kodak, HBO, and others. The judges have included such film notables as Saul Bass, Faith Hubley, Nina Foch, and John Canemaker. The major prerequisite for entry is that the film must have been done on a noncommercial basis by a student enrolled in a U.S. College, university, art institute or professional film school. The prizes are awarded in the following categories:

- Filmmaking
- Documentary
- Animation/Experimental
- Screenwriting
- Sound Achievement
- Film editing

If you'd like more information, write to: FOCUS, 1140 Avenue of the Americas, New York, NY 10036.

These are but a few examples. There are many more. There are festivals that are specially devoted to subjects such as the environment, medicine, industrial photography, traffic safety, folklore, science, submarine exploration, commercials, sports, and even a festival that accepts only entries for "Cheerful Films" (in Bordighera, Italy).

But even outside the festival circuits, all over the world, young filmmakers and video artists are being encouraged to produce and then exhibit their own films. I have watched the showcases spring up all over the country: The Collective for Living Cinema, the Millenium Film Workshop, The Kitchen Center for Video and Music, the cooperatives on both coasts, as well as the museums such as the Museum of Modern Art and the Whitney in New York, the latter very much concerned with expanding the art of video through its changing exhibitions.

Of particular interest to me has been the Film Forum in New York, founded in 1970 as a small, modest nonprofit showcase to encourage the experimental film, as well as the documentary and independent feature filmmakers. Under the guidance of its director, Karen Cooper, Film Forum has proven that there is a vital and interested market for the independent, and it has grown into the only full-time year-round movie house devoted entirely to the presentation of independent films in the United States. A short time ago, they moved into a newly constructed twin cinema in downtown Manhattan, and with major funding from the New York State Council on the Arts and the National Endowment for the Arts, they continue to offer a wide range of independently produced features, documentaries, narratives, animation, and experimental work. In past years they have premiered works such as *When the Mountains Tremble*, *Atomic Cafe*, Altman's *Health* and works by Wenders, Herzog, Fassbinder, as well as a previously unreleased classic, Fritz Lang's *Spiders*. For information, write: FILM FORUM, 57 Watts Street, New York, NY 10013.

We have already mentioned CINE (Council of International Non-theatrical Events, 1201 Sixteenth St. N.W. Washington, DC 20036) which represents another excellent outlet for screening new films. Not only does the annual festival have special categories for amateur and youth films, and not only does it award a "CINE Eagle" certificate to amateur winners, but it also sends selected entries abroad to represent the United States in overseas festivals in almost sixty countries. Thus, winning a film award at CINE can well garner several more awards in other international competitions.

On the West Coast, the Los Angeles International Film Exposition (FILMEX) has developed a yearly program that not only includes features, but also special programs of historical interest, as well as the world of the independent filmmaker, the animator and the documentarian. (FILMEX, PO Box 1739, Hollywood, CA 90028.

Possibly the biggest innovation on the festival circuit has been the blossoming of contests especially geared to video tape. Sometimes a part of other, larger film festivals, but more frequently on their own, these showcases have provided opportunity and prizes for the burgeoning medium. Now in its fifth year, the National Video Festival, presented by the American Film Institute and sponsored by the Sony Corporation, has covered everything from recent video acquisitions from the Museum of Modern Art to documentary tapes. television programming, and non-traditional forms and content.

The Videotape Production Association, reflecting the style of the older film industry, has instituted what it calls The Monitor Awards, covering a range of disciplines that would do justice to the categories honored by Hollywood. Among them:

- Cable
- Broadcast Short Subjects
- Music Video
- Documentaries
- Internal Communications
- Broadcast News
- Entertainment
- Computer Animation
- Commercials (Test)
- Commercials (Broadcast)

FILM ENTRY FORM

FILMEX

Los Angeles International Film Exposition

P O Box 1739 Hollywood, USA 90028 Telephone: 213/846-5530 Cable: ROSEBUD HOLLYWOOD

SUBMIT IN DUPLICATE
It is imperative that this Form be filled out completely and accurately!
Please attach an English synopsis, publicity materials, and stills.

Date: ______

Title of film (in original language): ______

English title: ______

Country of origin: ______ Year: ______ Date & place, 1st public screening: ______

Film festival presentations (list year): ______

Public presentations in USA: ______

Film gauge (check one): 70mm ☐ 35mm ☐ 16mm ☐

Screen ratio: Standard (1.33) ☐ Wide screen (1.66) ☐ Wide screen (1.85) ☐ 'Scope (Anamorphic) ☐

Sound system: Optical ☐ Mag ☐

Color: ☐ Black & white: ☐ Running time: ______

Footage or metrage: ______ No. of reels: ______

Is film subtitled in English? ☐ Original language: ______

Replacement value of print: ______

Will you permit the use of an extract for television promotion (3 to 5 minutes)? ______

Shipping Addresses for film prints ONLY
(Send correspondence to address above)

From within the USA
16mm only
Filmex
P O Box 1739
Hollywood, CA 90028

From outside the USA
all gauges
Filmex
c/o BBC International
P O Box 90793
Los Angeles, USA 90009

From within the USA
35 and 70mm
Filmex
c/o The Burbank Studios
4000 Warner Blvd.
Burbank, CA 91522

Producer: ______

Production Company ______
address ______
telephone ______

Director ______
address ______
telephone ______

Cast:
(Actor) ______ (Character) ______

Screenwriter ______
Cinematographer ______
Editor ______
Music ______
Art Director ______
Sets ______
Costumes ______
Sound ______

Film will be dispatched by: air ☐ sea ☐ mail ☐ diplomatic pouch ☐ on (date): ______

Film should be returned to: ______

American agent or distributor (if any): ______

I Understand that feature films will not be considered for the Exposition without synopsis and stills.

I certify that I hold all necessary rights for the submission of this film, and that I agree to abide by the Filmex Regulations. ______ (sign here)

In addition to these, there are also special awards for engineering achievement, for directing, editing, camera, sound, lighting, graphics, and post-production. So, even in our ever-growing field of video tape, the festival and award competitions are alive and well.

Of course, the competition is keen (but we begin with the assumption that you have something worthwhile to show). Furthermore, the idea of competition itself will be most valuable to you, for you will soon learn what is being produced and just who the new filmmakers and video-tape artists are. Your first award—indeed your first "Certificate of Acceptance"—may be just the encouragement you need. And you just never know when someone at Sinking Creek will see your work and become interested in you.

Many years back, I was invited to Washington to receive a CINE Golden Eagle for one of my films. As noted above, the festival has a young-filmmaker category and I watched the entries with some awe. I saw children who were producing work that was sophisticated, effective, and visually beautiful. While at the screenings, I watched the work of a twelve-year-old—one of the most ingenious films I'd seen all that weekend. Produced on 8mm, it was worth a comment, I thought. I found the young man sitting with his parents and said that I'd thoroughly enjoyed the film, told him to keep working in film, and that he was very talented.

About eight years later, I had just finished a lecture at the New York University Film School when a student of about twenty came up and said, "I don't know if you remember me..." And, yes, he was the same one I had met at CINE—now quite grown and very much into film. He told me that the bit of encouragement I had given him had convinced him to stay in the field. Actually, I don't know if I did him a favor—for I do not have an end to this story. I have not heard from him again. He may be a doctor or a lawyer, for all I know. Or perhaps he is still in film and someone has just said to him, "Oh, by the way, you were nominated for an Academy Award!"

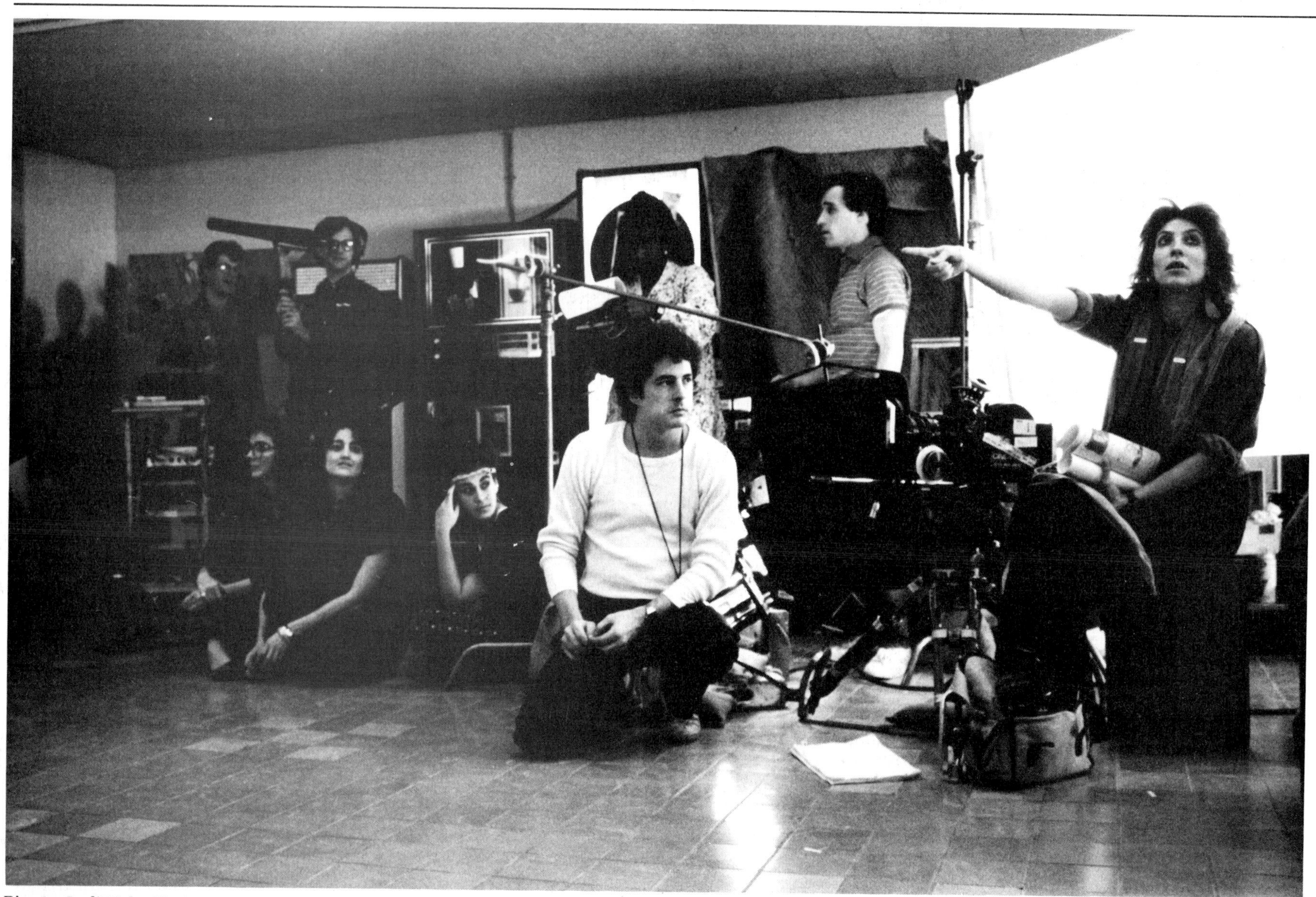

Director Lesli Linka Glatter on set during the production of her AFI Directing Workshop for Women project, Tales of Meeting and Parting. The film was nominated for an Academy Award.

CHAPTER 20

WOMEN IN FILM

"How Would You Like to Get into Movies, Baby?"

No one ever says, "Come on in." As a woman, you pound on the door and scream, *"Let me in!"*

—Nell Cox

Even in these "enlightened" eighties, it is no different from banking or finance. Or from any of the large corporations that manufacture automobiles, airplanes, toilet tissue, or chemicals. Or different from the service and utility industries, such as television, telephones, or power companies. The film industry is run by men—and if they can help it, it's going to stay that way. Every once in a while, an inroad is made into the sanctum sanctorum, such as the brief reign of Sherry Lansing as production head of a major studio, but winning a battle does not mean that you necessarily win the war. Even Ms. Lansing has left to form Jaffe/Lansing Productions and once again the hierarchy is dominated by men. With that depressing introduction to the chapter, let's take a look at the business as it has been, as it is now, and as it may be in the next few years, for women.

The past is easy. The women who "made it" in film were generally the actresses: Mary Pickford, Clara Bow, Joan Crawford, Marilyn Monroe, and any others who spelled "box office" for the moguls who ran the studios. The subtitle of this chapter, ironically given in this day and age, was a passport to the notorious casting couch, and the stories are legion in the industry about starlets who made their way into film by answering "yes" to that question.

There were few women playing any other role in the industry than "actress." Women just did not exist in the craft unions, with the possible exception of "women's jobs": script girl (sic!), wardrobe mistress, costume, production assistant, production secretary—or just plain secretary. There were few instances of women making it above the lower levels.

Of course, some women did "make it." The screenplays for Rudolph Valentino were written by June Mathis, and Anita Loos wrote the Douglas Fairbanks, Sr., comedies. Mary Pickford formed her own company with Charles Chaplin and Fairbanks. And, as far back as 1927, Hollywood had a woman director in Dorothy Arzner. Through the thirties and forties, Ms. Arzner was Hollywood's only woman director. Her credits included *The Wild Party, The Bride Wore Red*, and *Dance, Girl, Dance*. But she was only one—and not one of many. In an interview some years back, she was asked why she thought she was Hollywood's only woman director at that time. She answered, "I don't honestly know. Maybe producers felt safer with men; they could go to a bar and exchange ideas more freely. But I made one box-office movie after another, so they knew they could gamble a banker's money on me. If I had had a failure in the middle, I would have been finished. Today, of course, even the stars are all men. When men do put women in pictures, they make them so darned sappy, weeping all over the place, that it's disgusting!"

In later years, a few more women made their reputations in the medium: Leni Riefenstahl directed the German film of the 1936 Berlin Olympic Games (*Olympia*), among others, and Leontine Sagan did *Maedchen in Uniform* for Deutsche Film Gemeinschaft. Shirley Clarke worked both in the documentary and in the feature and her *Portrait of Jason* was produced under the most difficult conditions. If you were to look at a listing of the classic films in any catalogue, the first names of the directors would all read Fritz and Francois and Ingmar and Frederic and David—and if you happened to come across someone named Pat, you could be certain that it was *Patrick* and not *Patricia*! Nary a Mary, Josephine, or Vivian could be found.

But then an accusing male finger, now feeling a bit uncomfortable, points at things today and the still-male-dominated film industry, and says, "Aha, but look at how it's changed. Now we have Amy Heckerling and Elaine May and Joan Micklin Silver, and Claudia Weill and Susan Seidelman and Amy Jones..." True. But things have not really changed very much in the industry, even though there were shouts of "a new day a-comin'" back in the late seventies when women began to make their marks as directors, and more and more lower and middle-level jobs began to open up. At that time, too, the names of women began to appear more often as the producers of network television specials and in the award-winners circle for commercials. But—where the power really sat, in the top administration of major studios and in the "trenches" of directing, the figures were—and still are—quite appalling.

Back in 1979, six women members of Directors Guild of America (Susan Bay, Nell Cox, Joelle Dobrow, Victoria Hochberg, Delores Ferraro, and Lynn Littman) analyzed the records of the organization through thirty years of production:

- Of the 7,332 feature films released during that period, only 14 were directed by women.

- There were about 65,000 *hours* of prime-time television produced, 115 of them directed by women. Of that 115, 35 were directed by Ida Lupino, who owned her own production company.

But things have gotten better, they tell us. Let's look at the record once more—this time for the year 1983, when equal opportunity was the word, and lip service the credo:

- Of all the days worked on feature films during that year, only *two percent* were directed by women.
- Fifteen percent were written by women.
- Of nearly 700 members in the Producer's Guild, less than 100 are women.
- The networks fare no better. Only 10 percent of all studio executives are women.
- In this day and age of the hyphenated filmmaker, only *one* woman is a director of photography in the American Society of Cinematographers.

There are two more hurdles to overcome, and they are obvious ones to those of us who have been watching the trend for all these years:

- A woman will be judged much more severely than a man.
- She had better not fail. There will be no second chance.

There is "high visibility," the tendency to put women directors into jobs that are the stereotypical teen-age beach-party stories, and the very real reluctance that the men have to give money to women. If Michael Cimino directs a $34 million disaster (*Heaven's Gate*), you may be sure that you'll soon be reading that he is again working on a large project (*Year of the Dragon*) in spite of the box office failure. Just let a woman try it!

Unfortunately, the story is not much different in the world of the corporate film, and many women have survived and flourished by having male partners. For even here, money is still not given easily to women who produce and direct their own films. And the people who control the money are men.

What about the other crafts? What about cinematographers, for example? Well, in New York, Julianna Wang was the first woman to become a member of the union, but the road was rocky for the others who tried and failed. On the West Coast, Brianna Murphy was the first woman to crack the Cameraman's (sic!) Union back in 1973, and it was so unusual that it warranted coverage in the film magazines.

John Kuehl, one of the successful independent producer/director/writers, is head of her own production company in New York. She is shown on location with cameraman Elio Lupi.

Some women have always been at the top of the editing field: the late Verna Fields (*Jaws*, *American Graffiti*, and *Paper Moon*), and in her later years with Universal she was even promoted to Vice President. I've mentioned Sara Stein and Dede Allen before, and there are many more who "save it in the editing room." But, as one woman filmmaker friend puts it, "Of course women have been tops in the editing field; all the men went on to become executives!"

Essentially, then, the film industry is merely a reflection of society as it exists today. Much ground has been gained in the fight for equal rights for women, but unfortunately, sexism in one form or another, still exists. Even away from the "glamour" of Hollywood and New York feature films—in the everyday world of production of documentaries, educational films, television, government films, and on the client level, the door is only partially open, and old attitudes are changing quite slowly. It may take several more years for them to disappear.

Several of my own clients are women, and at first this seems to contradict the previous statements about their never really getting where the money or the power is. These women are usually in a supervisory capacity in public relations, advertising departments, and communications divisions. Their bosses are men, and many times a top job opens up above them, only to be filled by a man while they remain in middle-level positions.

In a casting session where several people sit in judgment, many male actors will still direct their audition readings to the male in the group, even if the woman at the far end is really the top executive present. And, even within the industry itself, the attitude is not much different, I'm afraid.

Claudia Weill tells a story about a time when she was director of photography on a TV Special and the only woman on the crew. No one had met anyone else before the crew call at 6 A.M. (Everyone, but everyone *does* get up early, as I've mentioned several times before.) In the station wagon, on the way to location, one of the men said, "Let's all get coffee." Now, the code in the industry—any industry—when someone mentioned coffee is that all heads immediately turn to the only woman present; in this case, the director of photography. After all, women have gotten coffee for conferences for years—and still do. Coolly, Claudia said, "Great idea. I'll take mine regular." No one else made the move to get the coffee. The crew went without it. Men don't really know how to get coffee. They never had to practice.

Producer/director Nell Cox on location with the New York City Fire Department for a motion picture sponsored by the Ford Foundation.

There are some positive developments. Possibly the most important is the fact that women have begun to fight, first in making sure to publicize the active prejudice of a male-dominated industry, and then through the formation of support groups, independent production companies, and even undertaking litigation where necessary. For example, not more than ten years ago, Women in Film had but 12 members in its Los Angeles chapter. Today, with chapters in New York, Boston, Dallas, Washington, Chicago, Atlanta, and other major cities across the country, plus chapters in seventeen countries overseas (Australia, Canada, Denmark, England, Japan, to name a few), the organization has mushroomed to the point where the chapter on the West Coast now has almost *1300 members*, with about 300 in New York. The group represents virtually every area of work in the industry: network and studio executives, grips, camera operators, producers, directors, performers, composers, editors and designers. Essentially, it advocates:

- Increased employment and equal opportunity for women.
- Depiction of women on film as fair and varied as that which exists in reality.
- Greater visibility of accomplishments by women.

- Networking—strengthened communication among women.
- Professional excellence by and on behalf of women.

To meet those goals, Women in Film maintains a job referral service, holds workshops and seminars for its members, invites guest speakers from the industry, and offers internship and apprentice programs as well as foundation grants for writing and completion of film projects. (For further information, write: Women in Film, 8489 West Third Street, Los Angeles, CA 90048.)

In 1974, the American Film Institute began a pilot program funded by Anna Bing Arnold and the Rockefeller Foundation specifically designed to provide a new opportunity for professional women. It's called the Directing Workshop for Women, and with a much more optimistic feeling than I have, perhaps, communicated in these few pages, Kaye Cooper-Mead of AFI comments about the industry in the eighties: "The climate seems to be improving for women in terms of finding representation with agencies and being considered for directing positions. The American Film Institute Directing Workshop for Women is attempting to improve conditions for women in the industry by providing them with the opportunity to direct narrative projects...which can then be used as visual examples to demonstrate their skills and talent as a director."

The workshop program is geared to "learning by doing," opening the student/director to a myriad of unfamiliar situations on a smaller scale than those faced by directors who work in the film and television industries. The activities include:

- Casting and directing some of the best known film and television actors in the industry.

the HOLLYWOOD REPORTER

Bri Murphy First Woman Accepted By IATSE Photogs

Bri Murphy, pr... of Sombrero Pictures Inc., is a m... 659 of IATSE, Internatio... first woman in th... qualify as a di... announced G... representative.

Sombrero, ... tion, has bee... production c... theatrical fe... a TV specia... a woman's...

Los Angeles Times

First Woman as Photo Director

Bri Murphy, president of Sombrero Pictures Inc., has become a member of Local 659 of IATSE, International Photographers, the first woman in the history of the local to qualify as a director of photography.

Sombrero, under Miss Murphy's direction, has been actively ... the prod... n... th... pr... aut... wor...

Fri., March 16, 1973

DAILY VARIETY DAILY

Murphy First Woman Director Of Photography

Bri Murphy, president of Sombrero Pictures Inc., has become a member of Photographers Local 659 of the Int'l Alliance of Theatrical Stage Employes, the first woman in the history of the local to qualify as a director of photography, according to b.a. Gerald Smith.

- Using state-of-the-art lighting and videotape equipment for shooting and editing.
- Scriptwriting and adaptation of existing material.
- Selecting and directing experienced production crews.

And—possibly the most important experience that the workshop provides:

- The opportunity to make mistakes and to learn from these mistakes in a non-threatening, supportive environment.

A look at the list of participants over the past workshop cycles indicates that the competition is keen, but it can be done: Lynne Littman (*Testament*) was a participant back in 1974. Others who made it through the program include actresses, television producers, writers, even casting directors: Susan Smitman, Lee Grant, Cicely Tyson, Karen Arthur, and my old friend, cinematographer Bri Murphy. In the 1984 competition for the Academy Awards, Lesli Linka Glatter's short film *Tales of Meeting and Parting* was nominated for an Oscar. (You can get further information by writing to American Film Institute, 2021 North Western Ave., Los Angeles, CA 90027.)

The eventual goal for most filmmakers seems to be the role of director—and this is no different for women than it is for men. It is an admirable goal, as I have stated before, but whether male or female, the chances of your becoming a director (especially as you finish film school or your first independent project), are very slim indeed. Kaye Cooper-Mead of AFI, in spite of her generally upbeat feeling about the field, adds, "The *climate* may be improving, but if you look at the job statistics that's another story. The job conditions are a *yes*. The actual jobs are a *no*!"

Bri Murphy, president of Sombrero Productions and the first woman to become a member of Local 659, IATSE, in Los Angeles.

The place to look, then, for women as well as men, is at the middle-levels of the film industry, where changes *have* been taking place much more rapidly than at the top. It is here that we have begun to see the impact of women forcing the issue, of confrontation with an industry that locked the doors for too many years. At first, we began to see (and still see to some extent) crews composed entirely of women, each job filled by women from go-fer to producer/director. But, as we moved from the seventies into the eighties, we have also noticed many more mixed crews than ever before. The unions have opened their doors—also as a result of both moral and legal pressures, so that we now have assistant camerawomen both in and out of the unions who have answered the questions for the industry, "Well, can they carry a heavy tripod up the hill?" (They can.) The sound department, especially in the documentary, has become a unisex category. And, women have somehow always made the best of Production Managers. The trick, of course, is to *get into* the industry—yes, for women as well as men, and then to fight the battles for the top.

There have been still other area of growth and maturing in the industry. Some festivals, organizations, support groups, and distribution companies were started as a part of the feminist movement, and are still open only to women who make their own films or tapes. Others have expanded to a point where they are now open to *both* men and women. For example, Women Make Movies, originally started in a church basement in New York, recently held its Fourth International Women's Film Festival in Washington, D.C.

The Women's History Research Center in Berkeley (2325 Oak Street, Berkeley, CA 94708)

wif

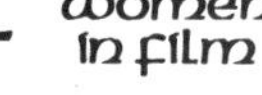

women in film

ATLANTA CHAPTER P. O. Box 52726, Atlanta, GA 30355

WOMEN IN FILM: OUR PURPOSE

The specific purpose in which the corporation primarily is to engage is to promote equal rights for women in the entertainment industry, to serve as a clearinghouse and repository for information on the participation of qualified women in the industry, and to make available to and educate the public, members of the industry, and women in the industry information about the availability of women in creative fields, discrimination, and other common problems women face in the industry.

Women in Film has grown into a nation organization with chapters in every large city of the United States.

continues to publish their directory, *Films by and/or about Women*, with information about:

- Films by Female Filmmakers
- Films by Women, about Women (by men)
- Experimental, animated, documentary films
- Listings that include Third World films, Social Protest, Female Portraits, Birth & Birth Control, Sexuality, Performing Arts, and Child Care.

In the first edition of this book, I wrote of New Day Films, which then distributed films made by their own members, all of them women. Today, ten years later, it has boomed, and it has now expanded to include all kinds of films about social change, labor history, mental health, sex education, women's rights, urban problems, and it is still made up of individual filmmakers, but it now has a membership that includes *both* men and women. (New Day Films, 22 Riverview Drive, Wayne, NJ 07470.)

The men who are reading this chapter should also take note of yet another trend: There are women who now own their own companies or who manage partnerships in the field of the television documentary and commercials, in the business film, and in the independent film. Some are partners with men. Others sell, write, research, and produce as well as direct.

In Washington, D.C., Meredith Burch is president of her own Meridian Productions, and though she agrees that it is still normal to find a male name on the corporate letterhead along with that of the woman who co-owns it, she has been an independent filmmaker—and a successful one—for a long time. Recently, she completed twenty General Motors historical vignettes called *Presidential Moments* as well as a documentary for the Gerald R. Ford Library on the subject of first ladies and first children. Does she find the corporate response to women difficult to handle?

"I find it very hard. But then, I think that everybody finds it very hard. I do find that the 'eye fixation level' at meetings and such—the eyes sort of move toward the men. Of course, on the creative side, everyone's very attentive toward the woman...but when it comes to the money part..." I found her silence descriptive and then asked her, "And when it comes to lunch. Do the waiters give the male client the check?" She laughed, "Yes, it happens. And I love it!"

Other women are making their way in the world of the independent film, funded by hard-to-get foundation grants. But then, it is not the easiest way to make films in any case. At Maddux/Boldt

Director Susan Seidelman on location for her film, Desperately Seeking Susan. After release of her successful low budget film, Smithereens, Seidelman was given a contract by Orion Pictures to produce her next film project.

Productions in New York, filmmakers Deborah Boldt and Hillary Maddux spent five years in the making of their documentary, *Miles to Go*, about eight women who go on a wilderness trip. They ranged in age from 27 to 72. The film was made on grants from foundations, corporations, and government agencies.

Deborah Boldt commented: "It was extremely difficult to raise money because it was our first project. We'd never made a film before, but we believed strongly in the idea and we brought a lot of energy and tenacity and conviction to the project. It took three years to raise the money to shoot—and another two years to finish. It has won seven awards since its release, including a special Academy Award of Merit (1984) and it has played theatres in a dozen cities."

Grania Gurievitch of Togg Films (New York) is another independent filmmaker who has worked for the past fifteen years on foundation grants, with films produced mostly for advocacy groups on subjects ranging from Mental Health, Child Abuse, Career and Family Planning, plus films for National Park Service.

Before becoming the first woman to crack the camera local on the West Coast, Bri Murphy formed her own production company (Sombrero Productions) and her work included documentaries, commercials, and features. When things were slow, she survived by working as one of the best production managers and script supervisors on the West Coast.

In spite of the progress, letters still come into companies owned by women beginning with the worlds, "Gentlemen" or "Dear Sir." Nell Cox has a form letter that takes care of the problem quite nicely. In spite of the fact that her company is called Nell Cox Productions, the "Gentlemen" letters still flow in from would-be filmmakers. The answer she sends, says in part: "Being a woman president of a corporation I find I am not moved to respond to letters addressed to 'Dear Sir' except to say to you that I think it's time you found some form of address that took into account the large number of women in the business."

And so, we are all looking for signs of change, even to finding a small name credit in a review in our local newspaper that says that a woman named Gillian Armstrong has directed a film called *Mrs. Soffel* (as well as other credits: *My Brilliant Career* and *Starstruck*). Or—that Susan Seidelman, discovered by the public and the industry with an $80,000 film (*Smithereens*), is rewarded with Orion Pictures backing and a budget of millions for *Desperately Seeking Susan*. Or—that even in Europe, other names join those of Mai Zetterling and Jeanne Moreau and Lina Wertmuller: a glowing review for a film called *Diary for My Children* directed by a Hungarian woman, Marta Meszaros. And, if Hollywood should call her, as it did for a short-lived love affair with Wertmuller, how long will it last? Susan Seidelman commented, "So few women directors get a second chance in Hollywood."

She is, of course, very right. And I, in turn, wonder if the names I've written about in this edition of the book will still be around when the next edition is published. Indeed, will I ever find need to revise the book and eliminate the chapter on Women in Film entirely? Will I call it, instead, *People in Film*, as it should be?

The best answer for now is a comment made to me by one of the most talented people in the film world, Faith Hubley. "We don't sit around talking about how hard it is to be a woman. We sit around talking about how hard it is to make a good film—and we go out and do it!"

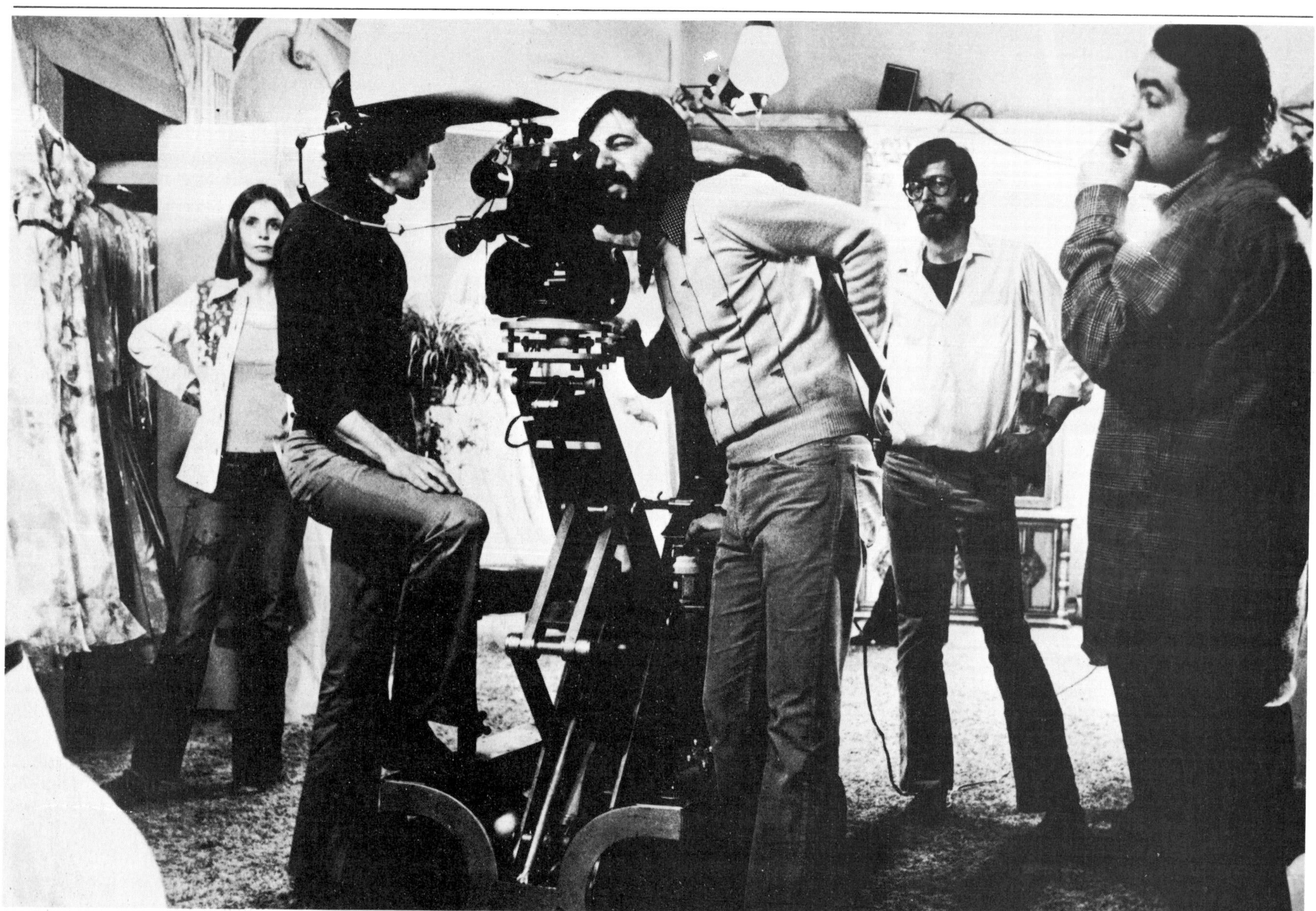

Most small production companies (such as Chuck Braverman, seen here shooting a TV Special), use free-lance personnel to augment their permanent staffs.

CHAPTER 21

THE FREE-LANCE MARKET

It's Either Feast or Famine

free-lance: . . . 3. a mercenary soldier or military adventurer of the Middle Ages, often of knightly rank, who offered his services to any state, party, or cause.

—*The American College Dictionary,* Random House, 1963

Most of the people in the film field are in the free-lance category, and thus this film field offers the largest job market. But it also provides some of the stiffest competition.

In the days of the large studios—which produced features as well as business films and commercials—production companies had staffs that were large and complete. In those halcyon days, Warner Brothers and Twentieth Century–Fox had salaried people ranging from contract directors to gaffers and other studio mechanics. Even the "industrial" companies such as Wilding (Chicago) and Jam Handy (Detroit) had weekly payrolls that included every craft in the film spectrum: make-up, camera, design, production, editing, even their own laboratories. As late as the early sixties, Wilding carried a staff of nearly four hundred people in Chicago, Detroit, New York, and San Francisco.

For the most part, this is gone—the victim of rising costs, increased production on location, and the development of lighter and more flexible equipment. As film moved out of the studios, the need for a large, permanent staff decreased. It was, after all, much more economical to travel a small nucleus of crafts people from home base and then hire the other technicians at the location than it was to face the huge studio payroll each and every week of the year, whether people were working or not. It also made more sense to utilize the best of the free-lance market without having to worry about "down time," when salaries had to be paid but the studios were "dark." Film companies throughout the United States—small as well as large—began to staff only in the critical areas, while using free-lancers to fill in the creative and technical gaps. Except for television, you will generally find that this is exactly how almost all production companies operate today.

The base structure of the film company generally consists of only a few people, possibly the partners in the organization, with everyone doubling in sales, production, and editing; many companies are, in fact, producing feature films with only a small permanent office staff and the *entire* crew contracted on a free-lance basis. But many highly successful companies are structured with a small basic unit. Occasionally a firm has as its nucleus a well-known cameraperson or director or business administrator. The rest are hired free-lance.

Beyond the savings, many producers feel there is much greater flexibility in utilizing free-lance talent. For example, some free-lance cinematographers are specialists in specific areas of photography. One of our own people —Herbert Raditschnig, who is actually free-lance but has been working for us so many years that we call him "our own"—is an expert in mountain-climbing and skiing photography. In fact, he has developed a rig that allows him to ski downhill *backwards* while filming the experts on their runs. Luckily he can also do other types of photography just as well. Imagine the plight of a production company that had a person on staff who could *only* do ski photography. Conversely, what do they do when they *need* ski photography and their cinematographer has never been on skis? It is almost impossible to keep one person busy all year, so generally producers call upon the free-lance experts, whether in photography, lighting, makeup, special effects, sound, production, graphics, or editing.

But another factor must be considered in this free-lance market. So far, we have mentioned that the *producers* prefer the system as an economical and flexible and creative choice. But, there are many free-lancers who prefer the life to any potential staff job! Many of them have made their reputations through the years, and make their living by going from job to job, producer to producer. They could never imagine themselves working for only one company for the rest of their lives. Almost all of the people who so graciously offered me advice and material for this book are, in fact, in the free-lance market—many of them by personal choice.

A second free-lance group—possibly the larger of the two—would *like* to get something permanent with one company, but free-lance through necessity. If there are only so many staff jobs available and if the market utilizes the huge pool of free-lance talent as a prime source, then many of these people must make their living as best they can—frequently in any job that can help pay the rent and provide the daily gruel until a reputation is made and wages are more generous.

You are probably thinking that free-lancing

can't be so bad. After all, you can choose your jobs, have plenty of free time between productions, and the flexibility of taking a vacation when there's no work around, be your own boss, deduct all sorts of marvelous tax advantages given free-lancers, have the wonderful opportunity of working for many personalities, experience a multitude of adventures . . . Right?

Well, *maybe*—but most of the time, *wrong!*

You must have a definite bent for free-lancing. Its fortunes fluctuate violently between starvation and overabundance. There are weeks or months without work and then suddenly everyone wants you at the same time. All in one week, a producer calls you to travel to Asia on a sports job, followed by a request from a company that *must* have you that same week to do a film on food in France—and that very day you have already accepted a job to film a series of junkyards up and down the East Coast. Sadly, you turn down the other two commitments. Once you have given your word to a producer, it is almost impossible to break that promise. Of course, certainly, there *are* ways. You can call the first producer to ask if you can be excused to go to Paris and you might even get an agreement that it's O.K. But, you may wonder, later, why you never hear from that first producer again. For that employer, the junkyards were more important than your glamorous trip. Free-lancers must develop a reputation for reliability among the people who hire them.

This brings up a term you will hear quite often in the free-lance field: "first refusal." It simply means that a producer is setting a tentative shooting schedule and is waiting for a firm commitment on dates; the offer of "first refusal" might be made to you instead of making a definite booking of your time. You are then *tentatively* booked on that project, but if a second job comes your way you have the option of calling the producer and, at that time, either a definite commitment must be given to you or you can be released for the other job. All this seems fine, and when it works it's very good. There are times when a producer will have committed himself to you —and then canceled the job just a week or so (or less) before production was to begin. In many cases, there is no way you can collect the money you would have been paid, had you worked—even though the producer may be morally obligated—and you are now too late to take that first job you were released from.

Then, of course, the feeling of "freedom" is also a fallacy. If you are not working, you had better be out looking. If you are gone, then someone else is called to fill the spot—and that means whether you were away on location or on a vacation in the Swiss Alps. Your freedom begins to play against you, for you are, as a free-lancer, a victim of when the jobs come up. Speak to any free-lancer who has worked for some years in this business, and ask about vacations, time off, personal needs—and you will find that free-lancing affects your personal life from beginning to end. Relationships are sacrificed, children and spouses are left at home for long periods of time, and vacations can become non-existent.

You must, furthermore, make your income during your busy periods. And you will find that, once you do develop a relationship with some clients and are beginning to work more and more, the physical wear and tear in these busy periods can become severe. Makeup artist Dick Smith describes it this way:

. . . you may be working seven days a week for months. It's exhausting, a very exhausting job. I'm now fifty-four—I find that one of my big problems is in keeping healthy enough to stand the pace. Much of the work being done now—particularly in independent film production—is on the basis of working twelve to sixteen hours a day. They're really brutal. So it's very rough on your health, it's hell on your social life, your home life. For instance, I never know from one week to the next what I'm going to be doing, so I've just given up buying theater tickets. It's very difficult to plan a vacation because two minutes from now my phone may ring and I may get a call that will set me packing to dash off on a job to Timbuctoo, which is exciting to a certain extent, but it does wreck your plans sometimes.

Of course, the well-known free-lancers in the field do begin to develop some kind of freedom of choice, for they are in demand all the time. Smith goes on:

I fortunately am in the position where I can turn down some of the things I don't like. So much of film is now done on location, and some of the locations are miserable. I turned down a film that someone wanted to make down in the jungles of Colombia. I just don't care for those creepy, crawly things and damp, wet, fever-ridden jungles. My young friend Rick Baker did a film several years ago in Brazil and nearly got drowned in the Amazon . . .

So much for the glamorous locations.

Free-lancing, however, is the place you

might very well begin your film career, and if you have the energy and the talent and the personality, you will probably find that it can be one of the most exciting (and frustrating) parts of your film life. In my own background I remember with warmth (and funny stories) the years of free-lancing. As with most pain, I don't really think about the difficult times, the months without income and the meals at a Horn & Hardart Automat (the McDonald's of my time), or of the constant round of job-hunting days. You will constantly be making the rounds of producers, continually renewing contacts, and forever showing your samples so that you can enlarge your range of potential job opportunities. Bit by bit, your résumé will begin to fill out and bit by bit you will have made your mark with the people who hire the crew—and suddenly you will begin to get a fairly steady amount of work from one or two sources, possibly just enough to keep you going until the next job crops up. And there will be times, especially at the beginning, when other work will have to fill out your income—whether in or out of film.

What do the producers look for in the free-lancer? Well, if I analyze the people with whom I've been working, over these many years, I might break things down into several prerequisites:

TALENT We must certainly begin with talent. Your talent may well lie in several areas, and at the beginning it will be difficult to prove. As you go on in the field, your specific talents will become more evident to the people who hire you. There are definitely many top-flight craftsmen in New York, but we use a soundman (Bill Shaver) who lives in Charlotte and a soundman (Don Matthews) who calls Los Angeles his home—and we travel them to any location in the world. The reasons are obvious, when we listen to the tracks that have been recorded under the most difficult conditions, yet sound as if they had been done in a controlled, high-fidelity studio.

Talented free-lance people generally find work no matter where they are based. Billy O'Connell (left) worked with the author as a gaffer for many years, even though he was based in Miami. Jon Fauer now shoots features, documentaries and commercials all over the world while making his home in New York.

So, too, with the lighting; it is no accident that we have a reputation for superb photography, even on complex locations. So, talent is the first factor. But I have come to believe, through the years, that the next most important prerequisite goes hand-in-glove with the first. Without either, a production can be a disaster.

AN AMENABLE PERSONALITY Time and time again we have ignored a recommendation to add someone to our crew—because we knew about his personality! The talent was there—frequently the very best in the field—and yet we went with another choice because the person recommended was known to be the worst traveling companion to take on location. Imagine being in the middle of a jungle with someone you had gotten to hate. Remember that, on location, you live together, eat together, sometimes share the same quarters in an underdeveloped country. You spend time in the heat together and in the cold—and the job can end with everyone madly in love with everyone else, or it can almost end in murder! Some years back, I saw a producer change cameramen because his first selection traveled throughout the country in a constant state of petulance because he couldn't get H-O Oats for breakfast and made everyone suffer because of it! Imagine, too, a crew member who might be hostile to the client, or to the people we meet on the trip, or to Customs officers, or to government officials in countries where people are suspicious of the "Yankees" to begin with. Think of what it might be like to discover—in a small, puritanical town where you are trying desperately to make friends so that the filming can go off smoothly—that your cinematographer or production manager or electrician is a roaring alcoholic after hours. Stated even more simply, just imagine that one of your crew cannot get along with people —including the producer and the director— and you will begin to see why the free-lancer who has talent *and* a flexible personality is the one who seems to be working most of the time.

RELIABILITY Perhaps this is a part of the personality syndrome, but I would like to break it out on its own, for very good reason. The term refers to much that goes on in the industry. Reliability was mentioned before in terms of being committed to the job—the people we know would never think of saying, "Yes," to a commitment and then trying to get out of it because "something better" had come up. We, in turn, have tried to let them go when it was a matter of our three shooting days versus a six-week job for them. We try to be fair in our own dealing, but this only comes from the fact that our free-lance people have been, in turn, most reliable when it comes to working with us.

On the job, reliability also plays a part in a number of ways, not the least of which is the fact that a crew member never misses a call "unless he is dead," as some of us like to say. That crew call is sacrosanct—whether it be for a 6 A.M. airplane (be at the airport at 4:30) or just the plain, everyday meeting on time at the station wagon to go out on location. Every producer can think of several examples in which people were never hired again because every member of the crew was downstairs, equipment loaded, engines started, and the free-lancer was still up in the hotel room watching the "Today" show or still having breakfast. Incidentally, we also try to communicate this reliability factor to our clients —and commercial producers do the same for their agency contacts who accompany them on location. It doesn't always work, but we try.

Since the free-lancer is always keeping his antennae out for future work, at certain times and in certain areas of the free-lance field the producer frequently gets a feeling that a "meter" is running. I have found this especially true in the area of free-lance writers, but it also exists among directors and designers and other people who consider themselves to be in the "creative" aspects of the film world. What I mean is, simply, that we get the feeling that we are entitled to only so much time for just so much money! This is not really a complaint, for no doubt that there is also that occasional exploitation of the free-lancer by the producer. In years past, when we used creative-type free-lancers more than we do now, we found that a call for an extra meeting with a client, or an additional production conference, would bring a retort such as, "Well, I have other clients, you know," or, "But we just had a meeting with your client two days ago—what does he want from me?" Of course, the meter was running and we had just about used up our ride. Our solution was to go completely "staff" on all the creative jobs (such as writer, director, editor) so that we could better service our clients.

GOOD SAMPLES AND CREDITS Here, in free-lance work more than anywhere else, it will be necessary to build your credits and to have something to show, if possible. After a while, the producers will know your work merely because you have already been on their crews. However, new people besides yourself come into the field every day, and small production companies rise up and then go down in the flames of competition—and all of these companies need free-lance people. So that, even if you begin to develop your steady contacts, you will have to prove yourself to *new* employers. Your résumé will grow, and hopefully so will your excellent reputation as a talent who is also a personable human being. Time and again we get telephone calls asking for recommendations among the various film crafts, and we are very quick to suggest that they hire the people with whom we have worked.

You will build your credits and experience as others have—slowly and carefully, taking whatever you can get and sometimes being paid quite poorly for it. A few months ago, I came across an ad in a trade paper that read as follows:

FILM PRODUCTION PEOPLE

Film Production people wanted for pre-production work on a quality 35mm theatrical science fiction film with guaranteed distribution, to be done on a very low budget. Model makers, set builders, costume people and general production assistants are needed. Little or no pay, long hours and hard work, pre-production will take approximately 3 months. You have to be crazy or in love with science fiction and/or film. You may starve but you will get lots of first class experience & the opportunity to work on a real film . . .

For the people who eventually work on that film, it *is*, nonetheless, a credit—and, who knows, it might well become a famous science-fiction film. And, more important, you don't really have to tell anyone at a future interview that you didn't even get paid for your work.

All of us in the film industry have survived those days of small beginnings. I asked several of my friends about their free-lance days. Barbara Martinsons, formerly a vice-president with Prentice-Hall Media, told us:

I decided to become a socially conscious film director, but I had no experience whatsoever, and, not surprisingly, no one would hire me. So I quit my job and went to graduate school to study film production.

In graduate school I looked at a lot of movies, learned how to splice pieces of film, and what a moviola was; that I'd never be an actress or a camera person . . .

Each job I got for the next three years lasted for the duration of the making of a short documentary film. I researched news footage and noted edge numbers once. I calmed the director of another film and had lunch with him a lot. I did sound recording for a documentary, synched rushes on an educational film, wrote some of a script for a short feature, and edited a thirty-second TV spot.

In some ways I seemed to be approaching the sensitive film director image I'd set up for myself a few years earlier. But I wasn't choosing my subjects and was not making the major decisions of shape and content. The work was good and I was learning a lot but the main challenge was to get hired again each time a job ended . . .

". . . to get hired again each time a job ended." And in those words, perhaps, we have the definition of the free-lance market. You will have to meet producers and convince them and sell yourself to them again and again. If you have something very special to offer, you may just find yourself beginning to work more and more while your credits get longer and longer.

I spent seven years as a free-lance director. As such, I had something very special to offer the industry: I had a beard.

Now, today, that is no great achievement and no one really cares. But back in 1950, when all this happened, a beard was a symbol of someone very strange—else why would he have a beard?

As a director, I suppose I was as good as many and perhaps somewhat better or worse than others—but *they* didn't have beards, and I began to discover something about this strange world. As I made my rounds to look for work, I found that one of two reactions set in, the moment I walked through the door:

- He has a beard, so he must be a "kook" or a Communist.

What would our sponsors say? And the advertising agency? And the public?

- He has a beard, so he must be artistic.

Actually, when you look at him, he might be described as "Christ-like." He's hired!

Now, I immediately lost 50 percent of the jobs for which I applied because I was a kook (or a Communist)—and I got the other 50 percent because I had to be artistic. Considering that these were superb odds in a field already overcrowded with young TV directors, I managed to keep busy for a long time—until one hot summer I shaved the beard because it itched.

Once again there was famine in the land.

Some business films are produced "in-house" by the corporation. Others are contracted out to professional production companies. In the film being shot here, Indoor World, a staff headed by Bill Early of Armstrong World Industries (right, arms folded) provided supervision and set design, while an independent company was hired to produce and finish the film.

CHAPTER 22

A PRACTICAL LOOK AT JOB HUNTING

Where It's Finally At

I generally try to find time for new filmmakers and young people just starting out in the field. One person had been recommended to me by a man who had done me a favor. Would I see him? Of course I would. Tell him to call. And he did.

The appointment with the young man was for 10:15 A.M. The appointed time went by. It soon became 10:45, and then 11 A.M. I assumed that he would not show up. But he did—promptly at 11:30—one and a quarter hours late. As he wandered slowly through the door, I expected some exciting story about being mugged on the way, but when nothing was forthcoming I asked sarcastically, "Did you get lost on the subway?" "Nope," he answered. "I took the bus—and you know how slow *they* are."

Of course, everyone reading this will be properly horrified and quickly say that it's a most unusual experience to find a four-year college graduate in communications who doesn't know enough to be on time, to call if he's going to be late, to apologize if there was no phone on the way. I would agree in a moment, if it didn't happen so often. But, countless times through the years, I have been astounded by the way many beginners approach their interviews. True, most of them have been on time—but, even so, that's about all I can say about their preparedness for meeting someone who might be a prospective employer.

Of course, this happens all over, in every industry. The interviewer begins to get the feeling, after meeting the interviewee, that the morning began with dear old Mom pushing her son or daughter through the mansion door and saying, "Go, darling—go out into the world. I love you, and everyone else will love you!"

Job hunting is tough. It's a constant series of rejections, piled one atop the other, day after day. The film business has its very nice people and its bastards, just as any type of life does. Possibly it may have a greater percentage of the latter than anyone else, and a great deal more temperament and ego than in any other field (except, perhaps, opera and the stage), but somewhere along the line you'll find a personality that clicks with yours, and before you know it you'll be working.

Fred Berner, a young production man in the industry, tells a story about his own first job. He had no technical skills, wanted a job in production—and knocked on a hundred doors. Nothing. Nothing happened. The hundred and first door opened to a scene of mild hysteria. It was a small production company and a crisis had occurred.

He was yanked inside.

"Do you know Westchester County?"

"Yes," he answered.

"Do you have a driver's license?"

Again, "Yes."

"Then, here's $50 and a Polaroid camera . . . a car is waiting downstairs. Here's the story board. Find me a location for this commercial—I need it by Wednesday!"

He did.

Timing is paramount. The person who knocked on that door might well have been a messenger, who would have found himself suddenly in the film industry. But it's not all luck—and it's not *all* timing. There are ways to go about finding a job.

THE JOB MARKET

We have made the point that there is much more to the film industry than the feature, the television show, and the commercial. Not that these areas are arid deserts for the beginner. Dave Garroway started his career as a page at NBC—and many others have done the same. But the odds are long, and most beginners run first to the networks for jobs. I would hate to see the waiting list at any of the network personnel offices, though there are occasional opportunities. The list below will try to cover all the areas of potential opportunity, including features, TV, and commercials. Look carefully at some of the other, lesser-known categories, for your first job may well lie waiting in a place you had never known existed.

FEATURES Briefly, most features hire on a per-job basis. About the only job opening that ever seems to occur is the gopher—and generally you'll have to know someone for even that. Keep looking at the trade papers, specifically for the "shoestring" jobs that advertise for people who want to work for nothing or for very little pay. Your enthusiasm may be the key to getting some experience that way.

TELEVISION The television industry is a slim market. It would not hurt, of course, to register with your local TV station, for you never know when a job will open, even on a temporary basis. Many stations hire summer replace-

ments from the colleges and universities and TV is a great way to get experience and to make friends in the industry. But in *film* areas (except for news and special events) television generally buys from the independent production companies. Television is an industry unto itself, and if it intrigues you (because of its own "glamour" and "excitement") I would suggest that you read *The Cool Fire: How to Make It in Television*, by Bob Shanks, formerly with ABC in New York (Vintage/Random House, NY, 1977). The entire book is devoted to television and he tells stories that are almost as funny as mine.

COMMERCIALS, DOCUMENTARIES, AND BUSINESS FILMS Production houses are now scattered throughout the country and many of them are turning out excellent films. Time and time again we have asked for samples from companies that are based in Cleveland or Dallas or Atlanta—and, with the usual New York–Hollywood snobbism, we have expected lesser work, only to be surprised. After all, Frederick Wiseman works out of Boston and Charles Guggenheim is in Washington, D.C. The beauty of working for a smaller company is that you will get a chance to do more than one job. In your first interview attempts, you will probably also find that people are nicer and more available than they are on both coasts.

There are several methods of finding out just where you might apply. The telephone book (believe it or not!) is a good place to start. Following that, you might do well to get a copy of the *Backstage TV, Film & Tape Syndication Directory*. It's published each year and is available from Backstage Publications, 330 W. 42nd St., New York, NY 10036, or Backstage West, 5150 Wilshire Blvd., Los Angeles, CA 90036, or Backstage Mid-West, 100 E. Ohio St., Chicago, IL 60611. The cost is minimal, but the information is invaluable to the job hunter. Not only does the book list companies in forty states, but it breaks them down both by category and by geographic location. As a result, you can find not only the producers who are in business in your particular city, but you can also get information about advertising agencies, music libraries, talent agents, unions, laboratories, and editing houses. Most important, the listings include the *names* of the people in the companies (and we shall discuss that important point later on). *Backstage Publications* publishes an annual listing of production companies ("*TV, Film & Tape Production Directory*"), available directly from any of their offices. *Television/Radio Age* (1270 Avenue of the Americas, N.Y. 10019) publishes an excellent listing of names and addresses in the industry. The book is called *Film/Tape Production Source Book* and includes the names of advertising-agency producers, TV film and tape commercial-production firms, and producers and distributors of public relations, business, and informational films.

IN-HOUSE CORPORATE COMMUNICATIONS You would probably be startled if you looked at a list of the companies which make their own films or which do their own audiovisual work in slide film and tape. We recently read that the Prudential Insurance Company was installing a network of over six hundred stations for an internal-communications system. The superb Sears Roebuck facility is illustrated on page 167. A large company in your own community may be doing the same —or, at very least, producing its smaller projects in-house while contracting out the larger-budget films.

When you begin to make your lists of potential employers, take a look at the *Fortune* magazine list of the five hundred largest companies in the United States. Write a letter to the companies' vice-president in charge of advertising or communications or public relations (a call will tell you the right title and the spelling of the name). You might find that the companies do, indeed, produce their own audiovisual material and that their staff is in need of a replacement. In addition, an excellent book lists every "association" in the United States and Canada—by name, subject, and geographic location, as well as giving the annual budgets and the names of the key executives. Many of the organizations listed have audiovisual departments; it might be worth your while to check the listings all the way from "Accounting" and "Aerospace" through "Zinc" and "Zoology." It's called *National Trade & Professional Associations of the United States and Canada & Labor Unions* by Craig Colgate, Jr., and Patricia Broida (Columbia Books, Inc., 1350 New York Avenue, N.W., Washington, D.C.). The price at this writing is fairly high, about $30.

GOVERNMENT FILMS The potential for jobs will vary from agency to agency, both on federal and state levels. Some groups contract all films to outside producers and others produce them in-house with staffs of their own, bolstered by an occasional free-lancer. The best book I've found is put out by the National Audio-

A PRACTICAL LOOK AT JOB HUNTING

Stephanie Chan, on location with Don Matthews. Once the author's youngest assistant, she is now a full-fledged producer of documentary films.

visual Center and is called *Directory of U.S. Government and Audiovisual Personnel* (National Archives and Records Service, General Services Administration, Washington, D.C. 20409). In it you'll find listed the audiovisual officers for each and every branch of the United States government. Over fifty departments are listed.

In our own business, we have made many of our first sales contacts by using this book, getting the name of the person in charge, and then calling to find out if an appointment can be set up. For those of you who might like to work in the civil service, it would be worthwhile to do the same. As in all governmental work, there is a large turnover on the lower levels—and it might be just the thing you're looking for as a start.

The state governments also have their own audiovisual people, sometimes scattered in departments that give no indication of communications potential. We've seen them in the commerce departments of Midwestern states (for travel and tourism), in the executive branches (for presentations and speeches), and in the departments that deal with social services (for dissemination of public-health information).

MEDICAL AND HOSPITAL FILMS Some medical institutions keep a small audiovisual staff available for their own in-house needs. They may need record photography in a particular department; in other cases, they use films for the training. Earlier, we mentioned that it was a hospital staff photographer (Rosemary Spitalari) who provided much of our most effective operating-room photography for the film *To Live Again*.

INDEPENDENT FILMMAKING Several times we have mentioned that this specific area of film production is one of the most difficult in which to make a living. Nevertheless, there are people who continue to survive in it—both on foundation grants and with support from various organizations such as television stations, political candidates, and corporations. Others start out with the sole purpose of producing a feature film that will eventually be distributed internationally and launch them on a lucrative career. This happens, however infrequently, but Scorcese and Malick and Silver and the Perrys have done it, and others will also succeed. This is not, in any sense, the "staff job" we've been talking about and it is a lonely road trying to raise the money, beat down the distributors, and then get the critics to give it a fair shake.

Some years back, I read a fascinating story. I tell it now because it once again gives us faith that determination is one key to success.

In the late seventies, the New York Film Festival screened a film by Barbara Kopple called *Harlan County, U.S.A.* It had taken the filmmaker four years, from start to final screening, and it told the story of the 1973 coal strike in Harlan County, Kentucky. It received good reviews and a great deal of recognition, but the most fascinating part of the story was Ms. Kopple's struggle to raise the $200,000 needed to produce the film. In order to maintain control of her project, she accepted money from foundations and church groups but refused offers that would have forced her to give up her authority. The two months of filming were financed with a Master Charge card, and at the time of the premiere, she was still very much in debt. However, her feelings might best indicate how all independent filmmakers feel about their

role in the business: "...you might as well bleed for something of your own." The blood she shed was rewarded with an Academy Award for the best documentary of 1976.

ADVERTISING AGENCIES They, too, are now located all over the country as well as throughout the world. Almost all of them have increased their billings considerably in the television area these past ten or fifteen years, and thus all have increased the size of their production departments. Before flying off to the "big city," however, it might be wise to check first to see if a large national agency has an office near you. If it does, find out whether it also has a local television production department.

The *Backstage TV, Film & Tape Syndication Directory* (see p. 162) does have agency listings for New York, Hollywood, and Chicago, and each gives the name of the commercial producers at each listed company. For the smaller cities, we would again suggest the Yellow Pages of the telephone directory, and a book that gives a complete advertising-agency listing throughout the country: *The Standard Directory of Advertising Agencies* (National Register Publishing Company, 3004 Glenview Road, Wilmette, IL 60091).

YOUR FIRST CONTACT

If I were to write, "Don't just show up at the office of the person you want to see," a hundred letters would arrive telling me that it was precisely that way that the first job was gotten. All right, then. Don't show up at *my* office without an appointment!

Most filmmakers are busy—and even if we're not busy, we like to tell everyone we are. I think it's inconsiderate, rude, gauche, unprofessional, and wrong simply to walk into a reception area and ask to see someone. There is a slight possibility that the executive will come out and fall madly in love with you and your background and offer you a job as executive producer, but the chances are slim. Most will not see *anyone* without a previous appointment.

wcet-tv

48

1223 Central Parkway
Cincinnati, Ohio 45214
(513) 381-4033

22 October 1976

Mr. Mel London
Vision Associates
665 Fifth Avenue
New York, New York

Dear Mr. London:

I would like to thank you for taking the time to see me in August. As a relatively inexperienced person just out of school, it was very encouraging to find people in the communications industry who were so supportive and helpful. I did find a job, and I think it is a good one, but it is not in New York City.

I am currently the assistant to the producer for a primary science series. The series is being organized and distributed by the International Instructional Television Co-operative in Washington D.C. The actual design and production will be done here in Cincinnati at WCET/48 which is where I am currently located. WCET has just opened a new and very well equipped facility which should make things that much more interesting. The series will be ready for air, both nation-wide and in Canada, by September 1977. If it is successful, we will do two more series aimed at different grade levels.

One way or another I may be looking for a job next September. If that is the case, I would very much like to approach your organization again. In the meantime, thank-you for your help and advice.

Sincerely,

Susan

Susan Lynn Schrier
Assistant to the Producer
Primary Science Project

Crosley Telecommunications Center
The Greater Cincinnati Television
Educational Foundation-wcet-tv48

One of the best letters received by the author in twenty years of seeing potential filmmakers.

The most important thing about your first contact with anyone is that you should know exactly which person you are going to see, *by name*. That is why I mentioned earlier that some directories and listings do give names of executives, as well as their titles.

THE LETTER Within the last few weeks, many letters have come into our office, as they usually do. The amount increases as the school year lets out and many of these letters are superb examples of what-not-to-do.

First of all, any letter that comes in addressed to "Personnel Director" is immediately opened by the receptionist; this is followed by a loud questioning: "Does anyone want to see another résumé?" The answer to this is obvious. The second letter that most people ignore is one duplicated on a Xerox machine. Are we on some kind of huge mailing list? What kind of potential employee would he or she be, if time cannot be taken to make a personal contact with our organization? Of course, there is an occasional attempt to personalize the impersonal by Xeroxing anything but the addressee's name, and then writing "Dear Sir or Ms," too. After a while, we get the feeling that all of the letters we receive can be put with the junk mail addressed to "Occupant Apartment 7B." Such job-hunting letters don't promise much to the recipient. We received one just the other day from a young woman with a fairly good background and a master's degree, who wrote to us by Xerox copy (though she took the trouble to sign her name in ink), promising that ". . . I have something unique to contribute to your organization." Well, she certainly did: she addressed her letter, "Dear Prospective Employer."

"Sir," "Madam," "Ms.," "Personnel," "Gentlemen" (and we took care of that last one in Chapter 20, "Women in Film")—all those impersonal openings are wrong. Absolutely, irrevocably, terribly wrong. What astounds me is the fact that at least 50 percent of letters come in addressed that way. Doesn't anyone teach how to write a good business letter anymore? If we receive ten letters a week, why do some of them elicit a response, while most are ignored? Just keep in mind that if a letter is addressed to me by name, I am the one who opens it—or at least, it gets to me to be read.

The best letters are generally short and to the point. Some of them speak of a follow-up phone call, suggesting that the interviewee would be most willing to come up at any convenient time. Some of the better ones understand that we might not have a job opening but that the writer would like to come up for advice, since just talking about the field and the tough job hunt can be of help, too. Essentially, there is a "flair" to the letters that we like—and no one can prepare such an overall general-use letter that will fit every situation. If you analyze the company you've written to, and if you can put in one personal line that makes us think that the letter has not gone out to three hundred companies in exactly the same wording, then maybe you will find us a bit more receptive.

Assistant cameraman Mike Rothenberg slates a scene for The Speaker, produced for the American Library Association by Vision Associates.

THE TELEPHONE CALL To put your mind at ease, know that it is not only the beginner who is sluffed off by the voice at the other end of the line he's dialed. Some people are just like that. It was the subject of an article I wrote many years ago for *The New York Times:* rudeness in business. Some people are just plain rude. Their secretaries are therefore rude, their children are rude, and their dogs are rude. Job hunting gets discouraging because of the rudeness and constant rejection. Certainly, you don't like being told, "He'll return your call," knowing full well that he won't, or, "I'll see if he's in," when she sits three feet from him and knows damned well whether he's in, or, "She's in conference," when we are all aware that she is reading the latest copy of *Newsweek* magazine and has totally forgotten how it was to hunt for that first job. Even in doing the research and the development of this book, my assistant and I (both of us professionals, with jobs) were many times treated as if talking to us would spread the Swine Flu. So it happens to us as well as to you. You simply steel yourself and make the next call. The experience will stand you in good stead. The more you talk to people on the telephone, the more you'll learn how to

get to the real person you're trying to contact.

Fred Berner used to set up his "office" in a telephone booth of the Hilton Hotel in New York when he was on the West Side, and in one in the Commodore Hotel when he was looking on the East Side. He kept a stack of dimes handy and made his appointments by calling the production houses and, when asked where he was from, he would answer that he was Fred Berner from the phone booth on the corner. Somehow, he found enough people with a sense of humor to let him come up for an interview. Eventually, after a series of small jobs, he became assistant director for an animated feature.

If you send out twenty letters, and you follow up with a telephone call one week later, it is just possible that two or three—or at least one—persons will be "willing to see you." Many such persons will remain names to you, however, and you will never get to them. Many of them legitimately have no time now to see you, and many of them may ask you to call back in two months or six months (and just possibly mean it). It's a good idea to keep a "tickler file" of your letters and calls, and their dates and times; the people to whom you spoke; and any other reminder material that will help you when you contact them again. After all, you may *have* to make that call two months later—unless, if you're lucky, you are working somewhere then and can throw away the list.

Above all, try not to get discouraged by the reception you get on the phone. Your tendency is, at such times, to ignore the calls you *should* be making, and the very next one might have been the interview you needed.

Which leads me to another important point: How much time did you spend in college studying? If you were working instead, how much time did you spend on the job? And now, if you're looking for a job, how much time have you spent at this? We've asked the last question of many people who came up to our offices for an interview, and the answers have ranged from "Very little" to "Very little." Possibly because the road is so difficult—and possibly because it gets even more difficult when you've been at it for weeks or months—the tendency is at last to slow down, to feel that if you've had two interviews that day, that should be quite enough.

If you're not out on an interview, you should be writing a letter, and if you've written all you can (which I sincerely doubt), then you should be telephoning. It is not too much to ask that you spend as much time looking for a job as you did studying. You may just find that you are getting more interview appointments —and this is what really matters.

Finally, we get to see you: a face replaces the letter and the résumé and the telephone voice.

THE INTERVIEW

Of course you're nervous. You walk into the office to see the person with whom you've made an appointment and the walls are decorated with gold medals, awards, funny posters, old-time movie stills, or autographed political photographs that you read nervously before being called in. ("To my good friend, Joe, from his good friend, Boss Tweed.")

Some people new to the field have actually anticipated these moments, and have, much earlier, practiced the technique of being interviewed. Whether in school, or among friends, or in special sessions with teachers or parents, they've tried to re-create what the interview might be like. Some have gone out on job hunts even though they were not quite ready to meet the "real" world—just for the practice. David Smith, another young friend just starting out in the field, told us that if he had ever known what this world of job hunting was like, he would have spent every spare moment at school trying to arrange for an interview—just for practice—so that he might have gotten to know the experience better and been more at ease.

Keep some things in mind when you arrive at that interview—most of all, the fact that we are not hiring your four-year education. We are looking at a personality. The questions we ask are to get *you* to talk—about yourself, about your film work, about your hopes and aspirations. Just as personality is a key factor in hiring a free-lance crew for a trip, so it is in any interview, for whatever purpose or field. We hire, primarily, from the gut. We have time and time again found that some of our successful applicants have actually lacked a few minor qualifications. Nevertheless, they have been hired because we felt the learning potential was there. Possibly the thing that "turned us on" in the first place was a bond in common with the job seeker. This happens more than any of us would care to admit! You certainly are much further ahead if the two of you are avid golfers or bread bakers than if there are no shared interests. Small talk frequently be-

Many large corporations have developed sophisticated and complex networks devoted to communications. Both in tape and film, these companies offer job opportunities to the beginner.

gins the interview, and we can probe, relate stories, and get to know you in a few quick moments.

Another thing that occasionally crops up is the question, from an interviewee: "What do you people do here?" Well, of course, we make films—but that is common knowledge. Printed in *The Backstage Directory* are listings of the *categories* of films that companies produce. Lacking those sources, I should think that a telephone call to a company which is willing to see you would uncover some information about them. How much time did you take to shop around for a college? How much time and how much effort go into buying your new car? We would like to hope that you were interested enough in us to find out about us *before* you got there. This also holds true for interviews with corporations or government agencies. *Before* you appear for the meeting, you should make it a point to find out just exactly what it is they manufacture or what service they provide. Today, with multinationalism a factor in the structure of many corporations, it would help considerably to look at their annual report before even calling.

At an interview, we hear other things, too, all the time, among them the phrase, "I'll do anything." We understand your desire to transmit your eagerness to the interviewer, but there are two problems inherent in that statement:

- First of all, you don't really mean it. You really wouldn't do *anything*; probably you could think of ten menial jobs you wouldn't do for very long.
- Second of all, and perhaps even more important, if the interviewer believes that state-

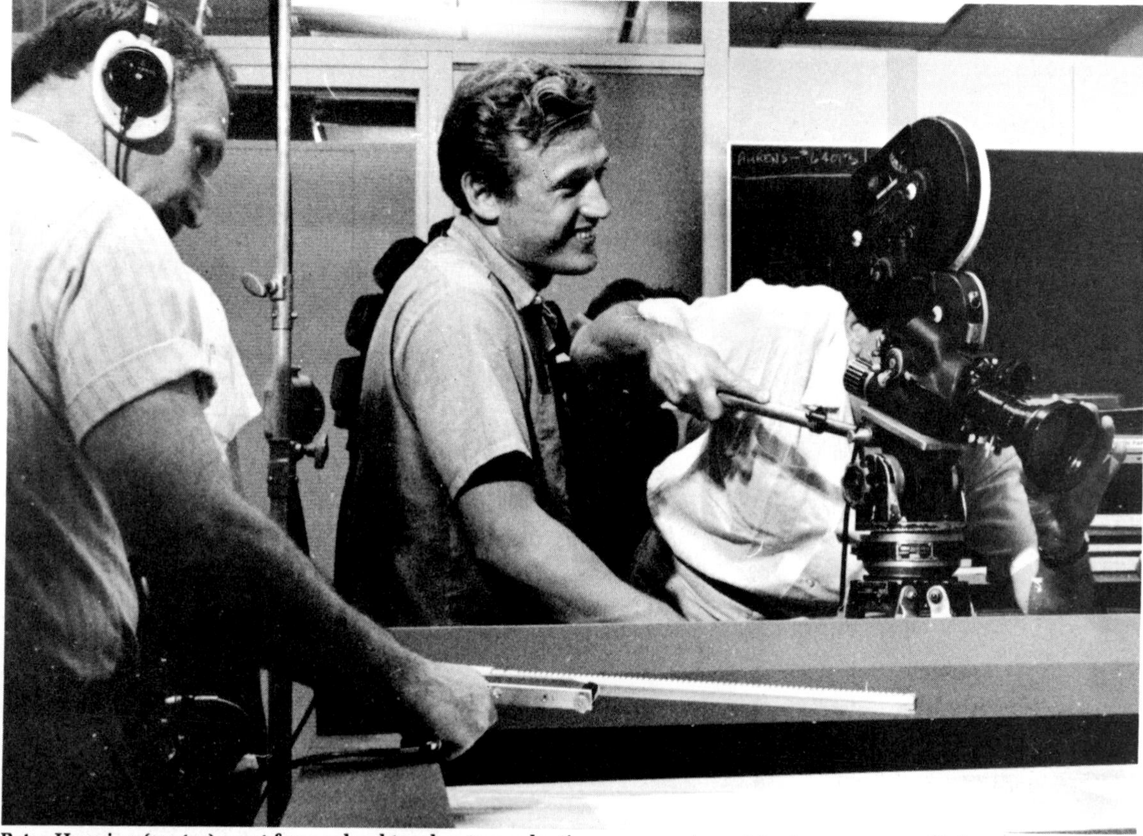

Peter Henning (center) went from school teacher to production manager to assistant cameraman. He is now one of the busiest director/cameramen in both film and television specials.

ment, he has no way to categorize you for a potential opening.

Are you interested in editing, photography, writing? "Anything" ends up meaning "nothing." It limits your potential in talking to the prospective employer.

You know what it is you want to do eventually. You have a pretty good idea of what excites you and interests you, now, in the film business. That is—or those are—the subjects you should be talking about.

Probably just as often as we hear, "I'll do anything," we also find that about 82 percent of all interviewees say, "I'd like to get into production." Fine. But let's look at that one, too. In the first place, get to know what "production" really means. Hopefully, the earlier chapter in this book (Chapter 4) will help. And perhaps you will discuss film with people in the field in order to help delineate the specific film areas that interest you most; we sometimes get the feeling that the quest for "production" means a quick entry into producing and directing, making a name in the industry, doing what Lucas and Spielberg and Sayles are doing. To expect a quick jump into that stratosphere is to equate graduating from law school with being nominated Chief Justice of the Supreme Court your first year out in the world. There can be only so many producers and directors in the field—and also just so many production jobs. We'd really like to know what film area interests you, and just where it is you might begin. Even the request for a job as a gopher would give us something on which to hang our decision.

Your interests might well be broader, too, than just one phase of film, especially in the early stages—and at your interview, certainly. We have seen new people who resisted jobs in any area except the one in which they eventually wanted to make their career. Your main object at this point should be to get your foot in the door—any door—and in any company that makes film. If a job is available, take it.

Women may well have ambivalent feelings about taking a job as a receptionist or switchboard operator. On the one hand, we might as well face the real fact that in this male-oriented world, it is generally the women who are answering those telephones (despite major corporate policy of not discriminating). However, you're right—it may be a dead end. Though you may get promises of moving up into the company, you may also find that most organizations want you to stay right at that front desk and keep your eyes from roving back where the "excitement" takes place. On the other hand, it *is* a foot in the door for many women, and it *is* a chance to meet people who work in film. What's more, in our own company three of our most valuable receptionists have moved into positions of responsibility—and, yes, two even got into "production." So use your judgment, and if your instincts tell you there just may be a chance, grab the opportunity. After a year, if you are still answering a busy switchboard, then perhaps it is time to move on.

Occasionally the question of handling some sort of technical equipment comes up in an interview; it might be in the realm of cameras or editing equipment or sound. This is a ticklish area, and I would strongly suggest that you *not* tell the interviewer you once read a book called *Getting into Film*, which told you to lie. I am merely suggesting that you never admit outright that you cannot do a job. Indicate that you might well be able to handle the job that is being described. It is a simple matter to say, for example, "I'm very mechanically inclined. I've fixed my car, myself, for years. I'm *sure* I can handle it." If you're bright, you'll learn to operate that equipment. Of course, I would not suggest that you indicate you can drive a car if you really can't. (And, incidentally, a license is almost a necessity in production. There are a thousand things for which you need "wheels.")

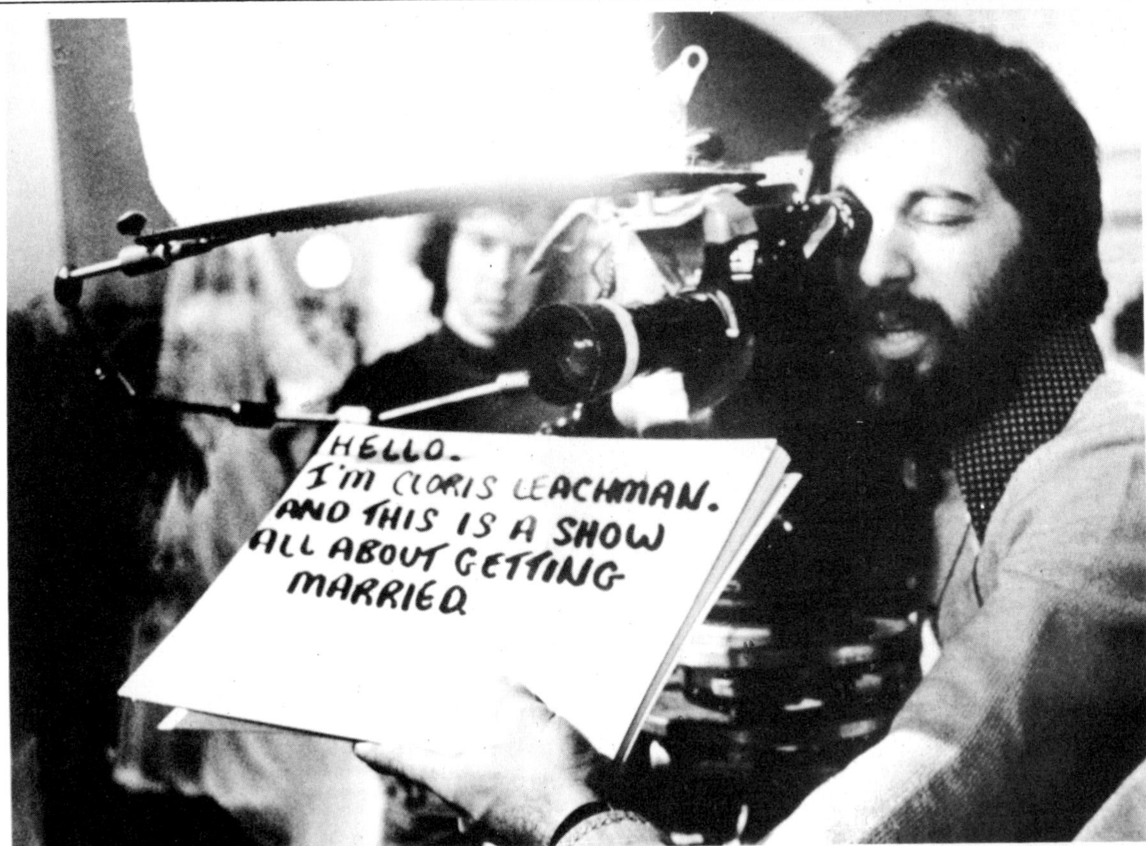

HELLO.
I'M CLORIS LEACHMAN.
AND THIS IS A SHOW
ALL ABOUT GETTING
MARRIED

After graduation from the University of Southern California, Chuck Braverman formed his own production company in Hollywood, where he now produces TV specials, commercials, and business films.

At the interview, *you* are expected to talk. The questioner wants more than offhand answers, and the more information you volunteer, the better it will look. Remember that this is (again) a business of personality; it comes up time and again when I describe the jobs to you. Getting along with people. Compatibility. Steadiness under tension. You have no better place to begin showing you have these qualities than at that first interview. Many times we have been so taken by job hunters that we have insisted they call if they get work and experience somewhere, or, at the least, let us know if we can answer any questions as they make the rounds through those next trying weeks. Remember, if we've given you an appointment and we're willing to spend the time to see you, then it must be *you* in whom we're interested. How do *you* think? How do *you* conduct yourself? How do *you* feel about film? We'd like to hear *you* do most of the talking.

One final word about the interview—and it just shows how much the world has changed, for twenty years ago it would have been the first thing in the chapter: What do you wear? How do you dress?

At one time, we would have read in Emily Post that "young ladies" should wear white gloves and not-too-frilly dresses and that "boys" should have their hair combed and wear a tie and white shirt. Today, we can give no rules. They vary from area to area and from company to company. In many places, you will be welcome wearing jeans. In other places, the women may wear slacks. And in still others, there *is* the absolute necessity of dresses for women, shirts and ties for men. You have to be the judge. You know the film area and the company to which you are going to apply. If it is a conservative organization or is in a part of the country where dress has not gotten to the blue-jean stage, use your common sense. But above all, be clean! No matter what you decide to wear, just imagine how we will project your eventually traveling with us, if you're a slob! In addition, the interviewer frequently thinks ahead to the time when you'll be meeting people: the clients of the company, other staff members, and the people out in the world that you'll be filming. You—as well as every other member of that production unit—will be projecting some kind of image. What kind are you projecting at the interview? Is it the right one for the company with whom you want to be working?

SAMPLES If you've made a film or tape sample, you are certainly much further ahead than if you have never worked on the production of a film. You have something to show and to talk about—although some film executives like to keep the sample for a few days and then screen it at their leisure. This accomplishes two purposes: it can be done in the early morning or late afternoon, without spending valuable daytime hours; and it saves the executive from having to confront you directly if the film is really quite bad.

Many films made in film school are, in essence, "compositions" that are done for much-needed practice. But they *are* samples of your work and they do show that you have been involved in the craft on a practical level. As door openers, they are probably one of the best devices.

The sample, moreover, need not be a reel of film. First of all, production may not be your selected area of work. Furthermore, some areas are easy to bring out in a film sample—editor, sound, camera, direction—while others cannot be seen in a sample film, for example, production management or chief grip. If writing is your chosen field, the sample certainly might well be a script or treatment you've done, rather than a finished film. Still photographs, graphic design, costume or stage design, a recording of your music, or a portfolio of your paintings or drawings would also be proper samples to show a prospective employer. Prospective employers will understand that you will not normally bring in a sophisticated, finished, well-produced film.

For those in the other areas of the field—electricians, grips, even sound people in some cases—it is much more difficult to show samples. Unfortunately, what really counts there is the building of reputation and reliability. These are areas in which staff jobs seldom open up, and so in hiring a new technician the personality you show at the interview is frequently a determining factor.

RESUMES They have become standard not only in the film business but in every industry and craft and profession in which people look for work—which means nearly everywhere. Many times, they are not even read, but are used for a file or just for something to say to a prospective employee: "Send me your résumé."

Résumés are improved by "creative writing" and they generally change as you become more successful. At the beginning, they tend to expand on the few things you've done, going on for as much as a paragraph about a job you performed on an independent film. This is fine, but as you get more and more experience you'll find that your résumé begins to become more staccato in its form. There are now more and more credits to list. This, too, is expected.

Above all, keep your résumé up-to-date and keep it simple. One page should be adequate. Going on for four or five is a waste of money and effort. Very few employers will read that far. Concentrate more on your *experience* than on your education. Remember how many of us feel that one year in the business is worth more than four years at college. (However wrong we may sometimes be.)

I have discussed the importance of personality and compatibility at the time of your interview. Your résumé is a better entrée at your first meeting if you also use it to list your interests and your talents outside the film field. Your background in sports, in art, in languages —even whether you have traveled extensively —are all areas of interest to those of us who hire new employees. Since timing is everything, just imagine our feelings if you were to come along as we were trying to build a crew for a film about river sports and your résumé told us you were an expert in the kayak. Farfetched? Not really. It has happened time and

The author's film crew takes a break among the mannequins at Lord & Taylor for the film, Your Future in Fashion. Back row: Ken Schlieman, Director of Visual Merchandising; Albee Gordon, Sound; Al Phox, Gaffer; Sheryl London, Art Director; the author. Front row: Jon Fauer, Director of Photography; Tina Gonzalez, Production Manager; Michael Barry, Assistant Cameraman.

again. In such a case, the hobby might get you the job and your film "background" might well fade into invisible ink.

OTHER DOOR OPENERS Barbara Martinsons, of Prentice-Hall Media, told us: "... at the beginning I tracked down every lead I could get. For example, 'Mr. Smith, you don't know me, but I understand that you have just received a grant to do a comparative study of education in suburban and inner city schools. I'd like to come and talk to you about a film sequence.' I pulled strings, no matter how slender: 'My Aunt Polly suggested that I contact you. You and she met on a cruise last winter, and she suggested that since you are connected with BBD&O you might have some helpful hints for me on breaking into film production . . . "

Of course, it helps to have a name to drop, but it isn't necessary that it even be your Aunt Polly who met the BBD&O executive on a cruise. (And note the approach that asks someone for advice!) It can be anyone. You will eventually make contacts in the everyday places of the film world—at festivals, for example, where the known and the unknown mingle for several days and small talk includes the production of new films, the experiences on the job, and funny stories. Furthermore, the guest lecturer at school, the professor who liked your work, the seminars run by professionals—all these are means by which to meet the people who work in film. Go to technical seminars and trade shows, such as the annual SMPTE (Society of Motion Picture and Television Engineers); they are well attended by cinematographers, editors, and executives. The special screenings held at museums, exhibitions, and universities may also bring you into contact with potential future interviewers.

Even the interview itself is a form of door opener that may lead to others in the industry. The first meeting might produce nothing of value except two or three more names of people whom "you might see for advice" or "for a job interview." Many times we see talents in you that lie in areas other than ones we can use—graphics or animation, still photography, technical ability—and we will recommend that you see someone else. In cases such as these, your next question should be, "May I use your name when I call?" And, generally, approval is given—it thus becomes much easier for you to break through the wall that protects your next target.

THE FOLLOW-UP

You tread a thin line between being a pain in the neck to someone and, at the same time, following up your first contact (whether it was on the telephone or in person). Some people say, "Get in touch with me in three weeks," and mean it. Others say it and forget it. Even if you are not told to follow up, it's a good idea to do so, for we get many résumés and many letters over the year and it's easy enough to forget someone who has made a good impression (we *quickly* forget the ones who have made a bad one).

Keep a calendar with notations about your visits and just when you think it might be wise to call back. Remember, it is generally all a matter of a talented person being there when the job opens up. Remember, too, the person on the other end of the line may have just received a call from a friend asking, "Do you know of a good production assistant who doesn't mind working twenty-six hours a day?" Chances are, you would have been forgotten, except for the fact that you had called that morning to check. And remember, you cannot just go out once and expect the world to remember you. Timing is everything, and those follow-ups must be made.

AFTER THAT FIRST JOB

The door may finally open a bit—and you put your foot solidly into it, looking around with glee at the new world it will open for you. But you are still not finished: the field is volatile, the company could be out of business in a few months, or someone may notice a certain resentment when you were asked to go for coffee the fifteenth time in two hours. (Remember, too, you never know when the people you met during your first job will be valuable to you when you are again out looking for work, with one extra credit on your résumé, of course.) Also, now employed, let's say your long trail of interviews took you to many offices and you met a great many people, some of them good and some of them bad. It might be a good idea to drop a line to the ones you liked—and who liked you. Tell them you've gotten a job and thank them for their encouragement and their time while you were looking. You'd be surprised at how we appreciate hearing from someone we've liked at an interview.

One of our recent interviewees was a young woman from Ohio State, who had made a sensitive and effective documentary about the last man who still paints Mail Pouch Tobacco signs on the barns across the country. We were terribly impressed with her, and it was one of those days when we were sorry that there was no opening in our company. A few weeks later, a letter arrived from her (see p. 164). It's one of the best we've ever gotten—and she'll be welcome in our offices again.

I've said many times that you may be asked to do menial work in your first job. It's worth repeating again. Nevertheless, that "beginning time" is also one of the best opportunities to learn and to grow. Brianna Murphy wrote this about her first job:

In conversation with some Hollywood night clubbers, I heard of a small non-union production company preparing a picture. They had a little office at General Service Studios. Uninvited and unannounced I went by to see if there was anything I could do. Little, non-union, no-budget production companies are always receptive to people who are willing to work and learn for little or no money. They put me behind a desk—I had no secretarial skills but there was much more to do. I called agents and actors, made appointments for crew members to come in, helped the production manager with the breakdown, scouted out wardrobe and props. I overheard all the pre-production conversations and became a sponge. Time neared to go on location and I was aware that there were jobs to be done that couldn't be paid for. The editor explained to me what notations he needed and what had to be observed and recorded for the director and the actors. Confident in my ignorance, I took on the jobs of script supervisor, wardrobe, props, make-up and hair—and still photographer. I was paid fifty dollars a week plus room and board on location.

And that's the way it is. This is a classic description of how someone moves from beginning to middle: doing everything and anything, never admitting ignorance, and then managing to learn the craft right on the job by listening, probing, helping. After a few years, Brianna saw the same thing in someone else. By now, a busy production manager, she wrote:

I recall, on one picture, we had a young man who worked as an equipment service manager—who was quiet and efficient during the production hours. I noticed that when we called a wrap (end of the shooting day), he didn't pick up and run like most everyone else. I asked him if he had more work to do, for my job was to be concerned about unnecessary overtime. He explained that he was off the clock but liked to listen in on the production conversations I had with the director. From then on, we invited him to sit in on our meetings so that he could listen better. On the next picture, he was a production assistant. Then some other company stole him. I'm sure he succeeded.

We all had different experiences in our first few years. The first job I ever got in the field was as a writer for network radio—my dentist's wife's friend had a son who was writing for network radio and needed an assistant. Could I write network radio? Of course I said yes. Then I learned how.

My move into film came when I met my ex-company commander from World War II on the corner of 68th Street and Madison Avenue in New York—an accident of time and place. I moved from television into film because he was president of a new and aggressive production company in Princeton, New Jersey.

Each of us in the field could fill a book of this size with experiences and stories and advice, and each of us would have a different word to say. This is the reason why I have used the sage advice of so many of my friends, for I could not have lived enough lives to experience everything in this exciting world of film.

Much of this experience can help *you* in your early probing search into motion pictures. The film world lives! Horatio Alger still stalks the streets of this incredible industry. What will it be like? Again, my friend Brianna Murphy says it better than I could: ". . . be prepared for long periods of unemployment, for some unfairness, for times of depression and disillusionment. Be prepared to work your fanny off and have the producer skip town without paying you. Be prepared to have to borrow the money to pay your answering service. Be ready to be rejected and insulted. Be aware that you'll make mistakes and they will not be tolerated. Ask yourself if this is the life you really want. The only security you'll find in this insecure business is that everything changes."

". . . Ask yourself if this is the life you really want." If the answer is, "Yes," and if you've gotten this far in the book, it obviously *is* the answer. Then there are only two more words to say to you. From me and from my dear, departed grandmother who gave me so many of the homilies by which I live:

GOOD LUCK!

SUGGESTED READING

For a long time, I toyed with the idea of ending each chapter with a list of the books that might give you additional information about the specific craft. There are, indeed, many books that can be valuable to you, but the new ones are upon us almost as soon as the old ones gather dust on the shelf. As a result, I have tried to include some titles within the chapters themselves, where I felt that the books might be important or where they were specifically recommended by one of our "consultants." In addition, I would now like to suggest that you get your additional reading from two primary sources:

MAGAZINES AND TRADE PUBLICATIONS

Keep in touch with the field through these sources. They are an excellent library of what is happening, what is current and important to you. New books are reviewed (by, for example, George L. George of Directors Guild of America), casting information and production calls are included, festivals listed, and even the industry gossip is a part of the reading fare. The advertising is informative, too—new equipment, as well as new techniques and developments, is critical to your learning process.

Some of the magazines and newspapers are: *American Cinematographer, Backstage, Computer Pictures, Film Comment, Film Daily, Millimeter, Sight and Sound, SMPTE Journal, Variety,* and *The Independent.*

BOOKS

There is an easy way to keep abreast of the new books, aside from the review columns in the list of magazines above. College and university bookstores, booksellers such as the Dalton and Waldenbooks chains, and even small booksellers in many cities all carry a fairly good supply of film books. Of course, many of them deal with the entertainment end of the business. However, the techniques of film and the craft books are also carried. For those of you who cannot find the information that you need, I have listed below three major bookshops that specialize in film literature, and a brief note or phone call to them will give you information about their listings. All of them will mail order your selections to you and, from time to time, they also publish book lists for their customers. Even the best-read film buff will find something new in their large selection.

Birns & Sawyer
1026 N. Highland Ave.
Hollywood, Cal. 90038
Tel: 213-466-8211

Normally this company does its primary business as a supplier of film equipment, but it also offers a large selection of film books with over 1000 titles in stock at any given time. Also available are technical books on the subjects of television and video tape, cable, and computer graphics. Other subjects:

- Acting
- Animation
- Business Practices
- Cinematography
- Costume Design
- Directing
- Documentary
- Editing
- Fundamentals
- Graphics
- Lighting
- Makeup
- Music and Scoring
- Reference
- Set Design
- Sound
- Special Effects
- Writing

Larry Edmunds Book Store
6658 Hollywood Blvd.
Hollywood, Cal. 90028
Tel: 213-463-3273

This is the largest bookstore of its kind—exclusively selling motion picture and theater books. It sells to colleges and universities and also to the general public. They do not have a complete catalogue, but book lists are available from time to time.

Cinemabilia
10 W. 13th St.
New York, N.Y. 10011
Tel: 212-989-8519

This is the largest film and theater bookstore on the East Coast and they offer a book list and a "Sampler List" for the asking. They carry just about everything in the field including history, criticism, techniques and crafts, screenplays, television, cable, videotape, management, and film magazines.

Two of the best in documentary film: Francis Thompson and Alexander (Sasha) Hammid. Their credits include a range of multi-screen and IMAX giant screen motion pictures, including Academy Award winner To Be Alive, films for NASA, and the acclaimed To Fly, originally produced for the Air and Space Museum at the Smithsonian, but now appearing all over the country.

ILLUSTRATION CREDITS

Cover Photo: Peter Rosenbaum

Page Number

1 Photo: Jon Fauer
5 Courtesy The World Bank
6 Courtesy Lenny Hirschfield Productions
7 Courtesy Lenny Hirschfield Productions
8 Courtesy Ohio Bell Telephone Company
9 Courtesy Methodist Hospitals, Memphis, Tennessee
10 Courtesy Methodist Hospitals, Memphis, Tennessee
12 Photo: Museum of Modern Art
Courtesy Robert Flaherty Study Center, School of Theology, Claremont, California
14 Courtesy Joe Longo
17 Photo: Allen Say
Courtesy Snazelle Films, San Francisco
18 Photo: Allen Say
Courtesy Snazelle Films, San Francisco
20, 21 © 1976 The Reuben H. Donnelley Corp., New York
23 Photo: Gordon
Courtesy Jock and Betty Lesie-Melville
26 Courtesy NBC and Landsburg/Kirshner Productions
29 Photo: Elaine Alder
30 Courtesy NBC and Landsburg/Kirshner Productions
33 Courtesy Writer's Guild of America, East
34 Courtesy Herbert Raditschnig
36 Courtesy NBC and Landsburg/Kirshner Productions
38 Courtesy Garrett Brown and Cinema Products Corp.
40 Courtesy NBC and Landsburg/Kirshner Productions
42 Photo: Allen Say
Courtesy Snazelle Films, San Fransicso
43 Photo: Allen Say
Courtesy Snazelle Films, San Francisco
44 Photo: Allen Say
Courtesy Snazelle Films, San Francisco
45 Courtesy MM Editing Systems
50 Photo: Edwin Langsam
52 Courtesy Malcolm Dodds Music
53 Courtesy Coca-Cola U.S.A.
55 Courtesy Emil Ascher, Inc., and CBS Records
57 Courtesy RCA Corporation
58 Courtesy Gershon Kingsley
63 Courtesy Braverman Productions, Los Angeles
65 Photo: Allen Say
Courtesy Snazelle Films, San Francisco
66 Courtesy Saul Bass & Associates, Los Angeles
67 Courtesy Carmen D'Avino
68, 69 Courtesy Saul Bass & Associates, Los Angeles
70 Courtesy Charles Goetz
71 Courtesy Digital Effects
72 Courtesy Joe Cirillo
75 Courtesy Cynthia Horton
76 Courtesy Screen Actors Guild
77 Courtesy NBC and Landsburg/Kirshner Productions
79, 81 Courtesy Dick Smith
80 Courtesy Cyclops Films
82 Courtesy Make-Up Artists

and Hair Stylists Local 798 (I.A.T.S.E.) New York
83 Courtesy Maurice Stein
84, 85 Courtesy Lester Polakov Studio and Forum of Stage Design, New York
86 Photo: Terry Chostner, Courtesy Lucasfilm Ltd. © Lucasfilm Ltd. (LFL) 1983. All Rights Reserved.
87 Photo: Museum of Modern Art Courtesy Janus Films
88, 89 Courtesy Lester Polakov Studio and Forum of Stage Design, New York
91 Photo: George Meluso
92, 93, 94, 95 Courtesy NBC and Landsburg/ Kirshner Productions
97 Photos: Keith Hamshere and Kerry Nordquist. Courtesy Lucasfilm Ltd. © Lucasfilm Ltd. (LFL) 1983. All Rights Reserved.
101 Courtesy RKO Pictures
105 Photo: Nancy Moran Courtesy Lucasfilm Ltd. © Lucasfilm Ltd. (LFL) 1981. All Rights Reserved.
106 Courtesy Robert Flaherty Study Center, School of Theology, Claremont, California
108 Courtesy Lenny Hirschfield Productions
109 Courtesy Braverman Productions, Los Angeles
110 Courtesy NBC and Landsburg/ Kirshner Productions
113 Courtesy Snazelle Films, San Francisco
115, 116, 117, 118 Courtesy Armstrong Cork Company and Batten, Barton, Durstine & Osborne, Inc.
122, 123 Courtesy Ohio Bell Telephone Company
125, 127 Courtesy Playback Associates, New York
126 Courtesy Ohio Bell Telephone Company
128 Photo: Susan Oristaglio
134, 135, 136 Reprinted from *The American Film Institute Guide to College Courses in Film and Television*, by permission of The American Film Institute, Washington, D.C.
140 Photo: Kent Rosner Courtesy Filmex, Los Angeles International Film Exposition
142 Courtesy Museum of Modern Art and The Film Society of Lincoln Center, Inc., New York
143 Courtesy Film Forum
144, 145 Courtesy Filmex, Los Angeles International Film Exposition
146 Photo: Basia Kenton
148 Photo: Neil Selkirk
149 Photo: Todd Weinstein
151 Courtesy Sombrero Productions
153 Photo: Andy Schwartz
154 Courtesy Braverman Productions, Los Angeles
160 Courtesy Armstrong Cork Company
164 Courtesy Susan Lynn Schrier
167 Photo: RCA Corporation Courtesy Sears Roebuck and Company, Chicago
169 Courtesy Braverman Productions, Los Angeles
175 Photo: Hella Hammid

Illustrations by Elaine Grove

Design Assistants: Paula Greif, Anne Winslow

Typography by Towne Typographers, Inc.
and Typographic Images, Inc., New York City.